6

7

8

Portraits by Edvard Munch on the front end-paper

1) Edvard Munch. Self-portrait with Skeleton Arm. 1895. Lithograph, OKK. G/1.192; Sch.31.

2) Frederick Delius. Drawing from *Verdens Gang*, 12 October 1891.

3) Vilhelm Krag. 1920. Lithograph, OKK. G/1.406-5; Sch.472.

4) August Strindberg. 1896. Lithograph, OKK. G/1.219a; Sch.77.

5) Gunnar Heiberg. 1896. Lithograph, OKK. G/1.217; Sch.75.

6) Arve Arvesen. c.1887-90. Oil on canvas, Private Collection.

7) Helge Rode. 1898. Drypoint, OKK. G/r.50-1; Sch.103.

8) Stephane Mallarmé. 1896. Lithograph, OKK. G/1.221-5; Sch.79.

Frederick Delius
and
Edvard Munch

their friendship and their correspondence

OVERLEAF:
Frederick Delius.
c.1890-91. Munch-Museet.
Pencil, OKK. T.127, p.25 reverse.

Frederick DELIUS & Edvard MUNCH

their friendship and their correspondence

John Boulton Smith

Triad Press   1983

ISBN 0-902070-26-6

NUMBERING OF LETTERS AND ABBREVIATIONS
The initial number used to identify each letter denotes the letter's chronological place in the total series sent and received. This is followed by either the letter 'D' or the letter 'M' to define the author and a figure denoting the number of the communication by that particular person. Thus '2.M.1' denotes the second letter in the whole series but the first one written by Munch. Letters written by Jelka Delius are numbered in sequence with those written by Frederick Delius. Munch's drafts of letters in Munch-Museet are not given an individual number in the series, but a suffix letter to follow the previous communication sent and received, and prefix 'Md.' followed by the number in order among the drafts. Thus Delius's postcard '47.D.34' is followed by Munch's draft reply '47a.Md.10'.

Two abbreviations have been generally used: 'OKK' and 'Sch'. 'OKK' stands for *Oslo Kommunes Kunstsamlinger* (Oslo Municipal Art Collections) and numbers appended to this prefix are Munch-Museet reference numbers. 'Sch.' followed by a number refers to Gustav Schiefler's catalogue of Munch's prints *Verzeichnis des graphischen Werks Edvard Munchs*.

Contents

	Preface	7
I	Early Lives	11
II	1889-1891	20
III	1892-1895	23
IV	1896-1898	29
	plates	33-40
V	1899-1902	49
VI	1903-1904	65
VII	1905-1908	78
VIII	1909-1918	99
	plates	105-112
IX	1918-1925	116
X	1926-1934	129
	Epilogue	141
	Notes to text	149
	Appendix A	174
	Appendix B	175
	Bibliography	178
	Index	183

Illustrations in the text
(all by Munch except p 118)

'Frederick Delius'	*Frontispiece*
'Funeral March'	46
'Evening'	54
'Phantoms'	96
Illustration from cover design of vocal score of *Fennimore and Gerda*	118
'The Kiss'	119
First page of Munch's draft letter to Delius	139
'The Scream'	177

To my wife, Margaret.

PREFACE

In 1963 I was working at the University in Oslo, engaged on researches into Scandinavian art. Some of this work was carried out in the new Munch-Museet (the Munch Museum), which had been opened that year in commemoration of the centenary of Edvard Munch's birth. When I was preparing to return ot England for Christmas I was approached by Johan H. Langaard, the first director of Munch-Museet. He told me that the museum had in its archives thirty-four letters and postcards from Frederick and Jelka Delius to Munch and that he felt that there should be some reciprocal letters from Munch in England. So far, however, his enquiries about these had elicited no replies. Could I help?

Back in London I approached the Delius Trust, who were extremely interested. Rachel Lowe-Dugmore, then the Trust's Archivist, took me to the 'Delius chest' in the Royal Academy of Music, from which she produced thirteen communications from Munch to Delius. She also introduced me to Dr Eric Fenby who again expressed great interest and he showed me the lithographic portrait which Munch made of Delius around 1920 and which had come to him on the death of Jelka Delius. Putting together both sides of the correspondence, which stretched from 1899 to 1934, and adding information from Munch's letters to his family, it became clear that artist and composer had been friendly from at least as early as 1896 until the year of Delius's death. I published articles on these findings in Olso in 1965 and in London the following year. Since then considerably more information has come to light. Ten drafts of letters from Munch to Delius have been discovered at Munch-Museet together with a further portrait sketch of the composer, made in 1922. Dr Lionel Carley, who succeeded Rachel Lowe-Dugmore as Archivist to the Delius Trust, has discovered in Oslo two much earlier drawings of Delius by Munch. These and references from other sources have established that the two men were acquainted as far back as the beginning of the eighteen nineties. Other light has come from letters of mutual friends, notably the Danish author Helge Rode and the Norwegian critic Jappe Nilssen. The complete correspondence and all other

7

available related material has been brought together in this book.

The correspondence is both fascinating and infuriating. Despite its long continuance it is often scrappy and repetitive and it is more frequently concerned with matter-of-fact arrangements than with discussion of ideas. A number of the letters and cards are useful in filling in details of the two men's movements and milieu, but much of the fascination lies in the gaps. What has survived makes it quite clear that quite a lot more has disappeared, but it does establish that artist and composer met from time to time over a period of at least thirty-five years and kept in touch through correspondence for longer than that.

I felt, therefore, that it would be most helpful to present the correspondence within a setting of the lives of Munch and Delius, with particular attention to mutual friends and other points of contact in their milieu. As I hope that this book will be of interest to readers on both sides of the North Sea, and as generally Norwegians are less familiar with the life of Delius and the British with the background of Munch, this should prove useful.

The correspondence has all been translated into English. Delius and Munch almost always wrote to each other in German, although Delius occasionally used Norwegian and once French. The German is often rather fractured, the spelling, particularly of names, is very erratic and the punctuation is frequently non-existent, and this has created problems over how to present the letters. In the end I decided that it was best merely to translate them and leave them as they stood, correcting no spelling and adding no punctuation, hoping that this would give some flavour of the originals. In my own part of the text the names are rendered correctly, to the best of my ability. At least the reader will not be irritated by the word 'sic' after every other name or by bracketed punctuation marks every few words. Lionel Carley tells me that he intends to use a similar procedure in presenting a selection from the letters in his forthcoming book, *Delius: a Life in Letters*.

The illustrations, with three exceptions, are all of works by Munch. Although contributions by other artists could also have been relevant, I felt that as the book is essentially a reconstruction of Munch's relationship with Delius this decision would be most appropriate.

Although the scale of this book is a modest one, research for it has been widespread and I am indebted to a great number of individuals and institutions for their help. First and foremost I am grateful to the Delius Trust and to Munch-Museet for allowing me to use, translate and publish letters and other documents in their possession, and for the full co-operation which both organizations have always given me. I am also deeply grateful to Munch-Museet for its generosity in lending me

8

photographs for almost all the illustrations. I am no less appreciative of
the support given me by the Norwegian Foreign Ministry and the
University of London's Central Research Fund, both of which have
financially helped me in making visits to Norway.

In England, I must start by thanking Lionel Carley. We have for
many years co-operated in our Scandinavian researches and his generosity in sharing material and in giving time has been unfailing. I am
also deeply grateful to other Delians, to Rachel Lowe-Dugmore, who in
her period as Archivist to the Delius Trust was equally supportive as
the present incumbent, to Eric Fenby, Robert Threlfall and Marjorie
Dickinson. Dr Carla Lathe has also helped generously, making suggestions and supplying me with information from her considerable knowledge of Munch's associates. Mrs Isobel Weber, the daughter of Eva
Mudocci, has given much valuable information about her mother and
encouraged me in every way. Anthony Martin has been most patient in
checking and helping with my translation from Norwegian and I am
equally grateful to the late Lisa Whitelaw for performing a similar
service with the German. Here I must also thank Clare and Horst
Ford-Wille. Lastly I most sincerely thank Jean McIntyre for her exper-
tise and patience in typing my manuscript and Lewis Foreman, my
publisher, for his imaginative co-operation.

In Norway, I am very grateful to past and present Directors of
Munch-Museet, Johan H. Langaard, the late Ragna Stang, Pål
Hougen and now Alf Bøe, and to Curators like the late Reidar Revold
and the present Gerd Woll. But perhaps I owe most of all, here, to the
present Principal Curator, Arne Eggum, and to his assistant, Sissel
Biørnstad, both of whom have shown infinite patience in helping and
advising my researches.

I must thank Dr Jan Askeland, Director of the Bergen Municipal Art
Collections, for reading my manuscript and Magne Malmanger, Principal Curator of Nasjonalgalleriet in Oslo, who has always supported
my Norwegian studies. I am also grateful to Leif Østby who, as editor
of *Kunst og Kultur*, has published my articles in Norway. Other Norwegian art historians to whom I am indebted include Ole Petter Bjerkek,
Hans-Jakob Brun, Trygve Nergaard and Bente Torjusen. Vivi Grefteg-
reff, for many years the librarian of Nasjonalgalleriet, has helped me to
find the answers to many questions, as has also the Universitets Bib-
liotek in Oslo. Waldemar Stabell has kindly provided me with material
about Eva Mudocci. I must especially record my appreciation of
Sigmund Torsteinson, previously Director of Grieg's home at Troldhaugen, the first Norwegian I met to quickly become enthusiastic to
make Delius's music better known in Norway. Over many years a

9

succession of cultural attachés at the Norwegian Embassy in London have given me full support and I should like particularly to thank Torbjørn Støverud, and his assistant, Ingrid Haugli.

I should like to thank the Danish Embassy in London and the Danish Foreign Office, in particular Flemming André Larsen and Bengt Petersen, for making investigations for me about Helge Rode. I am grateful to Mikal Rode, Helge Rode's son, for making available to me letters from Delius to his father and to H. P. Rohde for providing me with material about Munch and Denmark. The Swedish Institute has at all times been most helpful, as has Professor Stellan Ahlström, who on many occasions has given me information from his store of knowledge of Strindberg. I am greatly indebted to Mme Françoise Woimant, Conservateur en Chef chargée de l'estampe contemporaine of the Bibliothèque Nationale, Paris, for providing me with information about Munch's printers, while the Institut Français and the Goethe Institute in London have also kindly assisted me.

Finally I must thank all those other friends and colleagues in England and Scandinavia, too numerous to be individually recorded here, who have helped and encouraged me in so many different ways.

John Boulton Smith,
Bletchingley.
September 1982.

Chapter I.

EARLY LIVES

A LONG FRIENDSHIP BETWEEN TWO PERSONALITIES, EACH ACCEPTED AS AN important figure in his own art, is always something of considerable interest. Delius and Munch became acquainted some time around 1890 and they kept in touch until 1934, the year of the composer's death. This at first seems particularly remarkable as Munch had little connection with England and is only known to have had two English friends, the other being the violinist, Eva Mudocci. But of course Delius was a singularly cosmopolitan Englishman, coming of German parents and living most of his life in France. Add to this the particular love which Delius had for Norway and Norwegians and the fact that Munch spent much of his life abroad in Germany and France and one can readily see how it was cosmopolitan and Norwegian surroundings which provided the background for their friendship.

Although biographies of both men have been written many times, it seems appropriate here to indicate briefly their development prior to their meeting.

Delius's parents came from Bielfeld in Germany to settle in Bradford, where Julius Delius built up a business in the wool trade, becoming very wealthy and adopting British nationality. Frederick, or Fritz Theodor Albert Delius as he was christened, was the second son in a family of fourteen,[1] and was born in Bradford on 29 January 1862. Although Julius Delius was a business man and strict disciplinarian, he was a great lover of music and Frederick grew up in an atmosphere of chamber concerts and visits of distinguished performers such as Joachim and Piatti at his home. At first the staple musical diet provided consisted of the German classics, but the composer has said that his first great musical impressions were provided by hearing Chopin at the age of ten and Wagner slightly later. From an early age he played the piano, while violin lessons (from Mr Bauerkeller, of the Hallé Orchestra) started when he was six or seven. Apart from this musical background, his upbringing was that of a normal middle-class English boy, through a local preparatory school followed by Bradford Grammar School. Academically he did not distinguish himself, although he was brought up with more than one language, but he was enthusiastic over sport and outdoor pursuits, from which his liking for walking continued throughout his active live. His academic training was concluded with two year's study at the International College at Isleworth, just outside London, during which period he furthered his musical interests by attending concerts and opera in London and by composing his first song.

Despite his love of music, Julius Delius had no intention that any of his sons should take it up professionally, regarding it as an accepted fact that they would follow him in the wool trade. This assumption received its first blow when the eldest son, Ernest, defected to Australia and started sheep farming. Consequently, in 1881, Frederick was put firmly into the family business. However, as he showed no great aptitude for working on the firm's premises and as he was a good-looking young man, charming and an excellent mixer, it was soon decided to use him as a travelling agent to secure orders for the firm. After a period at the wool town of Stroud, in Gloucestershire, he was attached to a manufacturer at Chemnitz in Saxony. But in Germany Frederick was more interested in following music than wool. He was able to continue his violin lessons with the distinguished teacher Hans Sitt, and took advantage of the accessibility of Berlin, Dresden and Leipzig to enjoy the musical life there. It is hardly surprising that he was recalled home in some disfavour. In June of the following year Julius tried again, this time sending Frederick to Sweden. But after doing some business in Norköpping, a centre of the Swedish cloth trade, Stockholm and Christiania (as Norway's capital city, Oslo, was then called[2]), he escaped to the Norwegian mountains until summoned home by Julius in the autumn. The Norwegian mountains were to remain central to his life and art and his love affair with Norway may be said to commence at this time.

The next trip abroad was to the wool town of Saint Étienne, but the business part attracted him less than visits to Monte Carlo and Paris. In Paris he visited his uncle Theodor, who was living a life of sophisticated semi-retirement there and who in the future was to prove a great help to him. Theodor sympathized with his nephew, advising him to leave the wool trade, but not to break with his father.

In 1883 Delius was given the opportunity of another business trip to Norway. On this occasion he expanded his commitment to the country by learning sufficient of the language to understand the plays of Ibsen and Bjørnson, although he does not yet seem to have become acquainted with the artistic life of Christiania.

After these various forays, hardly convincing as business excercises,

12

however significant they may have been for the composer's ultimate development, Delius was able to convince his father of his unsuitability for the wool trade and to persuade him to try a quite different business tack. This proved to be the unlikely course of growing oranges in Florida. Florida was expanding fast at this time and an effective promotional campaign had encouraged a number of English to emigrate there. Likelihood of commercial success for enterprizing hardworkers must have encouraged Julius's hopes for his son while for Frederick it was an adventurous way of getting far away from Bradford and wool. Julius purchased the estate Solana Grove, on the St. Johns River and Frederick left England to take up residence there early in March 1884.

At Solana Grove Delius did not pursue the growing and marketing of oranges with any notable vigour, but the leisurely life and the beauty of the river scenery encouraged contemplation and thoughts of music. He was much impressed with the negro singing he heard, for example on the passing river boats, and the sound of voices in close harmony coming over the water was an effect which he later frequently tried to recapture in his music. The nearest town, Jacksonville, was only three hours journey by river, and in 1883-84 had a population of about 14,500. It was far enough south to be a winter tourist centre and visitors quadrupled the population during the season. It had a vigorous musical life, as Delius soon discovered, and he made many friends there. Outstanding among these was the organist Thomas F. Ward, who gave the young composer counterpoint lessons, which Delius later claimed were the best instructions he ever received.

After something over a year in Florida, Delius heard of an opening as a music teacher at Danville, Virginia and decided to go there. Here he seems to have had little difficulty in attracting pupils and for the first time in life he was able to earn a modest livelihood from music. As in Jacksonville, he soon made a number of friends, prominent among them being Robert Phifer, professor of music at the Roanake Female College (now Averett College), where Delius did some teaching. Phifer was the leader of musical life in Danville. He had studied at the Leipzig Conservatoire and no doubt confirmed Delius in his already formed opinion that he too must go to Leipzig to study. At Danville Delius again heard negroes singing, this time the hands in the tobacco stemmeries. One tune, which he had first heard in Florida, he now heard again; years later he was to use it for the theme and variations of *Appalachia*. Despite the many new friends and influences in America, Delius did not forget Scandinavia. Among the few small works which he wrote there two were songs to words by Bjørnson and Hans

13

Andersen, while musical friends in Florida included members of the Norwegian Mordt family who had settled there. One of these, Jutta Mordt (later Jutta Bell-Ranske) was to remain a friend for many years.

News had by now reached Julius Delius that his son had abandoned orange growing and was actually supporting himself by music. In consequence he was persuaded to consent to Frederick going to Leipzig to study music for eighteen months, doubtless encouraged by the thought that when qualified his son would be able to command more money as a music teacher.

Delius left America in June 1886, and after a short visit home to Bradford he proceeded to Leipzig in August to enrol at the Conservatoire. Here his principal teachers were Jadassohn, Reinecke and, once again, Sitt. But although he did work for some time at the formal disciplines, he soon became rather impatient with these. The most enduring legacy of the Leipzig period was through some of his new friendships. Frequently these were with Norwegians also studying there, such as the composers Christian Sinding and Johan Halvorsen and the violinist Arve Arvesen. In the summer of 1887 he revisited Norway, going walking on the Hardanger Vidde and in the Sognfjord area. On this occasion he experimented in taking down folk-songs (although he soon let this kind of fieldwork lapse) and began a notebook of musical ideas.

Back in Leipzig in the autumn, Delius for the first time met Edvard and Nina Grieg, who came to spend much of the winter of 1887-88 there. He and the Griegs quickly took to each other and a friendship was formed which was to last until their deaths. They celebrated a musical Christmas Eve in company with Halvorsen and Sinding, and on New Year's Eve the Griegs attended a party given by Delius.

Delius's time at Leipzig was nearing an end. Early in 1888 he was able to arrange a private performance of his orchestral *Florida Suite* in the restaurant Rosenthal, conducted by his teacher Hans Sitt and he finally left the city in the spring. In April he returned to Bradford, where he seems to have persuaded his father to allow him a trial period living with his uncle Theodor in Paris and working as a composer. Help in reconciling Julius to this course was provided by Grieg. After a concert given by him in London at the end of April, the Deliuses, father and son, entertained him to supper, and the composer strongly recommended a career in music for Frederick. Delius was able to leave for France with an annual allowance from his father, and although this was a reduced one it was to be supplemented by Theodor.

He spent the first few months in Paris at his uncle's home at 43 rue Cambon. Theodor lived in cultivated and sophisticated circles, numbering among his friends André Messager, who he introduced to his nephew. Delius enjoyed this existence, but gradually found that the social pleasures were hindering his composition. Towards the end of the year, after summer breaks in Brittany and Bradford, he took a cottage at Ville d'Avray, just outside Paris, where he could have more quiet time for composition. For the next six months his living was to alternate between there and the rue Cambon.

Although now settled in France, Delius maintained and deepened his connections with Norway. He kept in touch with Grieg and Sinding, sending both of them his new compositions for criticism. He even wrote to Grieg about the idea of living half of each year in Norway. Old Norwegian friends such as Arvesen came to Paris and Delius also made a number of new ones from among Scandinavian visitors there, such as Bergliot, the daughter of the writer Bjørnstjerne Bjørnson.

His new compositions showed a predilection for Norwegian and Scandinavian subjects (although America was also remembered in the tone poem, *Hiawatha*). In the Melodrama *Paa Vidderne* (On the Mountains) he set Ibsen's extended text for speaker and orchestra, dedicating it to Grieg. Although it was never performed in this form, a few years later Delius re-cast some of the same material as a concert overture of the same name. Five songs (1888) were dedicated to Nina Grieg, and were published by Augener in 1890 as *5 LIEDER (aus dem Norwegischen)*. These were settings of poems by five different Norwegian authors including, interestingly, one by Andreas Munch, great-uncle of Edvard. (Delius frequently made his settings of Norwegian poems in German translations, no doubt feeling that this would give them more chance of interesting publishers and performers.) Others were the *7 LIEDER (aus dem Norwegischen)* (1889-90), settings of Ibsen, Bjørnson and A. O. Vinje, also dedicated to Nina Grieg. In *Sakuntala* (1889), for tenor and orchestra, he was inspired to set a Danish poem, by Holger Drachmann.

It can be seen then that between his first visit to Scandinavia and the end of the decade, his initial attraction by Scandinavian countries and literature, and particularly Norway, had broadened and deepened. He had found something vital for his life and art and had acquired a large number of friends and acquaintances, thus making future friendships with congenial spirits like Munch easy and natural.

Edvard Munch, like Delius, came from a middle-class family, although, unlike the case of the Bradford wool-merchant, his father was not a wealthy man. But the family was an honourable one in nineteenth century Norway, a number of its members were servants of church or state while others achieved reputations in the artistic or academic fields. Some successfully combined both, and it is worth remembering that in Norway art (particularly literature) and politics were far more intermingled during the nineteenth century than in England. One ancestor, Jacob Munch was an engineer who also became Norway's leading portrait painter of his epoch; another, Johan Storm Munch was a bishop and a poet, while his son Andreas Munch was a poet and playwright, (this was the Munch whose poem *Solnedgang* (Sunset) was to be set to music by Delius); Edvard's uncle, Peter Andreas Munch was an outstanding historian.

Edvard's father, Christian Munch, was a medical man, deeply religious and with a great love of literature. He had worked for some years as a ship's doctor, before marrying and settling at Løten, about a hundred kilometres north of the capital. It was here that Edvard was born, on 12 December 1863. The following year the family moved into Christiania, where Christian Munch was a regimental doctor who also accepted a certain number of private, usually poor, patients. Although Dr Munch's army salary would have been good, he does not seem to have been very skilful in managing money, so the family were not particularly well off.

Munch did not enjoy the same healthy growing up as Delius, and fatal illness dogged his family. His mother died of tuberculosis when he was five years old. Of his four brothers and sisters, Sophie died of the same complaint when the artist was fourteen, Andreas died at the age of thirty, while Laura was later to become mentally deranged. Edvard himself was a delicate and sickly child and he worried about his health throughout his life, although in fact he was to live to an active old age. Small wonder that he should write: 'Sickness and insanity were the black angels that hovered over my cradle and have since followed me throughout my life'.[3] Themes of sickness and death were to feature large in his art, particularly during the crucial decade of the eighteen-nineties.

Despite these tragedies, Munch's family life was not of unrelieved gloom. After his mother's death her place was taken by her unmarried sister, Karen Bjølstad, who remained the centre of the family throughout her life. She was a kind and talented woman, who encouraged the artistic tendencies of the children and who was early convinced of Edvard's talent. Christian, the father, was a basically affectionate and cultivated man, and although he became more pietistic and moody after his wife's death, he does not seem to have been severely opposed to Edvard's artistic career, While Edvard was a young man his divergence from the family's religious beliefs and his bohemian associations caused considerable difficulties between them, but the degree of estrangement never became the great gulf which ultimately separated Frederick and Julius Delius. After Christian Munch's death in 1889, Karen Bjølstad kept the family together, and despite his living much abroad and his very different mode of life, Edvard retained a strong sense of family loyalty, keeping in touch with her and his youngest sister, Inger, throughout their lives.

After a school education somewhat interrupted by illness, in 1879 Munch was enrolled by his father at the Technical College with a view to becoming an engineer. However this did not prove successful, partly due to ill health, and Karen Bjølstad helped persuade Christian to allow the boy to leave and take up art seriously. In 1881, he became a pupil of the sculptor Julius Middelthun at the Royal School of Design. The following year he joined with six other young artists to take a studio in the centre of Christiania. At this time the 'new wave' in Norwegian art was dominated by a number of artists who were in close touch with Paris. They were particularly attracted by the type of French painting between the Barbizon School and the Impressionists perhaps best described as naturalism, work, by artists like Bastien-Lépage and Manet. These men included Christian Krohg, Frits Thaulow, Hans Heyerdahl and Erik Werenskiold. Munch's development owed something to most of these artists at this stage. Christian Krohg occupied a studio next door to the one taken by the young artists and advised them over their work. Munch was later to acknowledge his respect for both Krohg and Heyerdahl. Frits Thaulow ran an informal 'open-air academy' at Modum a little way from Christiania during the summers and Munch was painting at Modum at the same time. Thaulow (a distant relative of Munch) provided a strong link with French art, being a brother-in-law of Paul Gauguin, and Gauguin himself exhibited three paintings in the Christiania Autumn Exhibition of 1884, an exhibition in which Munch also participated. And it was also Thaulow who made it financially possible for Munch to make his first visit to Paris in 1885. (Delius was later to meet both Krohg and Thaulow, although he found the latter unsympathetic.)

Paris was to prove of the greatest importance to Munch and his art, but we do not really know just what impact this three week visit had on him. He wrote home that he had visited the Salon and the Louvre, but nothing of what he had seen of more modern French art. However, judging by his work of the time, he would certainly seem to have known something of Manet and Impressionism, whether discovered in Paris or through his Norwegian confrères.

During the eighteen-eighties Munch's art made rapid strides. At the beginning of the decade he was making tight little oil paintings, views

17

of Christiania and home interiors of members of his family. From about 1883, influenced by the naturalistic painters, his work became larger, much more confidently and freely painted. His range of subjects expanded, particularly in the direction of painting people, and he became very aware of the importance of light and atmosphere. 1885-86 were key years in which he painted his first mature masterpieces. His full length portrait of his fellow-painter Jensen-Hjell (1885), indebted both to Krohg and Manet, is masterfully accomplished. *Tête-a-tête* and the sketch *The Dance* (both 1885 and painted before his visit to Paris) capture a fleeting atmosphere with flecks of colour applied with broken brushstrokes. And in *The Sick Child* (1885-86), which he regarded as his real break-through picture, he experimented with impressionistic techniques to achieve the special atmospheric poetry for his tragic message. In this painting, intimately connected with recollections of the death of his sister Sophie, he for the first time realized what was to be the typical Munch subject; a poetic comment on the deep basic themes of mankind, in this case the confrontation of youth and death, distilled from actual visual experiences into a concentrated statement.

1886-89 may be described as years of consolidation. Technically his paintings did not become more daring than *The Sick Child*, but continued as realistic naturalism with impressionistic touches. Two probable masterpieces from 1886, *Puberty* and *The Day After* were destroyed by fire and although he repainted the themes later this does not tell us quite what the style of the originals was like. His subjects remained portraits, scenes with figures and landscapes. 1889 was another key year and its most important paintings include *Inger on the Beach*, the portrait of Hans Jaeger and *Spring*. The large painting *Spring* was another composition deriving from the sick child theme. In it, Munch declared: 'I took my leave of Impressionism and Realism'.[4]

During the second half of the eighties, a number of Munch's subjects were drawn from the world of the 'Christiania Bohemians', a world with which Munch for a time became closely involved. Basically these bohemians, taking their inspiration mainly from Paris, strove for expanded human rights and an increase in personal and artistic freedom. Their ideas on self-expression, free love, unimportance of family ties, and so on, cut right across the Protestant middle-class, and somewhat provincial, standards of contemporary Norway. The leader, Hans Jaeger, was a writer whose anarchist persuasions called for the overthrow of the existing social system. He received a two-month prison sentence for the publication of his novel *From the Christiania Bohemians*, all copies of which were confiscated by the police. Christian Krohg was another prominent member of the bohemians, editing their paper, *The Impress-*

ionist. His own socially critical novel *Albertine* (about the life of a prostitute) was also suppressed, although Krohg, who came from a highly-respected family, was merely fined. He retaliated by continuing his campaign with a huge painting of a theme drawn from the book (which ironically at a later date ended up in the national art collection). It was natural that a young progressive like Munch should be drawn through friends like Krohg into this bohemian circle, and Jaeger, in particular, was to exert a considerable influence on him. However, although he frequented the circle and adopted much of its restless bohemian life-style, a certain reserve and fastidiousness in his nature prevented him from becoming completely absorbed into it. For a few years Munch was pulled by Jaeger's radical doctrines into conflict with the traditional religious and social values of his family, thus causing difficulties and unhappiness between him and his father. The death of Dr Munch in 1889, without he and his son really becoming reconciled, gave the artist much pain and caused him to withdraw a little from the bohemians, although remaining friendly with individual members.

Munch's status in Norwegian art by 1889 was rather equivocal. The public disliked his more daring work and the portrait of Jensen-Hjell and *The Sick Child*, for example, came under attack when they were exhibited. Much of this was due to the impressionistic technique which would have looked unfinished to many eyes, blinding them to he fact that *The Sick Child* was the sort of theme highly acceptable in academic circles everywhere during the later nineteenth century. His association with the bohemians would also no doubt have helped him to a reputation as a wild man of art. Amongst informed artistic opinion, however, Munch was generally regarded as being very talented, although some disliked the way in which he appeared to be using his talents. In April 1889 he held a large one-man exhibition in Christiania, in fact a retrospective exhibition of his work, in support of an application for a state scholarship to study abroad. This application was supported by a number of established Norwegian artists, Krohg, Thaulow and Heyerdahl among them. It proved successful, although the award of the scholarship was qualified by the recommendations that Munch should find a teacher for life drawing in Paris and that he should submit examples of his work at the end of the year. The award, of 1500 kroner, was initially for one year, but it was renewed during the two succeeding ones, although not without protest by Bjørnson. The artist arrived in Paris about the beginning of October. He was to remain based mainly in France until the end of March, 1892.

Chapter II

1889–1891

THE FIRST CONCRETE EVIDENCE OF A MEETING BETWEEN MUNCH AND Delius so far to have come to light consists of two drawings made by the artist of the composer at the beginning of the eighteen-nineties. One of these is in a book of sketches most of which were made by Munch in St. Cloud or Paris between late 1889 and May 1890. This sketch (OKK T127 p.25, reverse) has been dated by Munch-Museet as 1890-91. It is a threequarter view head and shoulders portrait, sensitively drawn and a good likeness of the composer. (A further sketch in the same book — T127 p.45, reverse — could also possibly relate to this, but it is very slight and schematic and although the hair, moustache and collar are somewhat similarly positioned there is no real likeness.) The second drawing is reproduced in the Norwegian paper *Verdens Gang*, 12 October 1891 and initialled 'EM'. The head and shoulders are seen almost in profile. Although hair-style and clothes are similar to those in T127, the likeness appears slightly less striking. The drawing accompanies the review of a concert given by the Christiania Music Society on 10 October 1891, in which the concert overture [symphonic poem] *Paa Vidderne* by Delius was played. This piece was a re-working of his earlier Ibsen Melodrama and the occasion marked the first public performance of any orchestral work by Delius.[1]

A first meeting between Delius and Munch seems certain to have occurred either in 1890 or 1891, or possibly even as early as the summer of 1889. From late autumn 1888 until probably near the end of May 1889, Delius's principal base was the cottage he had rented at Ville d'Avray. Here he could work quietly, yet keep in touch with Paris, where he sometimes stayed in his Uncle Theodor's apartment. From June to September he was away on a visit to Norway. He travelled with his friend the composer Christian Sinding, going through Christiania and visiting Arve Arvesen at his family home in Hamar before arriving at Troldhaugen, the home of the Griegs just outside Bergen, in the middle of July. The party then proceeded to make a tour of the Jotunheim mountains. Munch was in Norway during 1889 until the autumn. In April he had his first one-man exhibition in Christiania and

20

applied for a state scholarship to study abroad, which was granted in July. Much of the summer he spent in Aasgaardstrand, a village on the Christiania fjord to which he was to become very attached, where he rented a house.

Delius returned to Paris in September, and in October he took an apartment in Croissy-sur-Seine, then a small town outside Paris, which had been much patronized by the Impressionist painters. Croissy remained his working base, with excursions to Paris, until his summer travels in 1890, which this year saw him not in Norway but in Leipzig during June, to be followed by Jersey, Normandy and Brittany, interspersed with times in Paris and Croissy. Munch came to France on his scholarship at the beginning of October 1889, and stayed in and around Paris until the following May when he returned to Norway. For some time he attended Léon Bonnat's art school in the mornings and by the new year he was living in St. Cloud, where he was to start formulating the new direction of his art. He went back to Norway in May, to spend the summer there, returning to France in November.

Delius continued his Croissy-Paris pattern of life through the winter and spring of 1891, until it was time for a summer visit to Norway, when he gave up the Croissy apartment. On this occasion he visited the Bjørnsons and the Griegs. He also spent some time with the conductor Iver Holter, who was to give the first performance of *Paa Vidderne* in October, and Delius prolonged his stay in Norway to attend this event before returning to France. Munch was in Paris during the early part of 1891, before leaving for Nice, and was back there again in May. He returned to spend the summer in Norway, leaving again in the autumn to travel via Copenhagen to Paris.

So the movements of the two men would appear to have provided a number of opportunities for their meeting, either in Norway or in France. Delius's enthusiasm for Norway led him to keep very much in touch with Scandinavian circles in and around Paris and at times he almost gives the impression of collecting any interesting Norwegians who turned up there. And he and Munch had a number of mutual friends and acquaintances who could have provided the link. For example, Arve Arvesen was now spending much of his time in Paris. Munch also knew the violinist and painted his portrait some time between 1887 and 1890, (private collection). Delius knew several Norwegian painters. In February 1889 he wrote to Grieg: 'Last Saturday Arvesen, a violinist and Soot, a Norwegian painter, came to me at Ville d'Avray'.[2] He also knew the artist Gudmund Stenersen who, together with Grieg, tried unsuccessfully to persuade him to join them in the mountains of Norway during the summer of 1890.[3] Eyolf Soot and Stenersen were both contemporaries of Munch. Soot had attended Léon Bonnat's art school, as did many Norwegian artists, and when Munch made his first visit to Paris in 1885, he and Soot travelled there together. Stenersen studied with Bonnat during the winter 1889-90, when Munch was also attending there. And in November 1890 Munch's aunt, Karen Bjølstad, wrote to him in France describing the Christiania Autumn Exhibition and singles out the paintings by Soot and Stenersen for comment, as if she thought that Munch would be particularly interested to hear about them.[4]

However, despite these and other possible connecting links, it is still not yet possible to determine precisely either when Delius and Munch first met or when the two drawings were made. Age of the sitter and clothing establish that they were drawn during the same period, although not necessarily at the same time. I think it likely that the drawing in the sketch-book (OKK T127) was made first, because of the dating of the other sketches in the book. The *Verdens Gang* drawing (the original of which has not survived) was not made in the same book, as there is no trace of a leaf having been removed. Most likely this second drawing was made in the summer or autumn of 1891 in connection with the concert, and Munch-Museet considers this to be the first occasion on which a drawing from Munch was commissioned by *Verdens Gang*. The commission may have come through Christian Krohg, who himself wrote for the same paper, or possibly through Munch's contacts with muscians like Arvesen or Hjalmar Borgström, both of whom he had painted prior to this. It seems likely that he would have made this second drawing from life, as Delius was in Norway that summer and autumn and Munch probably did not leave Christiania until November, but it is also possible that he might have made it when the composer was not present, basing it on the sketch-book drawing.

Most of the material in this chapter has of necessity been conjectural. However the two drawings remain as solid evidence of how early the long friendship was begun.

Chapter III

1892–1895

LITTLE EVIDENCE OF CONTACT BETWEEN MUNCH AND DELIUS DURING THE next few years has come to light. After returning to Paris in 1891, Delius settled in the city itself, taking an apartment at 33 rue Ducouëdic, in the Petit Montrouge quarter. This was to remain his home for the next few years. Munch, on the other hand, spent most of this period either in Norway or Germany.

In 1893 Munch's young friend and relative, Ludvig Orning Ravensberg, went to Paris to begin his career as an artist. On the first page of his notebook-diary is written Delius's name and his Paris address at 43 rue Cambon. Alf Bøe considers it likely that he was given the address by Munch,[1] although the handwriting of the entry is Ravensberg's. The fact that the address given is that of Theodor Delius rather than that of Frederick suggests that it had been given to Ravensberg by someone who had not been in touch with the composer recently. Unfortunately the diary does not help us with further reference to Delius.

During the same year, however, Delius was in Norway from July until September, sharing a cottage with Sinding at Drøbak, between Christiania and Aasgaardstrand, and visiting friends in the area. Munch's life-long supporter and biographer, Jens Thiis, has recorded his meeting with Munch, Delius and the Danish writer Helge Rode together at Aasgaardstrand at that time. In his *Minneord om Helge Rode*[2] Thiis writes that he met Rode the summer after the Dane had published *Hvide Blomster*,[3] and he suggests that the meeting took place in August 1893. He wrote that Munch had 'invited him there. Munch's German-English friend the composer Delius was also there'.[4] In a letter which he drafted to Delius much later, probably in 1929, Munch refers to a meeting between Rode, Delius and himself at Aasgaardstrand 'over thirty years ago' (see p. 136 below). This could refer to the 1893 meeting, but I like to think that the three men, who all became very friendly, also met at Aasgaardstrand towards the end of the nineties, and if I am correct the reference might equally apply to a later meeting (see pp. 58-59, below).

Clearly by the close of 1893 Munch and Delius must have been at least moderately well-acquainted, although their relationship would hardly yet have had the chance of filling out into the companionship which grew during Munch's extended stay in Paris during 1896-97. But this later comradeship was to grow in a circle of friends and acquaintances which had gradually been building up since the beginning of the nineties.

In November 1892, Munch had been invited to hold a one-man show with the Verein Berliner Künstler (Association of Berlin Artists). But his art proved far too radical for Berlin and shocked the society into closing it after only a week. However, this earned the artist a notoriety in Germany as a leader of the avant-garde and led to a succession of exhibitions there. He settled in Berlin, and began to evolve his crucially important *Life Frieze* series of paintings, which he was later to describe as 'a poem of love, life and death'.[5] Here he frequented the Scandinavian-slanted bohemian circle which congregated at the tavern nicknamed by Strindberg 'At the Black Piglet'. This circle included the writers August Strindberg, Stanislaw Przybyszewski and Richard Dehmel and from within it the art critic and historian Julius Meier-Graefe was to launch the cultural periodical *Pan*. A number of the circle's members also knew Paris and when in 1895 the group started to break up several of them went to France.

Strindberg in fact moved into Paris in the summer of 1894, to remain for some two eventful years. Here he frequented the same circle as did Delius.

Since moving into the Latin Quarter, Delius had been working hard. He had written two operas, *Irmelin* and *The Magic Fountain* as well as a number of smaller works. However he was still far from getting professional performances of his work, a notable exception being the performance in Monte Carlo of his syphonic poem *Sur les cimes*, another name for *Paa Vidderne*. By early in 1894 he was moving into a new phase of his life in Paris, becoming absorbed into a genuinely bohemian circle, at the core of which were Paul Gauguin and William Molard. Meeting places were at 6 rue Vercingétorix, where both men had studio apartments, and at the small *crémerie* of Madame Charlotte (Caron) at 13 rue de la Grande Chaumière. Facing the *crémerie* was the well known art school, the *Académie Colarossi*, and many artists took their meals at Madame Charlotte's. This circle was a cosmopolitan one, with Scandinavians and friends of Scandinavia well represented.

William Molard was the son of a Mantes organist, and his mother, Rachel Hamilton had been born in Norway. Molard's passion in life was music; he played the piano fluently if inaccurately and he also composed. Although none of these compositions are known to survive today, references to them by his contemporaries are usually not very complimentary.[6] He was also very interested in Scandinavia. His father had endeavoured to make Norwegian culture better known in France, and Molard was married to a Swedish wife, the sculptress Ida Ericson, whose daughter by a previous union, Judith, also lived with them. He could write in Norwegian. Molard had a clerical post in the French Ministry of Agriculture, which earned him just sufficient to devote his free time to music and to follow his sociable and bohemian way of life. For a number of years the Molard home was a gathering place for French and Scandinavian artists, writers and musicians and the Molards 'lived far from private lives, with visitors dropping in at all hours of the day, but mostly in the evenings when cheerful parties would often develop'.[7]

This circle was extended by the advent of Paul Gauguin, who became both neighbour and close friend of the Molards. After his first visit to Tahiti, from which he returned to France in August 1893, Gauguin settled in the rue de la Grande Chaumière, becoming one of the artists to frequent Madame Charlotte's *crémerie*. Some time at the turn of 1893/94 he moved to no. 6 rue Vercingétorix (also owned by his rue de la Grande Chaumière landlord), taking the apartment above the Molards. Gauguin liked the easy-going way in which the Molard's friends also looked in on him and soon commenced his weekly at homes, starting with little tea parties.

It is perhaps interesting to see some of the names of those who formed part of the circle at either 6 rue Vercingétorix or Madame Charlotte's *crémerie* (or both). Naturally this list includes both regular intimates and occasional visitors, and not all of them were there concurrently:

Artists
Ivan Aguéli (Swedish)
Ida Ericson (Swedish)
Pierre Bonnard (French)
Charles Boutet de Monvel (French)
Paul Gauguin ⎫
Albert Marquet ⎪
Daniel de Monfreid ⎪
Henri Rousseau ⎬ (French)
Emile Schuffenecker ⎪
Paul Sérusier ⎪
Edouard Vuillard ⎭
Paul Herrmann (German)
Alphonse Mucha (Czech)
Edvard Munch (Norwegian)
Roderic O'Conor (Irish)
Wladyslaw Slewinski (Polish)

Musicians
Frederick Delius (English)
Edvard Grieg ⎫
Christian Sinding ⎬ (Norwegian)
William Molard ⎫
Léon Moreau ⎪
Maurice Ravel ⎬ (French)
Florent Schmitt ⎭

Writers
Jacques Arsène Coulangheon
Alfred Jarry ⎫
Julien Leclercq ⎬ (French)
Paul Roinard ⎭
Vilhelm Krag (Norwegian)
August Strindberg (Swedish)

25

Judith Ericson-Molard has left us a vivid comment on this circle: 'Gauguin bubbles over with an inner richness, he is the *master* overshadowing all the others, even Delius — He didn't bear the mark of sordid poverty that was on all the artists of our milieu, both those who have succeeded since those days and those who didn't make the grade (with the exception of Delius who, obviously, is rich)'.[8] This is one of a number of occasions where Delius was referred to as rich by his friends during the nineties. In fact he was far from this, but he dressed elegantly, did not have to work for a living and received an allowance from home which, although very modest, must have seemed like riches to many of his circle.

Delius had known Molard at least as far back as April, 1890, although it was probably not until the turn of 1893/94 that he really became part of the Molard-Gauguin circle. Knowing Molard's enthusiasm for Scandinavians, Delius was always ready to bring his own Scandinavian friends into contact with him. For example he introduced Christian Sinding to him in 1892, and it seems possible that Grieg's connection with the Molard circle owed something to Delius. Grieg took to Molard, and Molard and Julien Leclercq together translated some of the composer's texts into French. The Norwegian poet and close friend of Munch, Vilhelm Krag, met Delius in 1893, (Delius set one of his poems to music about this time) and Lionel Carley considers likely that it was Delius who introduced him into the Molard circle.[9] A little later Delius may have performed a similar service for Munch.

Gauguin and Delius would probably have met around the turn of 1893/94, either at Madame Charlotte's *crémerie* or at the Molards, although he had known another of Gauguin's close friends a little earlier. This was the painter Daniel de Monfreid, who made a pastel portrait of the composer in February 1893. Although Delius probably never became an intimate of Gauguin, he greatly admired his work and was later to buy his great painting *Nevermore*. Moreover the tropical and exotic had a fascination for Delius as well as Gauguin, ever since his stay in Florida during 1884-85. One opera *The Magic Fountain* (1893-94 or 95) was on an American Indian subject set in Florida, while another, *Koanga* (started in 1895) is set on a plantation in Louisiana, with negro slaves as its heroes.

In August of 1894, August Strindberg arrived in Paris. It was by no means his first visit to France. During the eighteen-nineties the Parisian avant-garde artistic world was going through a period of considerable interest in things Scandinavian. One of its principal manifestations was an interest in Scandinavian drama, first Ibsen, then Strindberg. It started with Antoine's production of *Ghosts* at the *Théâtre-Libre* in 1890 and in 1893 there were no less than five productions of different Ibsen plays. Antoine produced Strindberg's *Miss Julie* in 1893 and the following year Lugné-Pöe produced his *Creditors* with the *Théâtre de l'Oeuvre* troupe. In December of 1894 the same company put on *The Father*, the first night being attended by Gauguin. By the time Strindberg came to Paris he had severed his links with the 'Black Piglet' circle in Berlin. At the same time his second marriage, with Frida Uhl, was starting to break up and they finally parted in November that year. In France Strindberg hoped to find new recognition and fulfilment. Not only were his plays being produced, but he prepared essays on a number of subjects for the Paris journals, painted pictures which he hoped to sell there, and generally hoped to find a sympathetic reception for his chemical experiments and his ideas on alchemy and mysticism.

Through mutual friends of Ida Ericson, Strindberg came into contact with the Molard circle towards the end of 1894[10] and spent Christmas with them. Indeed, Strindberg had known her some years earlier in Stockholm. Through this circle he became friendly with Gauguin, who introduced him to Madame Charlotte's *crémerie*. Gauguin and Strindberg saw a lot of each other during the first part of 1895, and the artist used a letter from the Swede to preface the catalogue of his final auction/exhibition in February at the Hôtel Drouot. Also about February Strindberg went to live in rue de la Grande Chaumière, just opposite the *crémerie*. Strindberg and Madame Charlotte seem to have got on well, and kept up a correspondence even after he had returned to Sweden. The paintings at her small restaurant included works by Gauguin, Mucha, Slewinski and Strindberg, and the *crémerie* also provided the principal setting for the author's comedy *Crimes and Crimes*.[11]

Delius probably met Strindberg towards the end of 1894 through the Molards and continued acquaintanceship with him through to 1896, when Strindberg left Paris in the summer, returning to Sweden. Delius appears to have known Strindberg fairly well, allowing for the author's difficult temperament and paranoid tendencies, as his short memoir of Strindberg (reproduced pp. 32, 41) speaks of dining together at Madame Charlotte's and of long afternoon walks taken in each other's company. Apart from mutual friends and Delius's enthusiasm for Scandinavians, a particular common interest must have been occultism and mysticism. Both knew the celebrated Parisian occultist Papus (Dr Gérard Encausse). Delius had met Papus by 1893, and in 1894 produced a booklet in collaboration with him, entitled *Anatomie et Physiologie de l'Orchestre*.

It has been claimed that Munch visited Paris twice during 1895, in

June and September[12] and a possible meeting with Gauguin on the earlier visit has been suggested.[13] However, Munch-Museet has no material in its archives which would confirm either of these visits and a letter written by Karen Bjølstadt on 18th June to Munch in Germany even suggests that he may not have gone to Paris at all: 'It is so good that you are coming home after all, and we certainly thought so, even though we had read in the papers that you were going to visit Paris and not come home to Norway this summer'.[14] In any case a summer meeting with Gauguin would have been impossible, as the French artist had left for Tahiti in March and before the end of June had reached New Zealand, from where he wrote to William Molard.[15]

However, if Munch did visit Paris in 1895, it would probably have been in connection with his graphic art as the French offices of the magazine *Pan* were now advertising some of his prints for sale. He might have been making some sort of reconnaissance for the long stay he was to make there during the two following years.

Chapter IV

1896-1898

BOTH DELIUS AND MUNCH SPENT THE BULK OF 1896 IN PARIS.
Delius was engaged on several major works, the opera *Koanga*, the first version of *Appalachia* (at this time for orchestra alone, subtitled *American Rhapsody*) and, possibly, on his 'fantasy overture' *Over the Hills and Far Away*. In the summer he visted Norway again, and in September he was in Karlsruhe trying (unsuccessfully) to interest the conductor Felix Mottl in one of his two completed operas. Delius in fact was at rather a difficult period, a period of implications of doubt and change. 'But now the Delius family were growing restless about what seemed to be an absolute non-return on all the money that had for years gone into maintaining a composer whose main works stayed unperformed and unsought after. Things came to a head when Theodor resolutely refused a request from his nephew for money to help get the new opera performed, with the consequence, it seems, that uncle and nephew fell out'.[1] Sir Thomas Beecham tells us, in addition, that Julius had cut his son's allowance by half, and that Delius was only able to keep going by financial help from an aunt in Berlin.[2] These events happened in the later part of 1895. By 1896 Delius must probably have realised that the chances of getting his music performed in France were as remote as ever and it was to be another year before his attempts for performance in Germany started to look up. By late 1896 he was seriously considering moving to London and had some hopes (unfulfilled) of a perforance of the *American Rhapsody* in Bradford. But in January of that year he had had a meeting which was to have the greatest possible importance for his future, although it was several years before the full significance was to become apparent. He had met at a dinner party a young painter, studying at the *Académie Colarossi*, called Helene ('Jelka') Rosen, whose family came from Schleswig-Holstein. At their first meeting they talked of Grieg and Nietzsche, two days later he visited her with a volume of his songs and a friendship was begun which was to lead ultimately to their marriage. So for Delius, although life during 1896 in Paris might on the surface be going on much as before, underneath were portents for change. For Munch, Paris during the

same period was to mark a real step forward in his work with a number of modest successes.

Munch came to Paris at the end of February in 1896 and remained based there until the summer of 1897. There were no doubt a number of reasons which persuaded him to move there from Germany at this stage. An important one must have been the growing importance to him of graphic art during 1894 and 1895. Paris was the undisputed world centre for modern printmaking, the place where, more than any other, forward-looking stylistic and technical experiments were being introduced. One has only to think of names such as Felix Valotton, Toulouse-Lautrec, Gauguin, Jules Chéret, Alphonse Mucha, Bonnard and Vuillard and many of their colleagues in the *Nabis* group on the artists' side, or Lemercier and Auguste Clot as probably the most technically brilliant and inventive of the actual printers, to understand the special draw towards Paris for a man like Munch.

Moreover the 'Black Piglet' circle in Berlin had broken up and the journal *Pan* was being taken over by a nationalistic Germanic clique with very different ideas for it than the original progressive and international aims of Meier-Graefe. Meier-Graefe himself had moved to Paris in the autumn of 1895 and when Munch arrived there was employed at Samuel Bing's new *Galeries de l'Art Nouveau*. Meier-Graefe, a close friend of Munch, would have been able to greatly help the artist through his many contacts. Here one could instance his publications of Munch prints and Munch's exhibition at Bing's in 1896.

A third reason may have come through Munch's large exhibition in Christiania in October 1895. This was his first exhibition in his home town for three years and it contained many of the pictures he had painted in Germany. Its reception was generally bad and demonstrated how far the artist still was from any kind of general acceptance in Norway. However Thadée Natanson, who with his two brothers edited the French avant-garde journal *La Revue Blanche*, was in Norway at the time, visited the exhibition, and contributed a piece about it in the November issue of his journal.[3] He concluded the piece by advising Munch to come to Paris. The artist must have been further encouraged to take this step when the following month *La Revue Blanche* reproduced his lithograph *The Scream* with his own accompanying text.[4]

This is not the place in which to discuss Munch's achievements in Paris during this year and a half but one can at least list them. First and foremost must come his development as a graphic artist, especially the woodcuts he now started to make, influenced particularly by Japanese prints and by Gauguin,[5] and his coloured lithographs. Then Munch exhibited his work three times during this stay. Two of these occasions were at the *Salon des Indépendants*, in both 1896 and 1897, where he showed ten paintings each time. He also held a larger exhibition at Bing's *Salon de l'Art Nouveau* during May and June 1896, which is believed to have contained about twenty-five paintings and fifty prints.[6] It was in connection with this last exhibition that Strindberg wrote his account of Munch's paintings which was published in *La Revue Blanche*.[7] (Munch also exhibited a few works in *L'Art Cosmopolite* in 1897, but this does not appear to have been a major affair).

Reaction to these exhibitions in the press was mixed, but some of it was sympathetic and one review, that by Edouard Gerard in *La Presse*,[8] he liked sufficiently to keep a cutting of it throughout his life, using it for exhibition introductions on two subsequent occasions. Later Munch was also to write of the French appreciation for pictures from the *Life Frieze* shown at these exhibitions.

Other modest successes which Munch could credit to this stay were the two lithographs he produced to advertise Lugné-Poë's Ibsen productions at the *Théâtre de l'Oeuvre*, *Peer Gynt* in 1896, and *John Gabriel Borkman* in 1897. He was invited by the dealer Ambrose Vollard to contribute a print to the first album in the series *Peintres Graveurs*, and he supplied the lithograph *Fear*, printed in black and red. He became acquainted with Stéphane Mallarmé, then the doyen of symbolist poets, and produced two portraits of him, a lithograph and an etching. A promising commission was one from *La Societé des Cents Bibliophiles* to provide some illustrations for a collector's edition of Baudelaire's *Les Fleurs du mal*. Unfortunately the president of the society, Monsieur Piat, died and the project was abandoned, although Munch did make some preliminary sketches for the illustrations.

All in all it is interesting just how many contacts Munch seemed to make in Paris, so many of them involved in the Molard-Gauguin circle, or in the circles round the literary/artistic journals such as *La Revues Blanche* and *Le Mercure de France*. And these were so often the circles in which Delius also moved. Exactly how Munch first came to meet Molard is not known. Lionel Carley thinks that the introduction may have come through Delius (*Delius, the Paris Years*, op. cit, p. 49). Bente Torjusen, however, considers (op. cit, pp. 197-8) that Munch probably got to know the Molards through their mutual friend, the Norwegian journalist, editor and publisher, Karl Vilhelm Hammer, who had often stayed with them.

We have four so-far discovered references to their connection. An early one comes in a letter Munch wrote home to his aunt Karen Bjølstad, dated 27 March 1896:[9]

31

'I am together with Delius and Vilhelm Krag these days — they both live near me — the Latin Quarter as it's called —.'

Shortly before writing this letter Munch had met Daniel de Monfreid, as the Frenchman recorded in his diary entry for 20 March 1896.[10] Delius and de Monfreid were now close friends and Lionel Carley tells us that: 'It was probably at Delius's suggestion that Munch then paid a first and unexpected call on the Monfreids, who were just settling down to lunch. Daniel was obviously taken with the newcomer, as he repaid the call in two days' time'.[11] On 31 March, Delius, de Monfreid, the Molards and the Schuffeneckers all attended the *vernissage* of the *Salon des Indépendants*. It is likely that they would have met Munch there, as he was one of the exhibitors.

During the summer Delius was in Norway, but back in Paris in the autumn he was seeing Munch again. On 8 December of the same year he wrote from there to Mrs Randi Blehr in Christiania: 'I am going to England in a fortnight for Christmas and hope to come to Norway next summer. I don't see many Norwegians here apart from Munch'.[12]

The most substantial picture of the circle is that given by Delius himself in his *Recollections of Strindberg*, published in 1920.[13] Some of the events narrated are also recounted in Strindberg's *Inferno*, the Swede's own account of this particularly disturbed period of his life, and can be compared with the composer's article. (The remainder of the article not included here in the text is given in Appendix A.)

'I met Strindberg in Paris in the early nineties at the studio of Ida Eriksen, a Swedish sculptress married to William Mollard, a French-Norwegian composer. Later on I met him quite frequently at the 'Crêmerie' of the Mère Charlotte, Rue de la Grande Chaumière (Montparnasse), where artists received unlimited credit. It was a little place of the utmost simplicity, where hardly ten people could sit down at a time and where one's meals generally cost one a franc, or a franc-fifty including coffee.

'Strindberg lived in a *pension de famille* just opposite at No. 12. Among the *habitues* of the Mère Charlotte at that time were Strindberg; a Polish painter named Slivinsky (Wladyslaw Slewinski); Mucha (Alphonse Mucha), a Tcheque designer of decorations and *affiches*; Paul Gauguin, the great painter; Leclerc (Julian Leclercq), a poet; the *maitre de ballet* of the Folies Bergère, also a Tcheque, and myself. I lived at that time at Montrouge, Rue Ducouedic, and generally took my meals at home, but occasionally lunched or dined at Madame Charlotte's to meet Gauguin and Strindberg. Or I would sometimes fetch Strindberg for a walk in the afternoon.

a) **Siesta.** *1883. Oil on paper mounted on panel. OKK.M.1055. Munch-Museet. Karen Bjølstad and Dr Christian Munch.*

b) **Military Band on Karl Johan Street.** *1889. Oil on canvas. Zurich, Kunsthause.*

a) *Edvard Munch's cottage at Aasgaardstrand.*
  (Photograph by courtesy of OKK.)

b) *13 rue de la Grande Chaumière, Paris; Madame Charlotte at the window above her **crémerie**.*
  (Panel by Mucha to the left, by Slewinski to the right.) (Photograph in the Royal Library,
  Stockholm, by courtesy of Dr Lionel Carley.)

a) Programme design for production of Peer Ibsen's **Peer Gynt** at Theatre de l'Oeuvre, Paris. 1896.
    Lithograph, OKK G/1. 216-12; Sch.74.

b) **Parisian Music-Hall.** 1890s.
    Black crayon, OKK. T.128-4. Munch-Museet.

a) **The Sick Child.** *1896.*
Etching, OKK. G/r. 43-2; Sch.60.

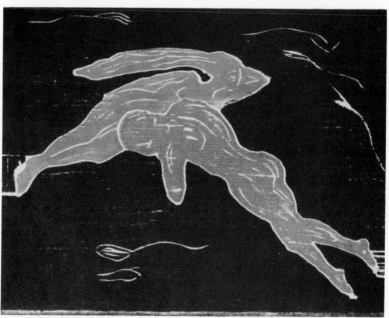

b) **Meeting in Space.** *1899.*
Colour woodcut, OKK. G/t. 603; Sch.135.

a) ***The Dance of Life.*** *sketch. c.1900.*
Indian ink, charcoal and crayon, OKK. T. 2392. Munch-Museet.

b) ***Moonlight.*** *1896.*
Colour woodcut, OKK. G/t. 570; Sch.81.

a) **Vampire.** *1895-6.*
Lithograph and woodcut in colour, OKK. G/t. 567-33. Sch.34.

b) **Madonna.** *1895-1902.*
Colour lithograph, OKK. G/1. 194; Sch.33.

FACING PAGE:
The Flower of Pain. *Cover design for Munch/Strindberg issue of* **Quickborn.** *1898. Watercolour, pencil and crayon, OKK. T. 2451. Munch-Museet.*

a)   **Violin Recital.** *1903.*
Lithograph, OKK. G/1. 254-23; Sch.211.
Eva Mudocci and Bella Edwards.

b)   **Self-portrait with Lyre.** *1897-8.*
Pencil, ink, watercolour and gouache, OKK. T. 2460. Munch-Museet.

'It was at that time Strindberg wrote his pamphlet 'Sylva Sylvorum'. He certainly was extraordinarily superstitious, for often on our walks he would suddenly refuse to go up a certain street on the pretext that some accident or misfortune was awaiting him there.[14]

'Edward Munch, the Norwegian painter, had just arrived in Paris and came to see me in my rooms in the Rue Ducouedic, and I asked him to accompany me to see Strindberg, who he had already met before, and who had now removed to the Hotel Orfila in the Rue d'Arras (actually the rue d'Assas). We found him poring over his retorts, stirring strange and evil-smelling liquids and after chattering for five or ten minutes we left in a most friendly manner. On fetching Munch next day to go to lunch he showed me a postcard just received from Strindberg, worded something in this wise, as far as I can remember: 'Your attempt to assassinate through the Müller-Schmidt method (I forget the real names) has failed. Tak for sidst.' It appears that the method to which he alluded consisted in turning on the gas from the outside, so as to suffocate the person within, or some such proceeding. And this was not the only time he suspected that an attempt had been made to assassinate him. Some time before, when Przbechewsky and his wife, old friends of his, arrived in Paris, he confided to me that they had only come to kill him.

'Shortly after Munch's supposed attempt to assassinate Strindberg I left for Norway, and on returning heard that he had left for Sweden. I never saw him again.'

The account of the 'attempted assassination' is born out be evidence from Strindberg. A postcard from Strindberg to Munch, postmarked 19/7/96,[15] reads as follows:

'The gas apparatus seems to be based on Pettenkofer's[16] experiment: blow out a light through a wall. But it works badly.

'Last time I saw you I thought you looked like a murderer — or at least an accomplice.'

Strindberg also writes of his enemies trying to poison him with gas in *Inferno*,[17] his 'fictionalised autobiography' of those years from 1894 until 1897. His particular fear was of the Polish writer Stanislas Przybyszewski (disguised in *Inferno* as the 'Russian' Popoffsky) and his Norwegian wife Dagny (née Juell). He regards Munch (described as 'the Danish painter') as a kind of emissary of Przybyszewski. Dagny Juell had been introduced to the 'Black Piglet' circle in Berlin by Munch, and had become something of its *femme fatale*. Her liasons probably included both Munch and Strindberg, but she finally married Stanislas Przybyszewski. They returned to Berlin in May 1896 after an extended visit to Norway, bringing with them their eight month old baby. Upon this Przybyszewski's previous mistress, and mother of three children by him, Marthe Foerder, committed suicide. Strindberg (possibly aided by inaccurate news from Munch, who was very close to Przybyszewski) persuaded himself that the Pole had killed his mistress and children with poison gas, and that he and Dagny had now come to Paris to do the same for him. In fact the Przybyszewskis were still in Berlin.

'I was poisoned, that was my first thought. Popoffsky had killed his wife and children with poison gas. He must have arrived. He must have sent a stream of gas through the wall as Pettenkofer had done in his famous experiment. What was I to do? Go to the police? No, for if there was no proof I should be locked up as insane.'

Evert Sprinchorn relates an amusing sequel to the story, recounted by another member of the circle, the painter Paul Herrmann, who Munch painted in the fine double portrait *Paul Herrmann and Paul Contard* (1897). When Herrmann visited Strindberg one day at the Hotel Orfila, the writer complained to him of the smell of gas although there was no gas stove in his room. Herrmann agreed about the smell, but traced its source to a dead and putrefying rat against the wall beneath Strindberg's bed.[18]

Although Delius's account seems therefore to be well corroborated, in fact he went to Norway that summer earlier than he states. While there he wrote to his old Norwegian friend from the Florida days, Mrs Jutta Bell-Ranske, dating the letter 15 July 1896: 'Since the beginning of June I have been in Norway, living on a farm in Valders and working on my new Opera — I shall leave Norway about the 24th or 5th August —'.[19] Delius could therefore not have visited Strindberg with Munch in July, and the date of the 'attempted assassination' is firmly established by the postmark on Strindberg's postcard. What exactly happened is for the moment a mystery. It seems to me likely, however, that Munch and Delius visited Strindberg together earlier in the year (Delius actually wrote that Munch had 'just arrived in Paris'), but that there was no accusation from Strindberg at that stage. Strindberg must have sent his postcard after a later visit from Munch, where the composer was not present. Subsequently, after Delius returned to Paris in the autumn and was seeing Munch again, the artist probably told him the story and showed him the card. Over twenty years later when Delius wrote his article (or possibly even dictated it to Philip Heseltine) the two events became telescoped, for what reason we do not at the moment know. This does not, however, invalidate the whole of Delius's article, which still remains a valuable document, much of its material corroborated from other sources.

Strindberg's 'Inferno' period in Paris was almost at an end. After the events narrated above, he left the Hotel Orfila, going to lodgings in the Rue de la Clef, near his beloved Jardin des Plantes, where he hoped to remain hidden while he finished his scientific researches. But soon his paranoia persuaded him that his enemies had found him again and near the end of July he fled from Paris to Dieppe, where his host was Munch's old mentor, Frits Thaulow. After a short stay there he returned to Sweden, where at Ystad he underwent medical treatment from Dr Anders Eliasson. Delius never saw him again, although there was to be one further collaboration between Strindberg and Munch.

Munch and Delius continued to see each other in Paris until December, when Delius went to Bradford for Christmas. Then for the next two years there is much less evidence of contact.

In January of 1897 Delius went to Florida, accompanied by another Norwegian friend, the boisterous and bohemian violinist Halfdan Jebe. He wished to see if the orange grove, Solana, which he had earlier farmed and then abandoned and which he still owned, could be turned to any advantage. While away, he visited old friends in America and worked on his piano concerto. Clearly he was not able to arrange anything very satisfactory about Solana Grove, as over the coming years there were to be a number of tentative proposals connected with it until it was finally sold in 1912 to the conductor Hans Haym, one of Delius's great early champions, for his son to operate.

Delius returned to Paris early in the summer, to find that Jelka Rosen, with help from her mother, had now purchased a house at Grez-sur-Loing. Grez was a tranquil and unspoilt village and the house was airy and commodious with a beautiful garden stretching down to the peaceful river. The village was something of an artist's colony. During the eighteen-eighties it had been dominated by Swedes, notably Carl Larsson, Karl Nordström and Strindberg, but in the nineties the company was more mixed, including English, Irish and Americans. Later, after Delius had settled there, there were to be more Norwegian visitors.[20]

No meeting between Munch and Delius is recorded during the summer of 1897. This is not surprising, as Munch was back in Norway before the end of June, while Delius moved out to Grez to live with Jelka during the course of the summer. This was effectively to be his home for the remainder of his life, although he was for some years also to retain rooms in Paris.

At Grez Delius was visited by the dramatist Gunnar Heiberg. Heiberg was the leading Norwegian playwright of the generation which followed that of Bjørnson and Ibsen. He was also a notable theatre

43

critic and in 1897 went to France as the Paris correspondent of *Verdens Gang*, where he became friendly with Delius. At this time he was also a close friend of Munch and an admirer of his work, belonging to the same bohemian circles in Christiania. Heiberg invited Delius to compose incidental music for his new play *Folkeraadet* (The People's Parliament), a satire on the Norwegian parliamentary system and its politicians, with digs at attitudes to nationalism and the current union with Sweden.[21] Heiberg returned to Norway and there are two letters that autumn from him to Delius, giving the composer information about the play and about the orchestra available.[22] Delius wrote most of the music at Grez, much of it consisting of variations based on the Norwegian national anthem *Ja, vi elsker dette Landet* (words by Bjørnson, tune by Rikard Nordraak). The use of the national anthem in a satirical context was very likely Heiberg's idea and with the undated letter he sent Delius an unspecified melody which may well have been it. In the other letter Heiberg wrote: 'The rehearsals begin on Saturday. And the intention is to put the play on in the middle of October.'

Delius went to Norway during October, to attend the opening of *Folkeraadet* on the 18th, completing the music on arrival by writing the short overture. Norway had already given the first professional concert performance of an orchestral work by Delius; now it had provided what was almost certainly his first actual commission to write an orchestral score. In this case, however, the work was to earn the composer more notoriety than praise. His use of the national anthem in a satirical context, particularly its minor key employment as a funeral march in the prelude to the last act, gave great offence in a country where nationalism was a popular issue, and the fact that this had been done by a foreigner was considered particularly bad taste.[23] After anarchic demonstrations in the Christiania Theatre, and withdrawal and reinstatement of the music, Delius finally withdrew it after the performance on 3 November, the day that the composer left Christiania for Copenhagen. The play on its own was quite well received and continued to run until 27 November, although public interest seemed to slacken a little after the withdrawal of the controversial music. Depite the general opprobium of Delius, his music had its supporters, notably the conductor of the theatre orchestra, Per Winge, the composer Johan Selmer, the critic Sigurd Bødtker and Christian Krohg, while the old Ibsen (who the composer encountered) was sympathetic. Krohg interviewed Delius for *Verdens Gang*, accompanying his article with a sketch portrait.[24] The feelings of one of Delius's supporters can be read in a letter, written to the composer some years later by the actress Milly Bergh: 'I am proud that when you did *Ja, vi elsker* — in the minor key

44

for *Folkeraadet*, I already understood how beautifully you worked and felt the individuality of the whole of your style . . .' .[25]

Munch would surely have been among Delius's supporters on this occasion, as these included so many of their mutual friends.[26] As he was in Christiania that autumn, it seems most probable that they would have met, very likely on a number of occasions. Although no absolutely direct evidence has yet come to light, this was certainly assumed by William Molard when he wrote to the artist from Paris in March 1898.[27]

'Since we last saw each other you have met friends from our circle in Christiania — Leclercq[28] and Delius — the latter has certainly had a real success in Norway and has kept the newspapers not a little busy; this has been fortunate for him, because at any rate attention has now been drawn to Delius's name up there and this can never do any damage. On the contrary — it is difficult in life to raise the superior being high enough above the bulk of humanity for him to be noticed and reach his appointed goal'. It is interesting that in the year when Delius wrote his funeral march for the satirical *Folkeraadet*, Munch produced his own important *Funeral March*, as a pencil drawing (OKK T. 392) and as a lithograph (OKK G/1.226). Both versions contain some grotesquely sardonic features.

Delius left Christiania at the beginning of November, making his way back to Paris via Elberfeld, in Germany, where the conductor Hans Haym was giving the first performance of his 'fantasy overture' *Over the Hills and Far Away* that month. (Haym was a contact through Jelka's close friend, the painter Ida Gerhardi). Although at the time this was to make less stir than the *Folkeraadet* music, it was ultimately to have much greater significance, as Haym's championship of Delius's music was to prepare the ground for the composer's growing reputation in Germany after 1900.

For Delius this was therefore a period of production and promise. He had within a short space of time achieved two public performances of his works. 1897 had seen the completion of *Over the Hills and Far Away*, the opera *Koanga*, the first version of the Piano Concerto (*Fantasy for Orchestra and pianoforte*) and the *Seven Danish Songs*. The words of the songs were all by J.P. Jacobsen, except for one by Holger Drachmann, and Delius set them first in their original language. Early the following year Ferruccio Busoni (who Delius had known since his Leipzig days and who had later met Munch, through the 'Black Piglet' circle in Berlin) started to show an interest in the Piano Concerto, but unfortunately this was not followed by a public performance. 1898-9 also had some notable compositions, the symphonic poem *La Ronde se Déroule*

and several of settings of Nietzsche, four songs and the *Mitternachtslied Zarathustras*, which last was later to be incorporated in *A Mass of Life*.[29] The choice of authors during these two years is significant. The writings of Nietzsche and Jacobsen meant much to both Delius and Munch, and the artist also knew Holger Drachmann and made a fine portrait of him.

Delius spent 1898 in France, living increasingly with Jelka at Grez-sur-Loing. Early that year there was a reconciliation with his uncle Theodor and when Theodor died shortly after this, he left his nephew a considerable sum of money. Delius was to devote the larger part of this legacy to finance a major concert of his compositions in London in May 1899.

During the time which he still spent in Paris, Delius continued to frequent the Molard circle. Daniel de Monfreid recalls Delius and the Molards visiting him in October 1898, in company with Edouard Gérard (the fiancée of Molard's stepdaughter, Judith[30]) and the graphic artist Achille Ouvré. (Ouvré was also known to Munch. He became well known for his illustrations and his portraits, which included one of Delius.) In November Delius visited de Monfreid again, and used 500 francs from his forthcoming legacy to buy a painting from among those which de Monfreid had recently received from Gauguin in Tahiti. This was the famous *Nevermore*, now in the Courtauld Collection, London. Surviving correspondence between de Monfreid and Gauguin informs us that Gauguin was pleased with this sale, partly because Delius had bought the picture because he liked it rather than for speculation, partly because he might want to buy another later and because it would be seen by Delius's well-connected visitors.[31]

After Munch returned home from Paris in the summer of 1897, he was to remain based in Norway for several years. His trips abroad were now to be visits, rather than living most of the time there, as had been his pattern since the end of 1892. The period started promisingly with his purchase in July of 1897 of the cottage at Aasgaardstrand, the village on the coast which meant so much to him. A few months after his return to Norway, Munch announced plans to publish a graphic portfolio with the title of *The Mirror*. Most of the lithographs and woodcuts in this series had been made in Paris in 1896-97 and were connected with the paintings of the *Life Frieze*. Then in September he held an important retrospective exhibition at Dioramalokalet, in Christiania, comprising (according to the catalogue) 85 paintings, 64 prints and 30 sketches and studies, almost certainly including *The Mirror* series.[32] Criticisms were mixed and rather confused, but they were by no means so universally unfavourable as on some previous occasions. It would appear that critics had now grown used to Munch's earlier, more realistic, pictures, although they disliked his more symbolic work of the mid-nineties. Nasjonalgalleriet purchased another of his paintings, the portrait of Hans Jaeger, painted in 1889.[33]

But 1898 and 1899 were to be mainly restless years. It was probably in 1898 that Munch met Tulla Larsen for the first time. Mathilde (Tulla) Larsen was the daughter of a well-to-do wine merchant, and was interested in the artistic life. An affair started between them and it soon became clear that she was as determined to marry the artist as he was to remain single.[34] This tempestuous affair caused Munch much restless travelling in Europe, at times with Tulla Larsen, at times in flight from her. Moreover the effect on his nerves caused him to drink more heavily, thus moving him nearer to crisis and breakdown. This hectic way of life, coupled with increased chest troubles, saw Munch in a bad state of health, and in the autumn of 1899 he entered the sanatorium Kornhaug, in Gudbrandsdal to recover his health and get the peace he needed in order to work.

Consequently it is not surprising that these two years were not his most prolific. Whereas for some years the artist had had important exhibitions every year, during 1898 and 99 he only contributed to a few collective exhibitions. 1898 was a lean year for paintings, and Munch's major work at this stage was in his prints. Some of these marked the last occasion, when he and Strindberg were to appear in connection with each other, although it involved no physical meeting. In the summer of 1898 the artist received a commission from the German periodical *Quickborn* for illustrations to a special issue devoted entirely to the work of himself and Strindberg. Strindberg contributed a new short novel *Das Silbermoor* (The Silver Swamp), while Munch furnished a number of assorted prints and drawings. Some of these were illustrations more or less closely connected with Strindberg, others were a variety of old and new motifs. The special number was published in January of the following year.

Among his travels, Munch visited Paris in May 1898, where he saw his old friends Stanislas and Dagny Przybyszewski, but there is no record of any meeting with Delius.[35] It had to wait until 1899 for significant evidence of renewed contact.

Chapter V

1899-1902

THE GREAT EVENT FOR DELIUS IN THE FIRST HALF OF 1899 WAS HIS
London concert, which took place on 30 May in the old St James's
Hall. The programme presented many of his best works (including
substantial excerpts from the opera *Koanga*), and an orchestra of 94
players had been engaged, led by Halfdan Jebe. The conductor was
Alfred Hertz, from Breslau, who had been conductor of the Elberfeld
Opera when Haym performed *Over the Hills and Far Away* in that city.
This was the first time that Delius's work had been performed publicly
in England (except perhaps for a few early songs), indeed it must have
been the first opportunity which the composer had had of hearing a
number of his compositions played by an orchestra. (However shortly
before leaving for London he had enjoyed a private, chamber-scale,
performance of *Koanga*, presided over by Gabriel Fauré, at Mrs Maddison's house before members of Parisian musical society such as the
Prince and Princess de Polignac. Fauré also gave Delius a number of
introductions to his own musical friends in London.)

The London concert attracted a 'fairly large and by no means
unappreciative audience'.[1] The reviews were generally favourable, a
number of critics expressing interest and commenting on the composer's originality, even if some were a little mystified, and reviews also
appeared in Germany. (This contrasts with the almost complete lack of
interest shown by Delius's parents, so far had their son grown beyond
their understanding.) However, although Delius was pleased with the
concert's reception, further performance of his work in England had to
wait for another eight years. Some of the composer's Norwegian friends
expressed their interest; Gunnar Heiberg, then in France, wrote to
Delius wishing him luck with the concert,[2] while Munch wrote later
congratulating him on its success.

After the concert Delius returned to France and shortly afterwards
completed his large orchestral nocturne, *Paris. The song of a great city.* In
the early summer there had been Norwegian visitors to Grez, probably
while Delius was in London. In early May, Jelka had received Tulla
Larsen there, together with a Mrs Mowinckel. A little later, but de-

finitely while the composer was away, Gunnar Heiberg spent a few days there. In June, Delius was planning his summer visit to Norway and wrote to Munch about it, sending the letter by Tulla Larsen, who was in Grez again. And before he left for Norway in July, he had been visited there by the Norwegian painter Alfred Hauge, another friend of Munch who had shared a studio with the artist in Christiania in 1895.[3]

In March Munch, who had remained in Norway over the winter, set off abroad once more. He travelled through Berlin and Paris to Italy, where he made a special study of Raphael with a view to decorative projects at home. On his way back to Norway he went through Paris again, probably in late May, but missing Delius. His summer was divided between Aasgaardstrand and Nordstrand.

The first surviving letter in the correspondence was one sent by Delius the following month.

Delius to Munch
(1, D.1)

Grez
12 June 99.

Dear Munch,

I am back again from England and I was sorry not to meet you in Paris — I am thinking of coming to Norway at the end of July to go some way into the mountains — Will you come with me to the Jotunheim or the Hardanger Viddern?[4] I could be quite a good guide — How are the etchings of the sick girl coming along?[5]

Write me a few lines to say whether I can count on you for the Jotunheim.

Farewell
Your friend
Fritz Delius.

Miss Larsens is here in Grez for a few days and is kindly sending this letter with hers.

Munch replied the same month from Aasgaardstrand.

Munch to Delius
(2, M.1)

Written in Norwegian

Aasgaardstrand
24/6/99

Dear Delius,

Thank you for the letter — of course I would have liked very much to go to the mountains — and we certainly would have got along well together — but unfortunately there are several obstacles. Firstly I don't know if I will be well enough — Perhaps you know that I have had influenza which has lasted a long time — then there is my work — which possibly will force me to stay here — In any case I hope we will meet — it may well be possible for me to go with you, if not up to the high mountains at least a part of the way —

I am living in my little house in Aasgaardstrand.[6] Unfortunately my guest room is not ready yet — otherwise you could have stayed here for a while — until you went off to the mountains —

50

This house of mine was really a brilliant idea — here I walk around in my garden in a free and easy way — just like in a little paradise . . . you must anyhow come down here for a few days.

— Your success in London has delighted me and I congratulate you from the bottom of my heart —

Write and tell me when you will be coming —

If you see the Mollards[7] give them my regards and tell them that I was so sorry I couldn't visit them — I felt so poorly and nervous that I couldn't ask them to come to me either. I did not meet anyone —

If only we could work out that plan with etchings[8] and music — and I.P. Jakobson.[9]

Until we meet again.

Your friend
Edvard Munch.

Two points in particular in this exchange of letters, pose interesting questions. The first, a simple material one, is whether Delius did visit Munch at Aasgaardstrand that summer. It seems to me most likely that he did so, and I should also like to think that at least one such meeting included Helge Rode as well.

Even more intriguing are the references to the 'sick girl' and the 'plan with etchings and music — and I.P. Jakobson'. Although Munch and Delius knew each other for the best part of a lifetime this is one of the very few times in the correspondence that give concrete evidence of their discussing each other's work, and the only time that implies a creative collaboration discussed between them. The nature of this collaboration has been discussed in earlier publication by Bente Torjusen, Lionel Carley and myself.[10] Although all conclusions are conjectural, the possibilities are sufficiently intriguing to make a summing-up desirable.

In the first place the fin-de-siècle was a period when synthesis between the arts was a common aim and innumerable examples could be instanced. Munch's paintings had been compared by writers to music, notably by Christian Krohg[11] and by Strindberg[12] and both the 'Black Piglet' circle in Berlin, and the Molard circle in Paris were composed of talents in art, literature and music. The Molard circle was particularly notable for its admiration for music, where, musician members apart, even painters and writers played musical instruments, Gauguin the mandolin and Strindberg the guitar. Gauguin confessed to Molard that: 'I have always had a mania for relating painting to music, which, since I cannot understand it scientifically, becomes a little more comprehensible to me through the relationship I discover between these two arts'.[13] Lionel Carley has told us that: 'One member of the circle, Charles Morice, collaborating with Gauguin on *Noa-Noa*, was planning in the autumn to draw from Gauguin's story "a sort of lyric pantomime or *ballet doré* ". Molard he felt would be the obvious composer for the work'.[14] (However, nothing seems to have resulted from this.)

So there is plenty of precedent for the type of synthesis suggested in Munch's letter and they probably discussed the idea during 1896-7 in Paris and possibly again on Delius's visit to Christiania in the autumn of the latter year. Dr Eric Fenby, who was later to be so closely connected with the composer, has informed me that Delius told him that he and Munch had often discussed a project similar to the one suggested here, but that to the best of his knowledge nothing practical ever came out of it.

The choice of work by Jens Peter Jacobsen would have been a natural one, as both Delius and Munch were deeply interested in his writings. Jacobsen was to be one of the writers whose work Delius used most frequently, and six of the *Seven Danish Songs* of 1897 were settings of his poems. Richard Hove has commented on how appropriately the music of Delius fits the mood of Jacobsen and how sensitive the composer is to the Danish language, and he also points out the similarity in mood of the music to some of Munch's paintings.[15] Other attempts have been made to demonstrate similarities between the work of Jacobsen and Munch, partly through the connections of the Norwegian writers Vilhelm Krag and Sigbjørn Obstfelder, both close friends of the artist. We know that Munch was fascinated by Jacobsen's best-known novel, *Niels Lyhne* (1880), the same novel that Delius was later to use for his opera *Fennimore and Gerda*, from his correspondence with the young American student of music, Kate Crawley around 1894-5.[16] Roy A. Boe has attempted to connect a number of Munch themes with *Niels Lyhne*, one of them the *Sick Child*.[17]

Munch likened his *Life Frieze*, his major preoccupation of the nineties, to a symphony. He liked to exhibit the pictures in such a way as to stress interconnection of subjects, and in hanging his work gave unity to the pictures of different format by creating a common background. For example, photographs of a Leipzig exhibition of the *Life Frieze* in 1903, demonstrate how the pictures are placed against a neutral band, which stretches along behind all of them.[18] For three or four years after his stay in Paris during 1896-97, Munch struggled to complete his print series *The Mirror*, on themes comparable to those of the *Life Frieze*, such as love, death and anxiety, a task in which he never fully succeeded. Friends from Paris like Delius and Molard knew something of Munch's printmaking projects, and Molard made a reference to them in his letter of March 1898 (referred to on p. 45), which demonstrates more fully than the query in the Delius letter the discussion of similar ideas within their circle: 'Are you continuing with your lithographic port-folio, in which you wanted to mirror the different phases of your life — soul-life — or have you been painting'. He goes on: 'I have written music to a play by Roinard called *Les Mirroirs* . . . I have regarded the whole thing as an exercise in composing simply with the idea that the music is to function as a foundation, a sort of backcloth before which the characteristic emotions of the play are to be played'.[19]

So with these precedents of art syntheses from the Gauguin-Molard circle before us, we can speculate a little on the nature of the proposed collaboration between Delius and Munch. It might have aimed at the form of an exhibition of Munch's prints, perhaps drawn from *The Mirror* series, or perhaps different subjects deemed to have a particular connection with Jacobsen themes, in either case very likely including the *Sick Child*. Against this background a selection of Jacobsen's writings would have been performed, at least some of them set to music by Delius and probably including the six of the *Seven Danish Songs*, as these were recent works. Other Delius music might have provided interludes between or backgrounds for recitation of other Jacobsen works. Arne Eggum has further suggested to me that they might have visualized a performance in a theatre, such as Lugne-Poë's *Théâtre de l'Oeuvre*, with Munch print subjects possibly interpreted by scene painters creating a mood for a performance of words and music. Munch had earlier sketched out some ideas for the production of a Danish translation of Maurice Maeterlinck's poetic play *Pelléas et Mélisande* and he was later to produce sketches for Max Reinhardt's Berlin production of Ibsen's *Ghosts* to create the mood for the scenery artists to aim at (see pp. 91, below). Delius, too, in his operas always sought to create an atmos-pheric mood and his final one *Fennimore and Gerda* (1910), in fact consists of eleven mood pictures in separate scenes, with pauses beween them to mark the passage of time (see also pp. 103-4, below). As an alternative possibility to the theatrical one, Arne Eggum has suggested that they might have considered producing a portfolio of Munch prints, Jacobsen poems and Delius music on interrelated themes.

The fact that both men use the word 'etchings' in their letter need not I think be too limiting. Although at the time they were written Munch was principally producing woodcuts and lithographs, there is no reason why he should not also have considered a collection of etchings and other intaglio prints as a few years earlier he had inter-preted many subjects in these media. But in any case I suspect that they employ the word loosely and use it to cover a wider variety of engraving techniques than pure etching (see note 8, above). But one can only speculate, and as it seems that nothing practical ever resulted from these discussions, it is hardly likely that much more concrete evidence of them will be discovered. But certainly strong similarities between mood and content can be found in Jacobsen, Delius and Munch. For example passages in the opera *Fennimore and Gerda*, where Niels sits brooding by the fjord, seems a close musical parallel to some of Munch's paintings in which a lonely figure is seen sitting on the shore, such as *Evening* 1891? (Private Collection).

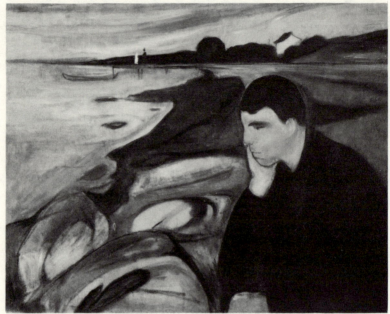

Evening. *1891? Private Collection.*
Oil on canvas.

There is more evidence of thematic similarity from about this time. Between September 1898 and February 1899 Delius was writing his symphonic poem *La ronde se déroule (The Dance goes on)*. The title page is inscribed:

'La ronde se déroule'
Symphonisches Dichtung
zu 'Dansen Gaar' drama von Helge Rode
von
Fritz Delius
1899

Below this are inscribed, in Danish, nine lines of the play:
'The dance of life, My pictures shall be called the dance of life! There will be two people who are dancing in flowing clothes on a clear night

54

through an avenue of black cypresses and red rose bushes. The earth's glorious blood will gleam and blaze in the roses, Claire. He holds her tightly against himself. He is deeply serious and happy. There will be something festal about it. He will hold her to him so firmly, that she is half sunk into him. She will be frightened — frightened — and something will awake inside her. Strength is streaming into her from him. And in front of them is the abyss'.[20]

Notice that Rode's character is an artist speaking of a picture which he will paint.

Delius at first hoped to provide an overture and some incidental music for Rode's play, which was published in 1898. No doubt his experience with *Folkeraadet* the previous year had encouraged him to feel that incidental music was for the moment a more likely way of getting his music performed in the theatre than with his operas. They had discussed the idea in correspondence. Rode wrote Delius a long letter about it in September 1898.[21] The letter is a tactful one, but he is not very encouraging about the scheme working.

'My dear Delius!

It is rather difficult for me to answer your letter. I wrote to lightly about the matter, preferring to talk about it when we met. The question had no real Actuality as 'Dansen gaar' and Dramas of the Mind shall and must have no Music. (Another thing is that every Drama kan and perhaps ougth to have an Ouverture and kan have Music between the Acts) . . .

'Now about 'Dansen gaar'. Suppose one had written an Ouverture to it and Music between the Acts one Difficulty was, that the Drama was accepted at the Theatre months before it was printed and no 'Solidaritet' therefore possible between Author and Musician. Probably the Theatre would say: We want no Music, it is unnecessary — more Work and more Money. And if it was a Foreigner who had made the Music, perhaps the[y] would further say: Why not at all events a Dane. We have young Komposers, who want to try their power.

'Now let me suppose, *you* had written this Music of course I would have felt very pleased. Of Course and I would have done anything I could to get it played. But I would have felt sorry if I had not succeeded. I have myself here to begin with had some Difficulties to get my plays performed and understanding, that your Music is a personal one, which not everybody likes at first, there *migth* arise Difficulties, which I would feel painfully especially on account of my utterly Want of Knowledge in musical Matters. These were some of my thoughts when I wrote. Now you see, I know nothing whether you have or have had a Mind or Time to write an Ouverture to 'Dansen gaar' but if you have felt it so and if that little Tone of Irritation in your Letter, which made me sorry, not least because I in certain Ways found it justified, was due to this, then I sincerely ask you: Do make it! Of course I shall be very glad, and I hope the Theatre will play it — I would find it very remarkable if they would not — An Ouverture is always played before the Performance (only Music between the Acts would be something ecceptional and therefore more difficult to get accepted) But here too I migth be wrong. The Theatre *migth* appreciate as I, that a Foreign Komposer took the Interest in a danish Drama.

55

'. . . As for the Future when (if) I write a Work which more than this *wants* Music we will talk about it. . . . And I migth write something which you would feel more than any Danish Komposer I know. This last is perhaps most probable.'

A further letter from Helge Rode was sent from Florence, where he was staying, the following February.[22] He had heard from Delius again. It seems as if the composer has written some music for the play, at any rate a prelude, as Rode writes:

'I understand well, that you want the Vorspiel to be played before the second or fifth Act. the (word undecipherable) in those perhaps having something musical in them. It has just been my Idea that the Music, the Song of Life was heard there, which in the other Acts is drowned in the Noise.
'Well let us hope, the Theatre can be brougth to understand it. You are quite right in not sending the Manuskript here. The Post is not quite safe. As soon as I leave Florence a Day or too before I shall write you my Adress in Kopenhague, and the Music and I shall arrive.'

Rode is not sure when the première of *Dansen gaar* will take place, although he hopes it will be this season. He talks a little vaguely about the possibility of his going to Paris later on, with the implication of perhaps seeing Delius.

Whether any prelude or entract by Delius was performed with the play seems rather doubtful. At any rate the work based on *Dansen gaar* was included in the composer's London concert that year; it had become the symphonic poem *La ronde se déroule*. This sounds too substantial a work to have been the mere Prelude which Helge Rode mentions, but presumably it used the same material.

New works performed recently in London would surely have been a natural topic for discussion at any meeting between Delius and Munch in the summer of 1899. Whether Rode was present or not, the fact that all three were good friends would have made a Rode-based Delius work of special interest.

This was the very time when Munch was working on his own important picture *The Dance of Life*. Munch's finished painting (Nasjonalgalleriet) dates from around 1900, and there is a sketch for it in Munch-Museet from about the same time.[23]

There are certainly similarities between the scene from Rode's play, where he states that his 'dance of life' is a picture, and Munch's painting. Both centre on a couple dancing in flowing clothes on a clear night, although in Munch's case the background is the Oslo fjord shoreline and moon, as against Rode's cypresses and rose bushes. Nevertheless the idea of the earth's blood gleaming and blazing in the roses is a Munchian type of metaphor, as for example in the *Flower of Pain* (watercolour, pen and ink, 1898, and also used that year for the

56

cover of the *Quickborn*/Strindberg issue), where the suffering artist's blood pours into the ground to fertilize a flower. Again the idea of a strong force flowing between the man and the woman is a Munchian one, although Rode has the man clasp the woman so firmly to him, while in Munch's *Dance of Life* it is rather the woman who firmly clasps the man. And the abyss which Rode sees opening before them is surely the same abyss which Munch fears when a man ties himself to a loving woman.

But these ideas were common at the fin-de-siècle; and many other writers and artists (for example Strindberg) make use of similar symbols. Besides, Munch's *Dance of Life* is a development of his own *Three Stages of Woman*, or *The Sphinx*, from 1894 (painting in Rasmus Meyers Samlinger, Bergen), where the same three types of women are used, although the solitary male figure is there shown in a different relationship to them. Arne Eggum has differentiated between the two: *Three Ages of Woman* (Woman in Three Stages) 'depicts a young man's conception of woman, *Dance of Life* depicts life in common between man and woman'.[24]

Arne Eggum has further deduced that, on a personal plane, *The Dance of Life* is a picture of Munch's affair with Tulla Larsen. As evidence he cites a draft letter of 1898, where the artist describes her as the woman of 'Three Ages' and suggests that the painting was conceived about this time. He continues to quote Munch on Tulla Larsen: 'I have seen many women who had thousands of shifting expressions — like a crystal, but I have met none that so pronouncedly had only three — but strong ones . . . It is exactly my picture of the three women . . . You have an expression of the deepest sorrow . . . like the weeping madonnas of the old Pre-Raphaelites[25] — and when you are happy — I have never seen such an expression of radiant joy, as if your face were suddenly flooded with sunshine — Then you have your hot face (i.e. the woman in red in the painting), and that is the one that frightens me. It is the sphinx, the face of fate — In it I find all the dangerous qualities of woman'.[26]

In 1901 Delius made a second version of his symphonic poem, now calling it *Life's Dance* and describing it as 'a tone poem', and he retained this title for the third and final version, which he completed in 1912. However the tone poem, although continuing to use the same two main musical themes, gradually grew further away from Helge Rode's play and Jelka Delius wrote of the 1912 version that (for the purpose of analytical notes) '. . . it is no good mentioning the Danish author as Fred's piece has quite detached itself from it . . . .'. 'He just said this: "I wanted to depict the Turbulence, the joy, energy, great striving of youth — all to end at last in the inevitable death" '.[27]

Although the Nietszchean theme of a dance of life was a fairly popular one around the turn of the century, it is certainly interesting to find Delius, Munch and Rode all using it at about the same time and the possibility of some cross-influence is a strong one. Rode would certainly have known Munch paintings on the theme of love, very likely including the *Three Stages of Woman*, when he wrote *Dansen Gaar*. Munch would probably have known of the Rode and Delius works while painting *The Dance of Life* and it is certainly suggestive that Delius changed the title of his work to *Life's Dance* not long after the artist completed his painting.

All of this would seem to make the idea of a meeting between the three friends, probably in Norway, towards the end of the eighteen-nineties a distinct possibility. Helge Rode, like Delius, visited Norway a number of times during the eighteen-nineties. We have noted how he, Munch and Delius met at Aasgaardstrand in 1893 (see p. 23, above) and there is also a postcard from October 1895 sent by Rode from Nordstrand to Munch in Christiania, arranging for the two of them to meet.[28] Much later, probably in March 1929, Munch drafted the letter to Delius referred to on p. 23 above, although we cannot be certain whether one like it was ever actually sent. The letter refers to a meeting between the three men in Aasgaardstrand 'over thirty years ago', but as Munch's memory later in life was not always precisely reliable, I think it could apply to a meeting any time during the nineties. However, the fact that the figure 'thirty years' seems fixed in his mind in 1929 suggests to me a date nearer 1899 than 1893, which would have been nearer to forty years previously. Moreover the subject matter which Munch refers to in the letter discusses ideas which we know concerned Munch in the later nineties, although they do not rule out an earlier date.

The relevant passage in the draft letter runs as follows:

'Do you remember how we — you, Helge Rode and I spoke in Aasgaardstrand over thirty years ago about things to come. We spoke about the transparency of the body and telepathy — It was what we have now, X-rays and radio and the wonderful waves which connect the whole world and the stellar system with us —' (46c, Md. 9, see p. 136). I do not know what Delius's views upon the subject may have been, but Munch was very interested in the idea of outside forces or currents which connected people with one another. For example in the coloured woodcut *Meeting in Space*, from 1899 he shows a man and woman floating towards each other in a mysterious, shadowy space, in which decorative sperms are also moving. Again, in the lithograph

Lovers in the Waves (1896) the head of a man and woman float on an endless sea (and perhaps will drown in it!). Or in his writings: 'Man and woman are drawn to each other. Love's underwater cable carries its current into their nerves. The cable strands bound their hearts together. The woman's hair has wound itself around him and penetrated to his heart'.[29] These sort of ideas were ones for which he was constantly seeking expressive form, notably in the later eighteen-nineties.

No more correspondence between Delius and Munch survives until 1903. But when this opens up again, its tone makes it quite plain that contact was maintained during the intervening years. There is also positive evidence of contact between them and mutual friends between 1899 and 1903. Some of this is from before the possible Aasgaardstrand meeting, as for example the letters from Gunnar Heiberg and Alfred Hauge (mentioned on pp. 49-50, above).

Part of another letter of this period from Delius to Helge Rode has survived in the possession of the Rode family. It does not make it clear when they had last met, nor does it mention Munch, but comments in it on Munch's close friend, the poet Sigbjørn Obstfelder and on Nietzsche are interesting. It was written, in English, from Grez on 22 September, 1900.

'I was so glad, my dear Rode, to hear from you again: it seemed to me that your not writing for so long meant that you would suddenly appear in Grez, however it is not to be so this year. I will hope you will come and fetch me next year, in that case I would also come to Italy with you — I was extremely sorry to hear of Obstfelder's death. Mrs Krogh told me of it. I did not know him well but he always struck me as being very refined and delicate. That Nietzsche is dead I was glad to hear it must have been terrible for this Colossus to be mad and have lucid moments. What a strange world we live in — Sometimes I think only a very few people think at all — Who understands Nietzsche? How many do you know? I am paralyzed when I realize how few there are and still this man was one of the world's greatest geniuses —'.

Here the letter reaches the end of a page, and the remainder has not survived. We have no way of knowing what else might have been included. It could be argued that 'your not writing for so long' suggests that they had not met for several years, but it is hardly conclusive.

Clearly Scandinavian friends tended to get in touch with Delius when they were in France. For example, a postcard survives from October 1900, from Delius in Grez to Jappe Nilssen in Paris.[30] The art critic and writer Jappe Nilssen was one of Munch's closest friends and lifelong supporters and he was also friendly with Delius for many years.

The postcard invites Nilssen down to Grez, giving the time of a train, and Delius also says that he will be coming to Paris on Saturday, en route for Berlin. A further letter from Jappe Nilssen to Delius concerns a possible performance of one of his songs in Norway. Although it is not dated, Rachel Lowe-Dugmore had deduced from the singer's career that it probably belongs to this time, between 1899 and 1903.

> Dear Delius,
> You once told me that you had composed the tune for Verlaine's beautiful poem "Le ciel est pardessus le toit si bleu, si calme . . .".[31]
> Knowing that your setting was excellent I mentioned the fact to Mrs Cally Monrad Reimers, who asked me if I could get hold of it for her. In that case she would sing it at a recital here in Christiania in spring and later in Stockholm and Copenhagen. And she is a brilliant singer in whose hands you can safely trust your composition, and she has the ear of the public as no other living Norwegian singer.
> Could you consequently send me your composition, you would render her and me a great service.
>
> Your friend
> Jappe Nilssen.[32]

Cally Monrad Reimers was also a friend of Munch who portrayed her on several occasions.

Between 1899 and 1903, the pattern of Delius's life remained much the same, namely most of the time spent living and working at Grez, with visits to Paris, where he still retained an apartment. These Paris visits were sometimes connected with artistic matters, sometimes with seeing old friends, and sometimes with women.[33] But these gradually decreased as the composer reached a more settled maturity with Jelka at Grez. He was now composing some of his major works. The definitive version of *Appalachia* (1902), the important opera *A Village Romeo and Juliet* (1900-01) and the minor one, *Margot la Rouge*, (1901-02), all belong to this period, together with a number of songs.

In 1901, two of Delius's *Seven Danish Songs* (orchestral version) were performed at the *Société Nationale de Musique* in Paris, the singer Christianne Andray and the conductor Vincent d'Indy. (These had been translated into French by William Molard.) They are reviewed by Debussy, who described them unkindly as 'very sweet songs, very pale, music to lull convalescent ladies to sleep in the rich quarters'.[34] Despite friendships with some individuals like Fauré, Florent Schmitt and Ravel,[35] Delius made virtually no impact on the French musical world. Although he continued to choose to live in France, the performance of the Danish songs was apparently the last of Delius's music to be heard publicly in Paris for a very long time and Delius's career went on to be built up in other countries.

In Germany Delius was finding his supporters and within a few years of the beginning of the new century his music was starting to enjoy a considerable success. In 1901 Hans Haym, who had premiered *Over the Hills and Far Away* four years earlier, performed the large orchestral nocturne, *Paris*, in Elberfeld; the following year Busoni performed it with the Berlin Philharmonic Orchestra, and, in 1903, Julius Buths gave a further performance in Düsseldorf. Richard Strauss read the score of *Paris* in 1902 and had some reservations about it, but the following year when Buths had made a two piano arrangement of *Paris* and Haym of *Life's Dance*, they played both to the German composer and Buths could write to Delius that: 'The impression they made on Strauss was definitely in your favour'.[36]

Although by 1902 Munch had had his supporters in Germany for the past ten years, it was in that year that his real breakthrough there came. For some years now Germany was to be the field for the major career advances of both artist and composer.

Jelka Rosen also had her artistic connections with Germany, notably her long standing friendship with the painter Ida Gerhardi. Latish in 1902 she was approached by Karl-Ernst Osthaus, the young Director of the Folkwangs Museum in Hagen,[37] very likely introduced through Ida Gerhardi, who was then painting a portrait of Osthaus. Osthaus offered to buy a painting of Jelka's, in the hope that she would introduce him to the great sculptor Auguste Rodin with whom she had been friendly for some time, and help him to purchase a work by Rodin cheaply.[38] Osthaus was very friendly with another German collector, Dr Max Linde of Lübeck, and the speciality of Linde's collection was the work of Rodin and Munch.

If Delius's life between 1899 and 1902 was growing more settled and leading on to the great works of his maturity, Munch's personal life was very much the opposite. 1902 in particular was a critical year, comprising on the one hand breakthrough towards artistic success, and on the other dramatic personal developments which further undermined his precarious stability.

The winter of 1899-1900 Munch spent in Kornhaug Sanatorium, in Gudbrandsdal, partly because of chest trouble, partly to secure peace from the pressures which the affair with Tulla Larsen was causing him. In the spring he made what he described as 'a very successful trip'[39] through Berlin to Florence and Rome, accompanied by Tulla Larsen. On this trip he spent some time resting at Airolo, in the Swiss mountains, the doctor having diagnosed a weakness in one lung, and he felt much better for this peace and quiet. After a stay in Como during July he returned to Norway, spending time in Aasgaardstrand and with a

61

large exhibition in Christiania[40] in the autumn.

Munch stayed for the winter of 1900-01 at Nordstrand, where he painted some beautiful views of the Christiania fjord. He did not go abroad the following spring, although his pictures were exhibited in Germany and Austria. During the summer he stayed painting at Aasgaardstrand, and in October he held another major exhibition in Christiania.[41] At both this and the 1900 exhibition, critical opinion was growing less hostile to Munch's work. His earlier realistic subjects were now deemed acceptable and moreover some of his newer works, like the Nordstrand landscapes, were not concerned with psychological, 'angst'-ridden subjects, which had always been disliked by most of the Norwegian art public. Between 1899 and 1901, Nasjonalgalleriet purchased four Munch paintings, significantly two landscapes, one portrait and only one 'theme' picture, the comparatively early and realistic masterpiece *Spring*.

In November he went to Berlin, staying in Germany for the winter and following spring. In March and April was the exhibition of the Berlin Secession,[42] and Munch was invited to show a large selection of his works, to be hung in the prominent position of the entrance hall to the exhibition. He exhibited 28 paintings, 22 of them from the *Life Frieze*. These were arranged in four sections, entitled *Budding Love, Love's Blossoming and Fading, Life's Anguish* and *Death*. His paintings were on the whole received well, and Munch was never to forget his gratitude to Germany for giving this opportunity to his most extended series of works.[43]

Munch already had a few German patrons and in 1902 he was to acquire more, of the greatest importance. Munch had known Albert Kollmann, a wealthy and eccentric business-man and mystic, since the nineties, but it was now that Kollmann really started to help him, buying works himself and working to interest others in Munch's art. One of these others was Dr Max Linde, a successful Lübeck eye specialist, who became a great Munch collector and close friend of the artist, looking after him and helping him to sort out his affairs. Assisted by Kollman, Linde published a short study on Munch that year, *Edvard Munch and die Kunst der Zukunst* (Edward Munch and the Art of the Future). A third important supporter was the Judge (Landrichstrat) Gustav Schiefler, who, apart from buying prints and helping Munch organize himself, was shortly to start work on the first part of his great catalogue of Munch's graphic works.[44]

These successes in Germany were to pave the way for Munch's international recognition, especially in the Germanic and Central European countries.

This period around the turn of the century was something of a watershed in Munch's art. On the one hand there are still new subjects on the sort of themes he had included in the *Frieze of Life* earlier in the eighteen-nineties, themes of love, fear and death. Here one could include such new titles as *The Red Vine, Melancholy (Laura), Death and the Child, Heritage, The Dance of Life, Golgotha* and *The Empty Cross*. However some other titles suggest a more philosophical, less pain-filled approach to the great forces of life, such as *Metabolism* and *Fertility*, and it is significant that Munch came to regard the former as a link with his later University murals, which are about 'the great eternal forces' as the artist put it. A painting like *Girls on the Jetty*, although linked with earlier puberty paintings, is a tender and more objective lyric poem, while the great landscapes of the period, such as *Train Smoke* and *White Night*, show a returning interest in nature for its own sake. Then there are a number of portraits of friends like Christen Sandberg, Holger Drachmann and Walter Leistikow, positive and relatively objective paintings or prints, revealing his constant gift for depicting individual character. It may be noticed too that in a number of his paintings of this period, Munch starts to introduce a lighter and brighter palette, partly anticipating his more drastic new experiments around 1907-08. His prints again show this diversity of subject matter, with works like *Harpy* in his old tradition of subjects relating sex to pain, others like *Meeting in Space* suggesting a concern with 'great eternal forces', or types like *The Old Fisherman* a rugged character study of an individual. A characteristic of these years is a continuing inventiveness in both lithographic and woodcut, and a virtuosic experimentation in combining different graphic media in the same print.

As was to be expected, Tulla Larsen features in a number of pictures from this time. There are several oil studies of her in Munch-Museet, while her red hair dominates the female characters in *The Dance of Life* and *Metabolism*, but he left no major oil portrait. The lithograph *Sin (Nude with Red Hair)* (1901), which is probably based on her, perhaps reveals his feelings most truly, particularly her dominating and possessive aspects which he feared.

Emotionally the years were very difficult, and as Munch was to write later: 'I have had some dangerously early autumn storms — they took away my best years — the midsummer of my manhood'.[45] Munch never got nearer to marriage than in his affair with Tulla Larsen, and his determination not to marry was bound to give rise to the greatest possible friction. When he entered Kornhaug Sanatorium during the winter of 1899-1900, he was trying to get a grip on himself, from the many pressures brought about by the affair and by his self-destructive drinking habits, as well as find a cure for his chest troubles. While he was there he wrote frequently to Tulla Larsen, and many drafts of these letters survive. 'They contain frequent and strong statements of his objection to marriage. He can accept it as a matter of pure form, with the reservation that for the sake of art, he must be free to do as he will — etc. He also wants their possessions to be owned in common between them, while it is clear that the rich Tulla Larsen is strongly in favour of an agreement under which they would each retain control of their own possessions after marriage'.[46] As a result of these arguments the two saw little of each other during the next two years. However Tulla Larsen seems to have made attempts to keep the connection going. Her liking for the bohemian circles made it easy for her to keep in touch with Munch through his friends, and Munch resented the way in which he felt she made use of them. Her attempts at reconciliation culminated in a half-hearted suicide attempt in the summer of 1902. Following this Munch returned with her to his house in Aasgaardstrand, where, in a futile quarrel, he accidentally shot himself in the hand, severing two joints of a finger on his left hand. This physically terminated the affair, but from it Munch developed an obsessive hatred of Tulla Larsen, arising from his feeling that she had betrayed and humiliated him. Later that year she went off to Paris with Arne Kavli, one of Munch's younger fellow artists, marrying him there in October 1903. This in itself was a humiliation, as she and Munch had talked about going to Paris just before the pistol-shot, and no doubt it accounts for Munch's uneasiness about visiting Paris in 1903. A major effect of the denouement of the affair was that a number of Munch's friends, who also knew Tulla Larsen, took her side, maintaining that the artist had treated her badly (with some probable truth). Two of these (also known to Delius) were Gunnar Heiberg and Sigurd Bødtker. This, combined with some continuing criticism of his work, convinced Munch that he was being persecuted by many of his countrymen. This insecurity encouraged his drinking and was to lead to a number of violent physical quarrels with other artists and writers over the next few years.

So in the late autumn, after an October exhibition at Blomqvist's in Christiania, Munch accepted an invitation to stay with Dr Linde in Lübeck. For the next few years Linde was from time to time to provide a tranquil temporary home for the artist. As Munch was to write to Jens Thiis: 'I beg you not to forget Dr Max Linde and his household — they helped me out of that chasm into which my fellow countrymen finally pushed me a couple of years ago —'.[47] In December Munch left Lübeck for Berlin and remained based there until the following March, when he ventured to France once more.

Chapter VI

1903-1904

THE YEARS BETWEEN 1903 AND 1908 ARE THE ONES FROM WHICH WE have the most surviving correspondence. Much of it is of a practical nature, and it is quite clear from what has survived that it is incomplete. Moreover, although there are implications of a number of meetings, there is only one which is positively factually established — the occasion on which Munch stayed with the Deliuses at Grez in 1903. These years are ones in which both artist and composer saw their reputations established in Germany. Munch now spent an increasing amount of his time there, while Delius also visited the country on many occasions in connection with the growing number of first performances of his work. Munch was no doubt gratified by the rapid growth of his own reputation in Germany and Central Europe, but he was also aware of the unique position of Paris as the world's art capital and of the desirability of promoting his reputation there as well. From 1903 to 1908 he exhibited each year at the *Salon des Indépendants*, with the sole exception of 1907. Here Delius was able to help him, as a friendly ally living not far from Paris, particularly as Jelka was now starting to exhibit at the *Indépendants* herself.

During the winter of 1903, Munch was in Berlin. Delius must have invited him to visit him in France, and Munch's first letter is a reply:

Munch to Delius
(3, M.2)   Hotel Hippodrome Am Knie Charlottenburg
                                                                            30/1 1903
Dear Delius,
    Many thanks for the invitation — I have a great longing for Paris and will probably be able to come — later — at the end of February — I should like to exhibit at L'Independants — I should be delighted to stay for a while with you then — it must be very beautiful — But I am afraid of a lady in Paris and expect new bad things — Write and tell me what you know — She has herself so many allies — Unfortunately my finger is not yet healed[1] — I don't think I·can come to Düsseldorf[2] how long are you going to stay there?
    Best wishes to you and Fraulein Rosen
                                        Your friend
                                        E. Munch

The next evidence comes from a letter home to his aunt, written in Leipzig where he was staying at the Hotel Palmbaum, Geberstrasse, dated 27/2 03[3],

'I will travel from here to Paris for a short time — when I shall exhibit some pictures — I will stay outside Paris with Delius and will keep myself hidden for understandable reasons —'

Munch's date of arrival at Grez must have been in late February or early March, as his German friend and patron, Dr Max Linde wrote to him care of Delius on 18 March:[4]

'Today I have written to Hr Osthaus. He will write to you either at Grez or Paris (post restante).'

Osthaus was becoming interested in Munch and it was probably during this year that he started to buy his works. Although apparently he did not buy many, as he wished to obtain them cheaply, he was to arrange a Munch exhibition at the Folkwangs Museum in 1906.

Jelka Delius comments on her own dealings with Osthaus in a letter to Rodin. She wrote to the sculptor on 18th March from Grez saying that she was in Paris the day before, taking her paintings in for the *Salon des Indépendants*, but that she had to catch the train back and so was unable to visit him. She warns Rodin about Hr Osthaus, who 'has not bought my painting (the one which he verbally bought in the autumn) and now he tells me that if I will help to get a Rodin cheaply he will buy something of mine'.[5] She goes on to assure Rodin that she would never stoop to this and that Osthaus 'is *very* rich and he must pay the price that you ask . . . He is very friendly with Dr Linde of Lübeck who owns eleven of your works. Linde will also come to Paris. But I think Linde is not aware of these little business peculiarities of Monsieur Osthaus.' She confirms that Munch is staying with her and Delius: 'The young Munk, very, very interesting Norwegian painter is here also. He is exhibiting at the *Indépendants*.' After saying that she has had the courage to send her large picture of 'this erotic garden', she continues about the difficulties of fulfilling her artistic aspirations, but 'Munk encourages me, as you do'.[6]

Jelka's nervousness at exhibiting can be understood as this was the first time she had shown with the *Indépendants*. On this occasion she showed five pictures, while Munch exhibited eight.

The *Salon des Indépendants* opened on Friday, 20th March, and Jelka went up to Paris for it. Delius would have accompanied her, and this would also be a likely date for the termination of Munch's stay with them. During the next six weeks there are a number of postal exchanges between Munch and Delius largely concerned with attempts to sell his pictures. Not all of these are dated and possibly several have disappeared, so their ordering has to be to some extent conjectural. The first is from Delius, not dated but sent from Grez on a Monday. As he says that they left (presumably Paris) the previous evening this would probably mark their return home from the opening of the *Indépendants*, and this would make Monday the 23rd March.

Delius to Munch.

(4, D.2)   Grez
                                          Monday (probably 23rd March, 1903)
Dear Munch -
We left yesterday evening at 5 o'clock — Behrend[7] writes to me that you can sell some engravings to Dr Robin[8] a friend of mine and brother-in-law of his and suggests that you should take your engravings there (;) he lives at *53 Boulevard de Courcelles*. He says that you must tell him the prices. Robin is a splendid fellow and extremely intelligent. Behrend tells me that the prices of your pictures are much too high and that with such prices you will certainly not make much progress in Paris — I think it would be wiser to set your prices rather less high. For example — The Tree and The Melancholy Woman 1,000 frs. and the large picture 2,500 and the small pictures 4 and 500 frs[9] Behrend loves your pictures and would like to help you. But he knows the conditions in Paris from A to Z. And knows how things have to be done and how not — Farewell now — Frl. Rosen sends her best wishes.
                                                   Your friend
                                                   Fr. Delius
Dr Robin
53 Boulevard de Courcelles
Mention my name and if Robin is not there ask for his wife —

Munch's next communication looks as if it were a reply:[10]

Munch to Delius.
(5, M.3)   Paris 24/3 03
Dear Delius!
Don't you think I should wait — until my etchings arrive before going to Herr Robin with my engravings?[11]
I have seen a studio near the Rue de la Sante — Is it too far?
                                        Remember me to Fraulein Rosen
                                                   Your friend
                                                   Edv. Munch

Delius replied the following Sunday; (although his letter is not dated, the sequence makes Sunday 29th March seem pretty certain.) One feels that he is not entirely pleased with the fact that Munch has not answered his question about prices.

Delius to Munch.
(6, D.3)   Grez Sunday (probably 29th March 1903)
Dear Munch
You did not answer my question about the prices of your pictures and everything, I

67

think, really depends on that — I think that Behrend cannot do much with such high prices and naturally I do not want to encourage you to rent a studio only *on this account*. But in case you are thinking of staying in Paris it seems to me more practical to have a studio and then why not in the Rue de la Santé[12] — When you receive the engravings — then go there at once[13] — I will be in Paris again in the middle of April —

I hope you are well
Your friend
Fr. Delius

Another communication must have arrived from Munch (which has since disappeared) almost as soon as this letter was posted, as Delius wrote again two days later:

Delius to Munch.
(7, D.4)   Grez
                                                                31 March (1903)
Dear Munch —
    What you write about Robin greatly astonishes me — There must be something wrong somewhere. Behrend has been in England I have just written to him and we will certainly put the matter right again so that something can be sold —
    I am glad that you have found a collector[14] Of course the prices are too low but you have to make some sacrifice to get in at all — afterwards you can *bleed* the dear people.
    I am glad that you intend to rent a studio — it is much better and then you can work. I will write and tell you the day on which I shall come in[15]
    Frl. Rosen and I send our best wishes —

Your friend
Frederick Delius[16]

Munch remained in Paris, but does not seem to have communicated with Delius for a few weeks. Dr Linde wrote to Munch there[17] and on 17th April the artist wrote to Karen Bjølstad that he would not be in Paris much longer and that he would shortly be going to stay with Dr Linde in Lübeck. He also tells her that 'I have sold a picture here for 500 Fcs —'.[18] By mid-April Delius was clearly wondering what had happened to Munch, as he sent a postcard:

Delius to Munch.
(8, D.5)
                                              postmarked GREZ 21 Avril 03.
Monsieur Edvard Munch
Hotel d'Alsace
Rue des Beaux Arts
Paris.
Dear Munch,
    How are you. Behrend wrote to me that you did not see Frau Robin but a secretary. Have you seen B again —? Write and tell me what you are doing — We are coming to

Paris for a fortnight at the end of the month. Have you a studio?

Farewell

Your friend

Fr D.

Frl R. sends best wishes

Berend had also by now written to Munch, apologizing for the misunderstanding over Dr Robin. He explained that Munch had been expected to send his prints to the doctor, not to take them personally, and that neither Dr Robin nor his secretary were prepared for his coming. He continues: 'Have you rented a studio where I can bring my friends to see your pictures?' and ends by congratulating Munch on selling a painting at *L'Indépendants*.[19]

It would appear, then, as if the attempt to sell prints to Dr Robin came to nothing. But this batch of letters, if rather scrappy are quite revealing. They suggest the balance and stability of Delius, settled with Jelka, compared to the restlessness and instability of Munch (except where his art was concerned) at this period. They show the trouble that Delius would go to to help his friends, and also his number of useful connections, and they reveal his patience. They also show — and this will be confirmed by subsequent letters — how much Munch relied on the friends who he trusted, and even made use of them, although not, I think, in a calculating way.

In the later part of the month Munch went to Lübeck to visit Dr Linde. From there he wrote to Delius and, although the letter is not dated, it seems clear that it was written before too much time had elapsed since Paris:

Munch to Delius.

(9, M.4)

Lübeck-Evangelisches Vereinshaus

Fischstrasse

(Undated, but probably late April or May 1903)

Dear Delius,

Am in Lübeck — will write to you more fully later — I was too fuddled[20] to be able to arrange my affairs — I can do that later in writing — Paris is splendid but it ruined my nerves — I will visit you in the autumn — Regards to Behrend —

Kindest regards to Fraulein Rosen

Your friend E Munch

In the summer Munch returned home, to Aasgaardstrand. In September he was again in Lübeck, when he painted Dr Linde's four sons (Behnhaus, Lübeck), going on later in the autumn to Berlin where, apart for a few days in Lübeck around the New Year, he spent the winter.

Delius remained mostly at Grez, where he was now working on *Sea Drift*. In the later summer he visited Basel, where a performance was given of his *Mitternachtslied Zarathustras*, the important Nietzsche setting which he had made in 1898. In September he and Jelka visited Holland and from there he sent a picture postcard of a Frans Hals painting to Munch, addressed to Aasgaardstrand:

Delius to Munch.
(10, D.6)   postmarked KATWIJKAANZE
                                                               1. SEP 03
                    Many greetings from us both
                            Fr. Delius

On the 25th September Delius and Jelka were married at Grez, and they sent a postcard to Munch:

Delius to Munch.
(11, D.7)   postmarked PARIS 3-10 03
Monsieur Edvard Munck
          Maler
Asgaardstrand
          Norvège
readdressed to Poste Restante
          Lübeck
          Duitsland
readdressed to Berlin Hotel Stadt Riga[21]
Dear Munch,
    How are you? And when are coming here again? I have just rented a studio at Avenue d'Orleans 110 and shall be in Paris rather more often this winter. Frl. Rosen and I have just legalized our relationship because we consider it more practical[22] — We have been in Holland but the weather was terrible — Do let us hear from you and fare well
                              Yours
                              Fr. D

Grez
1000 greetings and good wishes for your beautiful art.
                    Jelka Delius

The next group of communications comes from the end of 1903 and the beginning of 1904 and are largely concerned with Munch's attempts to exhibit in Paris. Several are undated and at least one seems to have disappeared, so that the order in which they are arranged here is partly conjectural.

The first, a postcard from Delius at the end of October, is clearly in answer to one from Munch, which has not been discovered:

70

Delius to Munch.
(12, D.8)
Postcard addressed to
Monsieur Edvard Munch
Hotel Stadt Riga
Mittelstrasse
Berlin
Allemagne

postmarked GREZ 28 (or 29) OCT 03

Dear Friend,

Lugné Poé's[23] address is, — L.P. Directeur du Théatre de l'Oeuvre Nouveau Théatre, Rue Blanche. I was glad to hear from you again and also that you intend to come to Paris again. I hope for the whole winter. You must also come here to Grez. We look forward to that I also have to go to Germany in January. Düsseldorf and Elberfeld[24] and perhaps also Berlin — When are you coming?

Best wishes from us both
Yours
Fr. Delius

Readdressed to Lützow. Str. 82. W.35

The next letter is from Munch:

Munch to Delius
(13, M.5)   Undated, but about Christmas 1903
                                        Sent from Hamburg[25]

Dear Delius,

I should like to exhibit my large frieze in Paris (a part of it was already exhibited 7 years ago at L'indépendants)[26] —

Do you know of a place? I had thought of getting one through Lugné Poë — Perhaps in his theatre? Could you speak to him — and how would you advise me on making accessible to the public — or selling — the pictures which are left in my studio in Boulevard Arago 65 —

In any case I shall exhibit some of them at L'indépendants — But what do you think? — Otherwise — Perhaps L'Art Nouveau[27] — I have had two big exhibitions here with the Secession and at Cassirer's[28] — with artistic success —

I am going to Weimar in January to paint Count Kessler[29] Perhaps I will go on from there to Paris —

The Vienna Secession is now arranging an exhibition of my collected paintings[30] — so all is going well in Germany — But I should like to do something in Paris —

How are you and your wife? I am looking forward to seeing both of you and your lovely house again — I am in Hamburg now and am going to Lübeck —

Best wishes to you and your wife
Your E Munch

Temporary address

The frieze needs a lot of space

Dr Max Linde
Lübeck

The next letter is a draft of a letter from Munch to Delius. Munch was in the habit of making drafts of letters to friends, which he

71

generally kept, and these are preserved in Munch-Museet. Sometimes these can be seen to form the basis of letters actually sent, in other cases we are less sure. This one would appear to be a preliminary draft for the previous letter (13, M.5). However, the reference to exhibitions in Berlin and Vienna suggests that it was written after 6th January 1904, when the Vienna Secession exhibition opened, and if this were the case this would be the draft for a new letter; (Munch's correspondence is frequently repetitive.) On the other hand I think Munch would have been quite capable of writing 'I have here large exhibitions . . .' when in fact they were only in preparation. So we cannot be sure, but I would still incline to think of it being written prior to 13, M.5.

The suggestions as to where to exhibit his pictures in Paris are largely the same as in letter 13, M.5 and it also appears as if Munch was toying with the possibility of giving up his Paris studio.

Munch to Delius.
(13a, Md.1)   Lützowstr 82
                                 Undated, but December 1903 or January 1904.

Dear Delius

I still have my studio in Paris — Can you do anything — or advise me how I should make the best use of my things — Perhaps an exhibition at Bing's?[31] — I will probably come to Paris in February — Perhaps something could be done in the meantime —

Do you know of a big place where I could exhibit my frieze —? Perhaps it could be arranged through Lugnë-Poé in a theatre — I have here large exhibitions in Berlin and Vienna[32] — and I am working hard in my studio — But it is not practicable to keep two studios going —

So you are tied up and I am still a free journeyman

But I always have feelings about the enemy — Woman I think you know Eva Mudocci and B. Edvards — They are here — Fraulein Mudocci is wonderfully beautiful and I almost fear falling in love — (one of thousands) What do you think? After the last affair with T[33] I am madly apprehensive — Write to me but don't send me 'the white cat'[34] again. At any rate don't tell me anything about that

Best wishes to you and your wife. Are you coming to Berlin and when?

This draft letter gives an interesting glimpse into Munch's wariness over women, prompted by his reaction to news of Delius's marriage. Although almost proud of his susceptibility to their charms, he clearly wishes the 'free journeyman' to remain free. It also mentions for the first time in the correspondence with Delius the name of Eva Mudocci, with whom he was to have one of his more notable romantic friendships and who was also known to the composer.

Eva Mudocci was born Evangeline Hope Muddock, of artistic British parents. Brought up as a child prodigy violinist, she later studied the instrument in Berlin under Joachim and Halir. In Berlin she met the young pianist Bella Edwards and the two formed a professional duo and lifelong friendship, performing mostly on the continent, particularly in Germany, Scandinavia and France.

They settled in Paris in 1903, in which year Eva probably first met Munch and Delius, although not on the same occasion.[35] She became very friendly with the artist and it is virtually certain that they had a love affair. Their closest years were between 1903 and 1908-09, although they were still in touch considerably later than that.[36] In this case Munch would hardly have cause to fear a 'predatory female' as Eva was also devoted to her career and to her close partnership with Bella Edwards. Munch made three celebrated lithographs of her in 1903, *The Violin Recital* (OKK G/1.254, Sch.211), *Madonna (The Brooch)* (OKK G/1.255, Sch.212) and *Salome* (OKK G/1.256, Sch.213), and there is also probably at least one uncompleted oil portrait of her by him from the same period (collection of Richard N. Tetlie, Washington D.C.). An extensive correspondence between them is preserved in Munch-Museet.

The next letter comes from Delius and seems to read as an answer to letter 13. Although it is dated 31st January 1903, it seems clear that he made a mistake and should have written December, as his letter reads: 'on the 21st January I have a concert in Düsseldorf' and other correspondence makes it clear that he went to Germany in the second half of January.

Delius to Munch.
(14, D.9)   Grez
                        31 Jan (but almost certainly December 1903)
Dear Friend —
    I have just received your letter and am very pleased that things are going so well for you in Germany — First of all I would advise you to exhibit some (5-6) of your best pictures with the *'Independants'*. I will then try and send as many people as possible there *Afterwards* (in May-June) exhibit your frieze, perhaps with Georges Petit[37] — L'art Nouveau[38] is no good for you — You must send me the dimensions as quickly as possible. and then I can look round in Paris for a suitable place. Nouveau Theatre[39] is no good either. It is rather dark and Lugne Poë (if I know him well) will not do anything for art. I am going to Paris in the middle of January and, as soon as I have the measurements of your frieze, will make careful enquiries — On the 21st January I have a concert in Düsseldorf. Perhaps, on your way to Paris you could pick me up and we could then travel back together. In any case send the measurements at once — Farewell. My wife and I send our heartiest New Year wishes and greetings —
                              Your
                            Fr Delius
P.S. Karsten decamped from here *in the night* without paying of course,[40] —

Munch's movements around the New Year are not clear. It seems

73

natural that Munch should have gone on from Hamburg to Lübeck. Yet we find Dr Linde writing to him from Lübeck on 4/1 04: 'As you can see, you have missed your friend Delius'.[41] This makes it sound as though a letter from Delius had turned up in Lübeck after Munch had left; (there is no question of Delius himself having arrived in Germany that early). Dr Linde's next letter is dated 10 Jan. 04? 'You had hardly left when the post arrived with money for you. I have sent two money-orders to you at the Berlin address'.[42] So Munch could have spent a few days in Lübeck, say from c.29th December to c.3rd January, or from c.5th to c.9th January. Alternatively, he could have come to Lübeck, gone briefly away and then returned.

In any case his next letter to Delius is addressed Lübeck, and it reads like an answer to Delius's letter (14, D.9):

Munch to Delius
(15, M.6)
HANSA-CAFÉ   Lübeck
Inh: HANS EILENBERGER   no date (but probably early January 1904)
Dear Friend!
    My frieze should really have a space of 14 × 14 m[43] — but could if necessary be reduced —
    Would it not be possible to have an exhibition at Duran Ruel's?[44] (But not the frieze)
    My work would show to great advantage there —
    In *L'Independants* the people gave me such a bad hanging position before and if they do it this time too it is going to be unpleasant[45]—
    When you come to Paris what is your address? I shall not arrive in Paris until February as I have to paint Count Kessler in Weimar[46]—
    It is very unpleasant having these Norwegians going around and running up debts — They harm others who have less money but who cannot live in this way—
    Gunnar Heiberg will probably completely ruin my old hotel in the rue de Seine[47]—
    Best wishes to you and your wife—
                                        Yours Edv. Munch
Temporary address.
Dr Max Linde
Lübeck

We hear little more about Delius's efforts to find Munch a large gallery in Paris at this stage. By the time of his next communication, the composer was in Germany. It is worth inserting here, however, a letter to Munch from Ludvig Karsten, who was in Paris, as it deals with business that is also referred to in the Delius letters:

Ludvig Karsten to Munch[48]

                                        Paris 20-1-04
Dear Munch!
    I have been to see Lemercier[49] and I can assure you that your stones are in safe

keeping despite the fact that the business is under new management. I did however have the impression that he would appreciate another little order. If there is anything else, I am at your service.

We had a brilliant retrospective exhibition here at Vollard's[50] of Gauguin, who as you perhaps know died in the autumn. The pictures went for relatively small sums such as two or three thousand francs. They were Vollard's property, probably aquired over the years for a few hundred francs each.

Incidentally do you know that Delius has married Mlle. Rosen!

L'Indépendants exhibition opens this year on 20th February and the sending in days are the 11th and 12th February.

If you would like to, and I think *you really should*, exhibit there this year, (you have after all a studio full of pictures) I will send them in for you. In that case you must *say exactly which* (paintings) and give prices and I will fill up the forms etc.

But you must please be good enough to send the entrance fee because I have only enought to manage for myself at the moment.

I am exhibiting there myself this year. One of these days I shall go out to Medon to look at some Van Goghs in a private collection.

There are not many Norwegians around this year. Even Heyerdahl has not turned up. I am living quietly and peacefully and am no longer on Mont-Parnasse. The Krohgs and the Diriks are here of course and entertaining their cliques with little anecdotes about each other.[51]

Is it so that you will be coming here in the course of the Spring!

Greeting
Yours
L. Karsten
66 rue de Seine

When Delius next wrote to Munch he had arrived in Elberfeld, going on there after the performance of *Life's Dance* in Düsseldorf on 21st January. Presumably he had checked on the safety of Munch's lithographic stones on his way through Paris to Germany.

Delius to Munch.
(16, D.10)
Postcard to
Herrn Edvard Munck
c/o Herrn Dr Lind   postmarked ELBERFELD 3.2.04
Lübeck
Dear Munck.

I have been here a fortnight and am staying for another 4-5 weeks. My opera 'Koanga' will be performed — Your stones are all present and are ready for your disposal in Paris. When are you going to Paris? Can you not come here first? Elberfeld is only 35 minutes from Cologne — Durand-Ruel would also be good — but it is expensive —

Many greetings from myself and my wife
Your friend
Frederick Delius

Hotel Bristol Elberfeld.

75

No more letters survive from 1904. However, no big Munch Paris exhibition took place and although the artist continued to flirt with the idea for several years, it was never brought off. On the other hand Munch did exhibit six pictures at *L'Indépendants*, which that year was held from 21st February until 24th March. As Delius was away in Germany, he would not on this occasion have been able to help Munch over this. However it may be that Ludvig Karsten fulfilled the offer he made in his letter of entering the pictures. It is just possible that Munch may have visited Paris himself in March before going to Weimar.

1904 saw a real upsurge of interest in Delius's music in Germany. Apart from the January performance of *Life's Dance* in Düsseldorf and the spring premiere of *Koanga* in Elberfeld, there were two notable concerts of his work in the latter town that autumn. These included two first performances, *Appalachia: Variations on an old Slave song* and a revised version of the Piano Concerto, as well as performances of *Life's Dance* and *Paris*. Although criticisms were mixed, there was no doubt that the serious commitment to Delius's music by conductors like Haym and Buths was beginning to take effect and this was to continue to build up. Haym was the conductor of both the autumn concerts in Elberfeld and he had also patronised the production of *Koanga* at the Stadttheater there in the spring. But the opera's première and its two subsequent performances were conducted by a younger man, Fritz Cassirer, who was now to be added to Delius's enthusiastic supporters. Fritz Cassirer belonged to the remarkable family of German-Jewish intellectuals who made such an important contribution to the cultural and academic life of Germany during the first part of the twentieth century.

Fritz Cassirer developed a warm friendship with Delius, which continued until the first world war, and in 1907 he was to conduct the first performance of *A Village Romeo and Juliet*, in Berlin, and the first London performance of *Appalachia*. Of no less importance was his assistance to Delius in making a selection from Nietzsche's *Also Sprach Zarathustra* to form the libretto for *A Mass of Life*, the largest and most ambitious of the composer's works for the concert hall. They spent part of the summer of 1904 together in France, engaged on this work, the composition of which was to occupy Delius through this and the following year.

Fritz Cassirer's brother, Bruno, and his cousin Paul, were closely connected with Munch's career during these years. The first surviving correspondence between Munch and Paul Cassirer comes in 1901. In this and the following year contact was important as Paul was both a leading German art dealer with a rather modern slant, as well as being Secretary of the Berlin Secession. The taste of the Secession's Chairman, the painter Max Liebermann was for a modified Impressionism, a taste shared by Cassirer. It is thus not surprising that in its early years (it was founded in 1896) Munch's art was regarded with some suspicion as being too radical. However Munch had his supporters in the Secession, notably the painters Walter Leistikow and Ludwig von Hofmann, who had been among those few who supported Munch as far back as his notorious 1892 Berlin exhibition.[52] With their help, and also that of Albert Kollmann, Paul Cassirer was won over to admire Munch, and these efforts resulted in Munch's successful exhibition with the Secession in 1902. For the next few years Munch frequently showed his paintings at Cassirer's gallery,[53] although this must have lessened after 1904, when Munch made a contract for the sale of his paintings with Commeter's, in Hamburg.

From 1904, however, Munch was to have closer contact with Bruno Cassirer when he concluded a contract with him for the sole rights to the sale of his prints in Germany. The drafting of this contract is the subject of considerable discussion in the letters to Munch from Dr Linde, and it is clear that Munch's patrons, Linde himself and Gustav Schiefler, were very concerned that the contract should not be too much to Cassirer's advantage.[54]

Despite common acquaintances and the fact that Delius was to make a number of visits to Germany in 1904 in connection with performances of his work, we have no concrete evidence of any meeting with Munch that year, although the artist also was in the same country for much of the time.

After wintering mainly in Berlin, Munch spent much of March and April in Weimar, where he painted the portrait of Count Harry Kessler. As an important patron of modern art, Kessler seems to have wished to attract Munch there, as he saw to it that the artist was offered a studio in the Academy of Art. After another visit to Lübeck he returned in mid-May to Norway, to spend much of the summer in Aasgaardstrand. After visits to Germany and Copenhagen (where he had an exhibition) in August, he was back in Norway for the autumn, with an exhibition in Christiania. Finally he returned to Germany in November, where he remained for the winter.

An important commission of the year was the frieze of paintings for the nursery of Dr Linde's house. Although Linde (probably with reason) did not consider the final subject matter as suitable for a children's nursery and consequently rejected the paintings, he purchased the latest large *Summer Night* picture instead as compensation and their friendship remained unimpaired.

Chapter VII

1905–1908

THE PATTERN OF THE CORRESPONDENCE DURING THE NEXT FOUR YEARS
continues in much the same way as in the two previous ones.

During 1905, Munch spent most of the year in Germany, with visits
to Prague, Norway and Copenhagen. He does not seem to have visited
Paris. Delius remained in France, at Grez but with visits to Paris, and
he also visited Germany. But there is no record of any meeting between
the two. Surviving correspondence is confined to the first five months
and is almost entirely concerned with Munch's exhibiting at the *Salon
des Indépendants*. It is evident that some correspondence has been lost.

The first item is a postcard from Delius which must be in answer to a
lost communication from Munch.

Delius to Munch.
(17, D.11)   postmarked GREZ 27 Janv 05
Postcard addressed to:
Monsieur Edvard Munch
Hotel Janson
Mittel-Strasse 53-54
Berlin NW
Allemagne
Dear Friend
    Have just written to Idependants and will arrange the matter for you.
                        Best wishes from us both
                            Your friend
                                Delius
Are you coming here soon — We should be very pleased.

The purpose of Delius's writing to *L'Indépendants* is made quite clear
in the next communication:

Delius to Munch.
(18, D.12)   postmarked GREZ 3 Fevr, 05
Postcard addressed to:
Monsieur Edvard Munch
Hotel Janson
Mittel Strasse 53-54
Berlin NW Allemagne
(re-addressed to Prague)

Dear Friend

I have just received the information that if you are already a member of the Society[1] you will have to pay 7.50 frcs for half a year's subscription and in addition an exhibition fee — which I can only pay for you when the pictures are handed in. The last sending-in days are 10th-11th March. The varnishing day 23rd March. My wife says that there is such great overcrowding that many who are not members of the Society will not get in.[2] My wife is exhibiting too. Shall we hand in your pictures as well? Do be sure to exhibit a couple of really good pictures — be a devil — ! Write me a card and tell me if I am to pay your membership subscription. Why don't you have a big Paris exhibition for once!

Best wishes from us both.
Yours
Fr Delius

The letter was re-addressed to Prague, where Munch had gone for an important exhibition of his work, arranged by the 'Manes' group of artists. This exhibition was a prestigious success for Munch, and he mentions it in his reply to Delius, written just after he had returned to Berlin.

Munch to Delius.
(19, M.7)   c/o Hotel Janson
                                              Mittelstrasse Berlin
          (Undated, but almost certainly between 7th and 9th February, 1905)[3]
Dear Friend,

Please be so kind as to pay my membership subscription for L'Independants — I will send it to you at once — I have just returned from Prague — where I have arranged a large exhibition[4] — and am waiting for money.

I shall perhaps send a larger picture too — my best things are now in Prague — It was splendid in Prague — I was the guest of the artists — and there were many parties — The mayor put his carriage at my disposal —

I have a great longing for Paris — I should also much like to visit you both in your very beautiful house but do not know if I shall get the time —

Do come to Aasgaardstrand for once[5]!

Well I will write again soon — In a few days I will send the money — but please see that I remain a member and lay out the money — Death to my enemies and greetings to my friends[6]

Your old
Edv. Munch

Please tell me how Fraulein Eva Mudocci is getting on — have you run into her[7]

Munch also wrote Delius a postcard about the same business but he probably did not sent it; at any rate it has disappeared.[8] The postcard was a Czech one, and the message seems to indicate his Prague exhibition. However, he gives a German address, so it was presumably written at the time of his return from Prague to Berlin.

Munch to Delius.
(19a, Md.2)
Postcard addressed to:
Mr. le compositeur Frits Delius
Grez (Marlotte)   (Undated but probably about the
Seine et Marne   same as letter 19, i.e. quite
Franckreich.   early in February 1905)
Dear Friend!
  Here I have a big exhibition in the whole of the gallery. Please be so kind as to lay
out the money for L'Independant for me
  — I am sending the money immediately —
                                Greetings   Yours   E Munch
Address Hotel Janson Mittelstrasse Berlin

Delius's next letter is clearly a reply to Munch's previous one (19, M.7).

Delius to Munch.
(20, D.13)   Grez
                                                                    11 Febr 1905
Dear Friend
  I have today sent 25 frcs to the Independants that is everything as you will see
from the enclosed letter.[9] I was very glad to hear that you were so successful in Prague
and hope you will be equally successful here. But one day you must put on a really big
exhibition here with all your best things.
  There will always be a room for you here at our house and we would be delighted to
see you here — We could then all go to Paris together for the exhibition. Frl Eva
Mudocci is in Paris, I know, but I have not seen her for a long time. She is charming.
                          Best wishes from us both
                                   Yours
                                 Fr. Delius

Munch has now sent some of his works to Delius, to place on
exhibition in Paris and Delius writes regarding them

Delius to Munch.
(21, D.14)   Grez
                                                           postmarked GREZ 26 Fevr 05
Postcard addressed to:
Monsieur Edvard Munch
Artiste-peintre
Hotel Janson
Mittel Str
Berlin Allemagne
(re-addressed 28/2 to Poste Restante, Hamburg).
Dear Friend — The sheets[10] have arrived but unframed — Write at once and tell
what you want done with them or it will be too late. 10th. 11th. 12th Feb[11] are the
days.
                          Most heartily
                                Yours
                              Fr. Delius

80

Munch replied from Hamburg, where he had gone at the end of February in order to paint a portrait.[12]

Munch to Delius.
(22, M.8)

GIEBFRIEDS HOTEL
Hamburg — St. Georg
c/o Giebfrieds Hotel
Kobbel 9 — Hamburg[13]
(Undated but probably early March 1905)
Dear Friend!

Please complete the list — Cassirer[14] has probably enclosed the titles and prices — the titles are probably on the back — You are sure to sort it all out —
1) Vampire 2) Madonna or Loving Woman 3) Strindberg 4) The Wave (Litho) 5) Le Soir Bois en 3 Couleurs Clair de lune Bois en 3 Couleurs and so on.

The Wave (la vogue?) Litho and Number 8 is not labelled I do not remember what it is Write a name in If there are no price-lists, then please fix the prices between 50-80 Frcs —[15]

I should like to come and see you perhaps next winter and paint something —

Best wishes to you and your wife

Yours Edvard Munch

Have you received the card — where I ask you to have the engravings framed and glazed cheaply —?[16]

Please remember me to Fraulein Mudocci do you know her address

There is now a gap of two months in the surviving correspondence, but there are certainly some communications missing here. At all events it seems almost certain that Delius put Munch's prints into the *Salon des Indépendants* and collected them when the exhibition closed.[17]

Frederick and Jelka Delius to Munch.
(23, D.15)

Grez
May 11 1905

Dear Friend

I have received the money today — thank you very much — I have had the engravings brought to my Paris flat. Are you not in touch with some dealer or other — if not which one would you like me to approach?[18] Write to me and I will look after this when I go to Paris. The weather is wonderful here. I do not believe in a war between Norway and Sweden[19] Europe has enough with Japan and Russia. My wife is writing the soup recipe herself.

Best wishes
Yours
Fr. Delius

Jelka Delius's contribution is written on the same sheet.

Dear Herr Munch,

You must pick the tender tips of the nettles, a whole basket full, chop them quite fine while still raw. Then one melts some butter and fries the nettles in it for about ¼

81

hour, then one pours over them weak stock or water adding salt to taste and let it all cook for about 1 hour. One puts a generous portion of cream and an egg (raw) beaten together into a soup tureen then stirring constantly one very carefully pours the hot soup on to it.

   Guten Appetit!

Yours
Jelka Delius[20]

This is all that has survived from 1905, and we know of no other direct contact between the two men that year, although it is not unlikely that they may have corresponded further.

Delius spent most of the year at Grez, completing *A Mass of Life*. He visited Germany in May and June for a performance of *Appalachia* on 13th June at the Lower Rhine Music Festival at Düsseldorf, conducted by Julius Buths, (at which time Munch was in Norway). It seems that he missed going to Norway that summer. At the end of the year his symphonic poem *Paris* was performed in Brussels.

Munch returned to Aasgaardstrand in the spring and remained in Norway until July. There he was much with Ludvig Karsten and painted his portrait. Unfortunately the two quarrelled and actually came to blows — the latest of a series of violent quarrels with Norwegians in which Munch had become involved. This year must have marked the nadir of his relations with Norwegians (apart from some faithful old friends), as after this summer he stayed away from Norway until after recovering from his nervous breakdown in 1909. In July he went to Denmark and in August had an exhibition in Copenhagen. In September he went to Chemnitz to stay with his friends the Esche family and paint portraits of them and their children, staying there (apart from a visit to Hamburg) until the end of October.[21] Henry van de Velde, the eminent designer and professor at Weimar, who had designed the Esche's house and who was also known to the artist, was in Chemnitz at the same time. About the beginning of November Munch went to Bad Elgersburg, near Weimar and he was to remain in the Weimar area for much of the following year. The principal reason for this extended visit to Weimar was a commission from the Swedish banker Ernest Thiel to paint a posthumous portrait of Nietzsche, of whom he was a great admirer. By 1905 Thiel had become one of Munch's important patrons, and on receiving the Nietzsche commission[22] Munch went to Weimar, where he could study the philosopher's writings together with the surroundings where he had lived.

This was a prolific period for Munch, and paintings in 1905 included a new version of *Girls on the Jetty* (Cologne), *Dance on the Shore* (Prague),

82

Two young girls on a farm (Rotterdam) and portraits of Gustav Schiefler, Ludvig Karsten and the various ones of the Esche family. He also made a number of new prints. Apart from the Prague and Copenhagen exhibitions already mentioned, he exhibited widely in Germany that year, as well as in Stockholm.

One further piece of information connecting Munch to Delius, which belongs to the end of this year, is preserved in Munch-Museet; a letter from Eva Mudocci to Munch, and it is worth quoting the relevant passage from it.

Rue Malebranche 11 Paris
Dec. 12 (1905)

Dear Edvard Munch!

. . . You asked about Delius — Yes — we have seen him — last spring he visited us together with his wife, and a few weeks ago they were here again[23] — I like her very much — she is so calm and good-natured and shrewd in a way — she has also I feel a kind heart — he is as always; a little older — a little more Mephistophelian! — they have invited us to their home several times, but we haven't been there yet — We played a piece of his music for him — which called for great effort from us because it was so terribly dull and we had to look as if we found it interesting! No! — That sounds too malicious of me! — I like him too — but not his music[24]. . .

One cannot help wondering if Eva Mudocci's comments on Delius's music might have had any effect on Munch, who does not seem to have been particularly conscious of his friend's compositions, at least not at this stage of his life.

1906 saw Munch again preparing to exhibit some works at the *Salon des Indépendants* and once again he was in correspondence with Delius about the arrangements. The exhibition opened in March and closed on 29th April. Munch was represented by six works, three paintings and three lithographs. The surviving correspondence opens with a letter from Delius, who was in Berlin. Presumably it reached Munch at one of the spas near Weimar where he was wintering, for although the artist did make several short visits to Berlin that winter, the letter suggests that he has been in touch with Delius but that they have not actually met recently.

Delius to Munch.
(24, D.16)

Kleist Strasse 38[11]
23 Feb
(no year is given, but events recounted in
the letter make 1906 certain)

Dear Friend.

I have been here in Berlin since the 8 January. A symphony of mine was performed on the 5th February and everything went off very well.[25] On Monday I am returning

to Paris and will take care of the matter.[26] You must send your pictures to the Independants at once. Grandes Serres. Cour la Reine. Sending-in days are 9. 10. 11. March: so you have still got time. I will pay for you —
Farewell — my wife sends her best wishes.
Your friend
Fr. Delius

Munch replied with a postcard at the beginning of March, addressing it in a particularly muddled form; however it did reach its destination.

Munch to Delius.
(25, M.9)
Postcard addressed to:
Monsieur Fritz Delius
Componist
Par Paris   postmarked WEIMAR 2.3.06
Grez sur Marne[27]
Seine et Oise
Marlotte
Dear Friend
     I have sent off 3 painting and 3 engravings[28] — The paintings are called — Les . buveurs — Paysages de Thuringerwald 2 pieces — Price for each picture 1000 Frcs — 3 Lithographs — Mr K. — Mr Henry van de Velde and Nietzsche — I leave it to you to reject the last one if you find it bad[29] —
     The works have been sent by express goods and will be there soon
Yours E M
The lithographs price 60 Marks each[30]

The slight delay over the arrival of the last postcard, caused by its muddled address, may well have caused Delius to write, asking what was happening. At any rate Munch wrote to him again a few days later, repeating his information.

Munch to Delius.
(26, M.10)   *HOTEL RUSSISCHER HOF*
Weimar   8 - 3 - 1906
am Karlsplatz
Dear Friend
     The pictures must be there by now and I hope you will find them —
     I have already written you a card about them —
     There are two landscapes of Thuringia, one (picture) 'The Drunkard' and three lithos — Hr. van de Velde[31] — Portrait Hr. K and Nitzsche[32] —
     The prices of the painting are 1200 Frcs[33] — The lithographs about 80 Frcs —
     Aren't you coming to Weimar soon?
     Many good wishes to you and your wife
Your friend Edv. Munch

On the bottom left-hand corner of the reverse of the letter Munch has drawn an ornamental monster's head, with a word issuing from its mouth.[34]

The pictures seem to have reached Paris safety and been put into the *Salon des Indépendants*, as the correspondence takes up again in April, when the exhibition was closing. The next exchanges are almost farcical and certainly demonstrate Munch's erratic way of dealing with his affairs. One must always bear in mind the pressures under which he was living during this decade, on the one hand the fast-increasing success, on the other the haunting insecurities and heavy dependence on alcohol, all this coupled with a peripatetic existence around Germany alternating between a succession of hotel rooms and more restful stays with well-wishing friends. Frequent changes of address alone leave one surprised that he managed to keep any effective business correspondence about his exhibition going at all.

Munch to Delius.
(27, M.11)
Postcard addressed to:
Herrn Fritz Delius
Compositeur
Grez sur Marne (Marlotte) (Hotel postcard with overstamped address)
Seine et Oise *'Hotel Sanssouci'*
Paris *Berlin W, Link-Strasse 37*[35]
postmarked BERLIN N.W. 15.4.06
Dear Friend

Please tell the forwarding agent to collect my works — and to store them until I give him instructions —

Please send me a card to tell me whether this has been done. Will you and your wife not visit me in Weimar some time.

Your friend E M —
c/o Hotel Sanssouci, Linkstr.

Munch also wrote another postcard, which he did not send.

Munch to Delius.
(27a, Md.3)
Postcard addressed to:
Hr. Frits Delius
Compositeur
Grez sur Marne (Marlotte) (Hotel postcard with overstamped address)
Seine et Oise Hotel Sanssouci
Paris Link-Strasse 37,
Berlin
Undated, but probably April 1906
Dear Friend

Please be so good as to tell the forwarding agent to store my works until I give more precise instructions

— I intend to arrange a bigger exhibition in Paris this winter — Will you perhaps help me — Will you and your wife not visit me in Weimar some time? Perhaps give a concert —

Yours E Munch

Delius received his postcard on 18th April and replied, promptly and practically.

Delius to Munch
(28, D.17)
Postcard addressed to:
Monsieur Edvard Munch (artiste peintre)
Hotel Sanssouci
Link-Strasse 37
Berline W.   Grez
Allemagne.   19th April
                                              postmarked 19/Avril 06

Dear Friend,

You have never told me who your forwarding agent is! You always write my address wrong! Where are you going to this summer? I shall come to Berlin again in September. I have not yet been to Paris. How are you. We both send our best wishes.

Yours friend
Fr. Delius

About this time Munch drafted a longer letter to Delius. It could have been intended as a reply to Delius's last postcard (28, D.17), which would make it April, or it could possibly be after their next exchange (29, D.18 and 30, M.12) at the beginning of May. I favour the earlier date; it might be that he had drafted it before he heard from the *Indépendants* (30, M.12) and that their communication made sending it unnecessary.

Munch to Delius.
(28a, Md.4)   No address
              Undated, but probably late April (although
                            possibly early May) 1906

Dear Delius

I have no forwarding agent but I thought that you had engaged someone — I have lost the papers [36] — Will you tell me what is to be done —

Perhaps you could write to someone about this matter — I have written to Mitchell and Kimbell Marche St Honere but I don't know whether it is all right without the papers — Perhaps it has to go through the forwarding agent of *L'Independants* — (There's a forwarding agent Delibes)

Pecuniarily and artistically and also physically I am all right — Unfortunately that dirty business with Fraulein L — 3 years ago[37] gave me such a nervous shock that my nerves are still not in a fit state — I am almost unable to associate with people — and

86

it is bad as I have now so many friends in Weimar — in Jena[38] too I have many
friends — Won't you come over there some time —
   Here I am having great successes but would like some time to have an exhibition in
Paris — It might be possible perhaps to find premises —
   I am now looking for a place where I can work in peace and quiet —
   Those 4 years of torture with Fr. L and the splendid final result have inflicted a
hellish wound upon me —
   It has greatly amused the other dear friends[39] —

The next two communications crossed in the post.

Delius to Munch.
(29, D.18)
Postcard addressed to:
Hern Edvard Munch
Artiste Peintre,
Hotel Sans Souci
Link Strasse
Berlin Allemagne
(re-addressed to: postmarked GREZ 1 Mai 06
Mutiger Ritter, Bad Kösen)
Dear Friend.
   Up till now I have been waiting for news of your pictures because I have not heard
anything[40] I presume that you have written to your forwarding agent yourself.
Independants was closed on Sunday. I hope you are well. Perhaps I will come to
Norway this summer[41].

                          Best wishes
                     Yours Frederick Delius

But before he received this postcard, Munch heard directly from
L'Indépendants. He sent their communication with a covering note off to
Delius:

Munch to Delius
(30, M.12)
(written on both sides of a printed visiting card and enclosing the notice from
L'Indépendants. The envelope is a printed hotel envelope from the Hotel Kaiserhof,
Jena in Thuringia.)
Addressed to:
Mr. Frits Delius
Compositeur
Grez sur Loing   postmarked JENA 1.5.06.[42]
Seine et Oise (Marne)   (on the back of the envelope Munch has
Marlotte   written the address:
Paris   Edv. Munch
                                                          Mutiger Ritter
                                                          Bad Koesen
                                                          Sachsen Weimar)

87

Dear Friend

I have received this — I supose it means that the secretary will send the things to the forwarding agent —

That loathsome woman business quite ruined my nerves at the time — and I am still not well[43] —

Your friend
Edvard Munch (printed on visiting card)
Hotel Mutiger Ritter
Bad-Koesen
Another curious address[44]

Enclosed is a printed notice with the following text:

SOCIÉTE DES ARTISTES INDÉPENDANTS
22nd Exhibition — 1906

Important Notice.

Owing to an unforseen circumstance we are obliged to close our exhibition on Sunday 29 April at 6 p.m. — In consequence, removal of works will therefore take place on *Monday 30 April* and *Tuesday 1st May* from 9 a.m. to 6 p.m.

The Society's exhibitors are informed that, *after this time works not removed will be placed in the repository at their own expense.*

The Secretary
A. Séguin

A handwritten postscript is added:

'I have made a note for your pictures to be delivered to Mrs. Mitchell[45] to whom I am sending the same notice

Compliments
A. Roitier[46](?)

The pictures must have found their way back to Munch all right, although whether through the agency of Delius or not we cannot say. However a postcard written by Munch, but not posted seems to round this episode off.

Munch to Delius.
(30a, Md.5)
Postcard addressed to:
Mr Fritz Delius Komponist
Grez sur Marne
Seine et Oise
Marlotte
Frankreich

Bad Koesen
Saxen-Weimer
(Undated, but probaby May 1906[47])

Dear Friend

Many thanks for your trouble — The French are probably angry with my painting again[48] — Even so I feel that the most daring works must be exhibited in L'In-

88

dependants — Do you think it would be possible to arrange a large exhibition in Paris
— Do you think the premises of L'Independants are for hire in the autumn? —
I will give you two of my prints — Which will you have? —
Greetings Yours
Edvard Munch.

The tantalizing question is, did Munch send some such letter, containing the offer of the prints? Delius did own some Munch prints, certainly in the latter part of his life and it is likely that he acquired them earlier, as later on there was much less opportunity of direct connection between the two men. I suspect that Munch in fact did give him some.[49]

In May, Delius's *Sea Drift*, for baritone, choir and orchestra, one of his loveliest works, received its first performance at Essen, conducted by Georg Witte. Critical opinions in the German musical press were mixed, but conductors were keener. Apart from those already mentioned, one now finds Max Schillings (to whom *Sea Drift* is dedicated) and the young Carl Schuricht among Delius's supporters. Delius went to Germany for this[50], but there is no record of a meeting with Munch who seems to have remained in the Weimar area.

In the summer Delius and Jelka went to Norway. During the second half of June he left his wife painting at Aasgaardstrand, while he went further down the coast to Fredriksvaern. On 1st July, Jelka and Ingse Vibe (Müller),[51] another friend of Munch's sent the artist a joint postcard:[52]

Maleren Edvard Munch
Bad Kösen
Sachsen Weimar
re-addressed to
Weimar
Hotel Russischer Hof   postmarked AASGAARDSTRAND I VII 06
  Many greetings, when will you come? I am trying to paint here. It is so beautiful!
Jelka Delius.
  I am a good deal with Fr. Vibe, my husband is going to the mountains, he is not
here. —
  (Jelka has written on the plain side of the card, Ingse Vibe on the picture side — a
view of Aasgaardstrand.)
  You must come soon, then we shall have a fire in the fireplace and 'palmefest'.[53]
Many affectionate greetings from your friend I.V.
  I shall *not* go to Modum, so will you come down here soon?

Delius arrived back in Aasgaardstrand shortly afterwards and himself wrote to Munch:

Delius to Munch.
(31, D.19)
Postcard addressed to:
Herrn Edvard Munch
Russischer Hof
Weimar Tyskland[54]   postmarked AASGAARDSTRAND 7 VII 06
Aasgaardstrand
Dear Friend
   I am very disappointed that you are not here. It is splendid here and lovely
weather. I am going into the high mountains for some weeks and then I shall be
coming back here for some weeks and hope to see you then. Yesterday I called on
your sister and aunt[55] in your lovely little house. The garden is very fine also the
flower bed. My wife is here too and we both send you our best wishes.
                              Your friend
                              Fr. Delius

Delius left again on 8th July, leaving Jelka in Aasgaardstrand,
travelling through Christiania to the muntains of Rondane. He returned on the 25th, to find news that Munch was staying in Germany
that summer and would not be returning to Norway. He wrote again:

Delius to Munch.
(32, D.20)
Postcard addressed to:
Herrn Edvard Munch
Russischer Hof
Weimar
Tyskland
(re-addressed 5/8 Ilmenau)   postmarked AASGAARDSTRAND 2 VIII 06
Dear Friend,
   I am sorry that you are not coming here this summer. We will be very glad to see
you at our home in Grez.[56] We are coming to Berlin in September. An opera of mine
will be performed. Perhaps you will come there.
   Best wishes from us both.
                              Yours
                              Fr. Delius

The opera was *A Village Romeo and Juliet* (1899-1901), probably his
greatest work in this form. Fritz Cassirer had set his heart on putting
this on at the new Komisches Oper in Berlin, and had hoped that it
would be produced in the autumn of 1906. However various difficulties
ensued and at the beginning of November he was advising Delius not to
come yet. Delius does not seem to have been put out, as he was in the
middle of composing *Songs of Sunset*. But by the end of November the
difficulties had been cleared and Cassirer could write that 'a performance ought to be possible at the end of January'.[57] (In fact the first
night was 21 February 1907.) So Delius did not in fact go to Germany

during the autumn of 1906, but remained in Grez after his return from Norway.

Munch spent the remainder of the year in Germany. His feelings about being misprized and persecuted in Norway were now reaching disagreeable proportions and Germany could provide appreciation, friends and work. In fact he was to stay based there for the next two years. During the summer he received an interesting commission from the theatre director Max Reinhardt. Ibsen died in 1906, and to commemorate this Reinhardt decided to open his new intimate theatre in Berlin, *Kammerspieltheater*, with a performance of *Ghosts*. Reinhardt was determined to create the appropriate atmosphere, and he asked Munch to produce sketches on which his décor could be based. These Munch did (several of these are now in Munch-Museet), and Reinhardt was delighted with the results, going on to commmission paintings to decorate the foyer of *Kammerspieltheater* (*The Reinhardt Frieze*) and sketches for the décor of a production of *Hedda Gabler* the following year. Although Munch remained based in the Weimar area for most of 1906, the work for Reinhardt necessitated visits to Berlin. He attended some of the final rehearsals for *Ghosts*, exhibited his sketches for the play at the time of its performance and attended the party to celebrate the production's success, where he met the stage designer Edward Gordon Craig.[58] By the beginning of 1907 he settled in Berlin again, where he remained for the winter. Besides his work for Reinhardt, he painted a portrait of Walther Rathenau, who had been one of his very first German patrons.[59]

From 1907 and 1908 there are only two surviving communications between Munch and Delius, one from each year, but they imply considerably more contact.

Delius went to Berlin early in 1907. At the beginning of February he invited Munch to a little party there:

Delius to Munch.
(33, D.21)
Postcard addressed to:
Herrn Edvard Munch
Kunstmaler
Hôtel Hapsburger Hof,   49 Neue Winterfeld Str. *4th Floor*
Am Anhalt Bahnhof   *Wednesday*
                                     postmarked BERLIN 6.2.07

Dear Friend
    Do come to us *this evening* 8½-9.0 o'clock. A few friends are coming including Bruno Cassirer. Sandwiches, wine, beer etc Shall be extremely pleased to see you again.
                        Best wishes
                        Fr Delius

Clearly Delius has been in touch previously and Munch knows that he is in Berlin. I should think it likely that Munch went, despite the shortness of notice, particularly as his dealer Bruno Cassirer was going to be there. The nature of the note even suggests that some such meeting had been discussed before. It is very tantalizing to know nothing about further contact that year, particularly at a time when both men were involved in work for theatres, and there are so many questions one would like to ask. Did Munch see *A Village Romeo and Juliet*? Did Delius see Munch's work for Reinhardt? Did they discuss their ideas about stage designs at all? The two men's ideas on the importance in creating mood in stageing seem very similar. The critic of *DIE MUSIK*, reviewing the first performance of *A Village Romeo and Juliet* wrote: 'He carefully calls his work an Idyll in pictures and indeed simply presents us with mood-paintings';[60] And Reinhardt had asked Munch to provide sketches for *Ghosts* to set the mood and atmosphere: 'Up to now Ibsen's stage interior has been shockingly neglected and abused. However I believe that it constitiues an essential part of the multiplicity which lies between and behind Ibsen's words and which not only surrounds the action but also symbolizes it. . . . I am firmly convinced that with your particular help we will be able to adjust the people and scenery to each other in such a way, that we well illuminate as yet unfathomable depths in this splendid work . . .'.[61] And the mood-pictures of both Delius's opera and Munch's Ibsen interpretations were to be presented in a manner which was basically expressionistic and realistic, not abstractly symbolic.

However, later in the year their paths led physically in rather different directions, Munch remaining mostly in Germany, while Delius started to establish his reputation in England.

The premiere of *A Village Romeo and Juliet* was on 21st February and there were two subsequent performances, all conducted by Fritz Cassirer. The reception was mixed. The critic of *DIE MUSIK* did not like the work, although he admitted 'that there was no lack of the usual applause at the première' (see note 60). On the other hand the composer Humperdinck was impressed and wrote to Delius accordingly.[62] So with these performances of his opera in the capital Delius must have felt himself well established in Germany. Moreover 1907 saw the appearance of the first monograph on him, also in Germany, by the musicologist Max Chop.[63]

In the spring Delius visited London. With the exception of a few songs, his work had not been heard in England since the 1899 concert but now, no doubt encouraged by news of the composer's growing reputation in Germany, English conductors started to take an interest in his music, notably the redoubtable Henry Wood. In October he performed the Piano Concerto in London, with Theodor Szántó as soloist, and it was well received. This was followed the next month by the first English performance of *Appalachia*, under Fritz Cassirer. The impact on the musical world must have been considerable as in the following year at least seven major works[64] were performed in England, in some cases more than once, under conductors like Wood, Thomas Beecham, Granville Bantock, Landon Ronald, Arbos and the composer himself, although Delius was not a very skilful conductor.[65] In October 1907, Delius met for the first time Thomas Beecham, then at the beginning of his meteoric career. Beecham has written: 'The first performance in England of *Appalachia* is one of the half-dozen momentous occasions I have known over a period of more than fifty years',[66] and a large part of his life was thenceforth devoted to making himself the leading interpreter and promoter of Delius's work.

But perhaps the biggest impact of Delius's arrival on the English musical scene was that of the impression his music made on young composers. There practically a whole generation seems at this stage to have been affected to a greater or lesser degree. First there were the five, known as the 'Frankfurt Group' from them having studied there together: Balfour Gardiner, Percy Grainger (himself Australian), Norman O'Neill, Roger Quilter and Cyril Scott. Apart from these, Granville Bantock (an older man more of Delius's generation), Arnold Bax, Havergal Brian, and Ralph Vaughan Williams were among those impressed, while a little later even younger men like Philip Heseltine (Peter Warlock) and Geoffrey Toye were also to come under the spell. For some of these Delius was only a stage in their development; others became close and lasting friends, notably Balfour Gardiner, Bantock, Grainger, O'Neill and Heseltine. At this stage Delius allowed himself to become a little more involved with the organization of musical life than he was generally to do, and in 1908, launched in company with a number of his new-found friends, the Musical League, intended to promote the performance of new English music. Its President was no less a person that Sir Edward Elgar, while Delius was its Vice-President.[67] But despite its worthy aims, the League did not succeed in attracting sufficient support to have a long life. It achieved a Festival in Liverpool in 1909, largely comprised of the work of English composers, but thereafter it faded out. Delius was hardly the man to want to be involved in the practical tedium of organizing promotional activities and in any case his feelings about the English musical scene tended to see-saw in relation to the fortunes of his work there. In a letter to Granville Bantock he wrote: 'The Musical League I suppose is dead

. . . I am afraid artistic undertakings are impossible in England — The country is yet not artistically civilised — There is something hopeless about Engish people in a musical and artistic way, to be frank, I have entirely lost my interest and prefer to live abroad and make flying visits — '.[68]

So the new successes in England, although very important, as they meant that Delius now had two countries where his works were performed, did not radically alter his way of life. Flying visits were now made more frequently to England as well as keeping in touch with Germany, but the backbone of his life was still composing at Grez. During 1907-8 he wrote the orchestral works *Brigg Fair*, *In a Summer Garden* and *A Dance Rhapsody* (No.1), completed the *Songs of Sunset* for soloists, chorus and orchestra and started work on his last opera, *Fennimore and Gerda*.[69]

Nor did he forget Norway, and in the summer of 1908 went on an extensive walking tour there, accompanied by Thomas Beecham.[70] A particularly sad event must have been the death of his old friend and supporter Grieg, who died on 4 September 1907. Grieg, although in poor health, had been on the eve of leaving Bergen for England, where he had been going to conduct his piano concerto, played by Percy Grainger, at the Leeds Festival. The new friendship with Grainger had meant much to old Grieg,[71] and was also a link with Delius. Delius must have much regretted that Grieg had been unable to meet him, because of health reasons, when he visited Norway in 1906.[72] His debt to the Griegs had been considerable, and he continued to correspond with Nina Grieg after her husband's death.

Among friends from the Christiania bohemian circles to which Munch had belonged, Delius was still in touch with Milly Bergh who wrote to him late in 1907, congratulating him on the London successes of the Piano concerto and *Appalachia* (about which she has read in a London paper). This is the letter, referred to on pp. 44-5, in which she recalls appreciating his music at the time of *Folkeraadet*, and she continues 'since then you have cleared up all that is vague and obscure mostly because you have put your art and your work above everything else in the world —'.[73]

For Munch 1907-9 were climacteric years. Professionally things continued to go well. His pictures continued to be on exhibition, he was still working on the *Reinhardt Frieze* and his patrons were active; for example Ernest Thiel bought a number of paintings during 1907. But as Munch himself wrote at the time: 'My fame is growing. My peace of mind is another matter'.[74] Arne Eggum has perceptively written: '*Self-Portrait in Weimar* (Self-Portrait with Wine Bottle)[75] tells us more convincingly than words can that Munch felt he had entered a blind alley as far as his art was concerned. Taking over Munch's role in France, the fauves had gained attention as young revolutionaries with their use of strong colours, and the young Brücke artists in Dresden wanted to put his name on their banner. But Munch could not reach a decision either to join the young German group of artists or to prepare a major exhibition in Paris. He could have obtained a studio in the capital of the grand duchy of Saxe-Weimar and become a "court painter", but he couldn't make his mind up about this either'.[76] In the letters of the past few years, we have constantly heard Munch raising the idea of a large exhibition in Paris with Delius, but nothing ever came of this.

Munch was certainly well aware of the importance of exhibiting in Paris and he was conscious of the new art there. In September 1907 when he was exhibiting at Paul Cassirer's Gallery in Berlin, the exhibition also included works by Cézanne and Matisse. And about this time Munch began to experiment with new techniques, notably breaking up the surface of his canvases with long hatching strokes of pure colours in paintings like *Cupid and Psyche* and *Death of Marat*, both from 1907.[77]

But underlying all this was Munch's mental state. The end of the affair with Tulla Larsen in 1902, and his subsequent quarrels and imagined humiliations, still preyed on his mind, indeed they became a crescendo in 1907-8. Because of his bad nerves he drank increasingly to deaden them, this led to more quarrels and thus more drinking to decrease the effect on his nerves. This vicious circle he came to attribute increasingly to the 1902 incident. Munch had attempted to break out of this pattern, notably in the time spent at the Thuringian spas and Weimar, but without lasting success. In 1907 he made another attempt, going to the seaside health resort Warnemünde, on the Baltic, a 'German Aasgaardstrand' as he called it, where he hoped to lead an active and healthy life by the sea, and work out new ways for his art. There he spent the summer and autumn, wintered mostly in Berlin, returning to Warnemünde for the spring and summer of 1908.

On the one hand his Warnemünde paintings were monumental pictures of a new vitality, like the great *Men Bathing* painting (1907, Ateneum, Helsinki), a hymn to man and the sun which looks forward to the Oslo University murals. On the other, he tried both in painting and writing to get to the bottom of his obsessions with the Tulla Larsen affair. From about two years after the end of the affair, Munch had started to show his hatred of her and her supporters in a number of malignant caricatures. Frequently she appears in company with Sigurd Bødtker, usually depicted as a poodle, and Gunnar Heiberg, shown as a toad or pig. Christian Krohg is another old associate who also

95

appears in some of these caricatures. Tulla Larsen is also visualized by Munch as other unpleasant characters, for example Hedda Gabler, in a sketch for Reinhardt's production of that play, and he also made innumerable written notes and sketches about her.

Phantoms. *1905. Drypoint, OKK. G/r.108; Sch.224.*
(Tulla Larsen, as Salome, receives the head of the artist from the dog-executioner in the presence of a toad-like Herod and his consort.)

In 1905 he spelt out his feelings that the woman betrays the man and ends by murdering him in the first version of the *Death of Marat* (OKK M.351 — at first called *The Murderess*). It shows the prostrate dead man and standing woman both naked and quite recognizable as himself and Tulla Larsen. It is a powerful picture, painted initially in an impressionistic, realistic way. However, at a later stage (Arne Eggum thinks in 1907 or 1908), Munch thickly over-painted on part of it a table with a still-life comprised of fruit and one of Tulla Larsen's hats (a distinctive feature of hers). Between 1905 and 1908, Munch made other painting and lithographs on this basic theme of savage war between the sexes, including a new version of the *Death of Marat* (OKK M.4 — sometimes referred to as *Death of Marat II*).[78] This is painted in his new experimental technique.

It is interesting to compare the savage sex war which Munch, who never worked out a sound, lasting sexual relationship with a woman, paints with Delius's attitude to love in his works of the period. Delius, who had in the past enjoyed many love affairs at different levels, was now successfully married to an understanding woman. In works like *Sea Drift* and *Songs of Sunset* he sees love as a golden state which passes all too quickly leaving a lingering and yearning nostalgia.

In February 1908, Munch made a short visit to Paris. He did not get in touch with Delius and the exact purpose of the trip is not clear. However, it seems likely that reasons may have been to arrange for exhibition at the *Salon des Indépendants*, or to sort out works of his which may still have been stored there. That year the *Salon* was from 20th March to the 2nd May. In March he was back in Warnemünde, and he wrote to Delius from there some time during the course of the exhibitions:

Munch to Delius.
(34, M.13)
53 Am Strom
Warnemünde
undated, but some time between
20th March and 2nd May, 1908.[79]

Dear Friend,

I was in Paris for a few days and should have liked to visit you but I soon had to get away again — I shall probably soon make a little trip to Paris again —

Please give me the address of the 'Lynx' bureau (newspaper notices) 'Makers of Famous Men'[80] I would like to see what the French say about my picture 'La Mort du Marat'[81] — It is by the way only an experiment and makes no effect at all if it is not well hung — But I think that the paintings which do not go anywhere else must be exhibited in L'Independants Tell me whether my works are well hung — and where? — in which room? —

The decorative picture is a sketch for a whole frieze in the 'Kammerspiel'[82] — Please give me the address of Wilhelm Molard too[83] — I have been living here in Warnemünde for a long time — a German Aasgaardstrand — away from bad memories and false Norwegian friends —

With best wishes to you and your wife —

Your Edvard Munch

Death of Marat seems to sum up Munch's final feelings on the violent conclusion of his affair with Tulla Larsen. In the actual event Munch had gone into hospital to have his bullet wound operated on. Tulla Larsen had taken up with the painter Arne Kavli and subsequently, encouraged by Gunnar Heiberg and Sigurd Bødtker, gone off to Paris with him. Thus, symbolically, she has murdered Munch and left him dead. The artist gave the picture an allegorical title of a famous Frenchman murdered by a woman and sent the picture to Paris after Tulla Larsen (admittedly five years later), thus achieving a kind of symbolic revenge.[84] Remembering that the painting was also executed in Munch's newest experimental style, rather like the new French art of *Les Fauves*, one can understand why he was so interested in the French reaction to it.

Unfortunately the French reviews seem to have given it little attention, merely placing Munch with Braque, Derain and Marie Laurencin among 'all this battalion of practical jokers'.[85] Munch must have been very disappointed and, indeed, this seems to have been his last major attempt to interest the French through the *Salon des Indépendants*. He did send pictures there twice more, in 1910 and 1912, but on these occasions only what seems to have been a token representation.

Munch says in this last letter to Delius that he hoped to be making another short trip to Paris soon. But this did not materialize. During the summer he continued to work at Warnemünde. Then in the autumn he travelled via Hamburg and Stockholm to Copenhagen, where he was going to have an exhibition.[86] In Copenhagen he became involved in a prolonged bout of drinking with the Norwegian author Sigurd Mathieson, which precipitated a breakdown. With the help of his old Danish friend Emanuel Goldstein, he entered himself in the psychiatric clinic of Dr Daniel Jacobson for treatment at the beginning of October. At the end of that month he wrote to Jappe Nilssen:

> 'The crunch had to come some day . . . But when it did, it was fairly dramatic — after a trip to Sweden followed by four days in a mass of alcohol with Sigurd Mathiesen, I had a real blackout and also some minor form of heart attack, I believe. My brain had become damaged by my continued obsessions. I am having shock treatment and massage and I feel very well in the peaceful atmosphere here — surrounded by extremely kind nuns and a very capable doctor'.[87]

Munch remained under treatment in Copenhagen between seven and eight months, but still continuing to work. He was to emerge cured, with a period of his life ended, and returned to live permanently in Norway in the spring of 1909.

Chapter VIII

1909–1918

LETTER 34 IS THE LAST EXTANT LETTER FROM MUNCH WHICH WE CAN demonstrate that Delius received. But a number of letters from Delius or Jelka to Munch have survived and we can see from these that the two men continued to correspond and meet. And from the last six or seven years of Delius's life we also have a number of Munch's drafts of letters to the composer, some of which are among the richest in the whole series.

But for nearly ten years after Munch's admission to Dr Jacobson's clinic, very little evidence of contact survives, the only concrete piece being one postcard from Delius in 1913.

The months in the clinic did cure Munch, partly through the treatment and partly through his own determination. He said that 'The way in which I finally decided to cure myself was a fairly brutal one . . .',[1] and it meant in fact giving up alcohol and his old way of life. He wrote to his friend Sigurd Høst: 'My motto has become "Steer clear of everything". I now confine myself to nicotine-free cigars, non-alcoholic drinks, and non-poisonous women (either married or unmarried). You're going to find me an extremely boring uncle'.[2] He had partly exorcised his obsessions about the predatoriness of woman in paintings like the *Death of Marat* from the Warnemünde days and he completed his process with his fable *Alpha and Omega* and the lithographs which illustrated it.[3] But most of his work while at the clinic, and he had lost nothing of his power and skill, was of less introspective subjects — fine portraits of Dr Jacobson, of Helge Rode, of some of the nurses and of himself, and vivid studies of animals in the zoo.

Munch kept in touch with friends while he was in the clinic, but these tended to be his old staunch Norwegian friends (who had not become involved in the Tulla Larsen affair), like Jens Thiis, Jappe Nilssen and Christian Gierløff, old Danish friends like Emanuel Goldstein and Helge Rode and patron-friends like Dr Linde and Ernest Thiel, all of them real intimates.

While he remained in Copenhagen, events in Norway started to swing in his favour. In 1908 Jens Thiis became the first director of

Nasjonalgalleriet, in Christiania. Later that year Munch was made a Knight of the Order of St. Olav, an important Norwegian decoration. And in 1909 Jappe Nilssen and Jens Thiis organized a major retrospective exhibition of his work in Christiania. The exhibition was a great success, and Thiis purchased five paintings for Nasjonalgalleriet, thus encouraging the collector Olaf Schou to present the gallery with sixty works by Norwegian artists, including several by Munch.

Consequently it was not difficult for his friends to persuade him that the time was now ripe for his return to Norway, and this took place in May, 1909. On the boat going back Munch's cousin, the painter Ludvig Ravensberg, urged the artist to take part in the competition for the decoration of the new assembly hall of the University in Christiania, which was to celebrate its centenary in 1911.

Munch decided almost at once to enter for the competition[4] and for the next seven years the University murals were to be his major task. His path to its successful conclusion was by no means an easy one, for although Munch now had more supporters in Norway than ever before, there were still many opponents to his work including, for a long while, the University authorities in Christiania. It was not until 1914 that the University finally decided to accept Munch's paintings, which were ultimately installed and unveiled in 1916.

Munch regarded the University mural decorations as one of the two major extended projects in his life's work, a complement to the *Life Frieze*, and portraying 'the powerful forces of eternity'.[5] The theme is the vitalistic one of mankind as part of the great eternal forces of nature. Initially Munch submitted two designs for the competition, *History*, which was accepted, and *Towards the Light* or *The Mountain of Mankind*, which was not. Whereas *History*, with its old man passing on knowledge to the young boy, is concerned with the continuity of the life of ordinary people, *The Mountain of Mankind* is a more philosophical idea, bearing some similarity to those expressed in Nietzsche's *Also sprach Zarathustra*. (Munch's original design has been destroyed, but we know it from a sketch, OKK .778.) Munch had earlier dealt with a more pessimistic expression of this theme in 1897, in the lithograph *Funeral March* (OKK G/1.226, Sch.94) where the tower of upward-struggling figures culminates in a coffin. In *The Mountain of Mankind*, the figures struggle upwards and ultimately one, the superman, emerges through a cloudy belt to stand proudly greeting the sun, as did Nietzsche's Zarathustra. In the paintings of the completed decorations, Munch followed more the tone of *History*, with 'the great eternal forces' nourishing ordinary people rather than supermen; no doubt this was partly due to the nature of the murals as public art, but it was also that his work was now becoming freer from his pessimistic brooding of the nineties and more concerned with external themes of landscape and working people. But the idea of *The Mountain of Mankind* continued to fascinate him and he was still working on it well into the nineteen-twenties. However for the commanding central wall of the University's hall, he now took Zarathustra's sun, left out the prophet, and painted it rising over the Norwegian coastline in a burst of incandescent energy, its life-giving rays awakening and warming the figures of men and women who turn towards it on the adjacent walls. This life-confirming sunburst calls to mind the exultant paean with which Delius's own great Nietsche-inspired work, *A Mass of Life* opens.[6]

In view of the fact that *Also sprach Zarathustra* was such an important work for both Delius and Munch, it is frustrating that the letters give no indication of their discussing Nietszche together. 1897, the year in which Munch made the lithograph *Funeral March*, was one in which he and Delius were in touch. The two men corresponded and probably met not long after the first performance of Delius's *Mitternachtslied Zarathustras* in 1899. Munch stayed with Delius at Grez only a few months before the work was performed again, in Switzerland in 1903. Again Delius finished composing *A Mass of Life* (on which he had worked with Frtiz Cassirer, a near relative of Munch's German dealers) only shortly before Munch received his Nietzsche commission from Ernest Thiel in 1905, and the two men were frequently in touch during the following year when the artist was executing his Nietzsche portraits. So although the only reference in the correspondence to Nietzsche is when Munch asks Delius not to send the lithographic portrait to the *Salon des Indépendants* if he does not think it good enough (p.84, 25, M.9), it would seem incredible for them never to have discussed the philosopher's work, particularly *Also Sprach Zarathustra*. Delius could write: 'I consider Nietzsche the only free thinker of modern times and for me the most sympathetic one — He is at the same time such a poet. He feels Nature. I believe, myself, in no doctrine whatever — and in nothing but Nature and in the great forces of Nature.[7] And this seems near to the 'great eternal forces' in nature which were the subject of Munch's University murals. I doubt if Munch ever heard *A Mass of Life*, although I think that Delius, in view of this enthusiasm for his friend's work, may well have seen the University murals on one of his later visits to Norway. At all events we have no evidence of what either thought of the other's grappling with Nietzschean subject matter.

The acceptance of the decorations by the University set the final seal on Munch's recognition as a great painter by Norway. The years discussed in this chapter were very rich ones in his production. His themes were now generally less introspective, mostly of man and nature seen more objectively and optimistically. They include landscapes, portraits and subjects of men and animals at work in outdoor settings. Frequently they are on a large scale and the success of the University murals clearly encouraged Munch to think more of further opportunities to create a public art. Colours and technique are also new, developed from the experiments the artist had been making at Warnemünde, before his breakdown.

On his return to Norway, Munch wished to keep clear of the Christiania area. He consequently settled at the little town of Kragerø, some distance down the south coast. The landscape and the people there appealed to him and the productive years there were probably the most contented of his life. However, as he became involved in the large scale paintings for the University, he required more space for working and so he bought or rented other properties, first the Ramme estate at Hvitsten and then Grimsrød manor house (with 24 rooms) on the island of Jeløy. Both of these were back up the coast, nearer to Christiania, so presumably his dislike of the capital was gradually being overcome for the sake of convenience. He divided his time between Kragerø and these other properties. Finally in 1916 he moved back to just outside Christiania, purchasing an estate at Ekely, which was to remain his home for the rest of his life.

During this period Munch's reputation continued to rise in Germany and other European countries east of the Rhine. His work was shown in a constant stream of exhibitions, of which the Cologne Sonderbund Exhibition in 1912 was probably the most important. Here his 32 paintings were given a separate room (Picasso was the only other living foreign artist accorded the same distinction there), and he was presented like Cézanne, Van Gogh and Gauguin as a pioneer of modern art. Sketches for the University murals caused a great interest when he exhibited them in Germany, the University of Jena actually putting out feelers towards acquiring the finished paintings if they were rejected in Christiania, and this acclaim was one of the main factors which finally decided the Norwegian university to accept them. In 1913 Curt Glaser began his study *Edvard Munch*, which was published in Germany in 1917.[8] Munch's work also started to appear in New York at this time, six paintings in a Scandinavian exhibition there in 1912 and eight prints in the Armory Show the following year, which also went on to Boston and Chicago.[9] Only in Paris was he making no headway, and his small representation in the *Salon des Indépendants*, with one painting and four prints in 1910 and one painting and two prints in 1912, suggests that he had no great hopes in that direction.[10]

Munch still travelled abroad, but these trips were now short visits rather than extended stays. In 1911 and 1912 he visited Germany, and in the latter year also Paris; in 1913 he visited Germany three times and also Paris and London (his only visit to England), where he made a lithograph of Westminster Abbey.[11] In 1914 he revisited Germany and Paris. But there is no record of any meeting with Delius. Then came the first world war, and while it lasted Munch seems to have refrained from travelling outside Scandinavia. His exhibitions during the war years were also almost entirely confined to the Scandinavian countries, although there were a couple in Germany, both of graphic works.

For Delius, too, these years were fruitful and successful, although the first world war affected the course of his career more than it did for Munch, who lived in a neutral country. Performances of his works were now fairly regular in both England and Germany, and there were also a few in America, although his music did not firmly establish itself there at this stage.[12] *A Mass of Life* received its first complete performance in London, under Thomas Beecham, in 1909; in December of that year Hans Haym performed it at Elberfeld; in 1911 Haym gave another performance and it was also performed in Vienna. In 1910 England had its first taste of a Delius opera with Beecham's production of *A Village Romeo and Juliet* at Covent Garden. Delius had dedicated his *Songs of Sunset* to the Elberfeld Choral Society; it received its first performance in London in 1911 and was performed again at Elberfeld in 1914.

The years were also rich with new compositions. Between 1908 and 1914 virtually all his principal works, whether with or without words, were inspired by the North, usually Scandinavia. The opera *Fennimore and Gerda* (1908-1910) is subtitled: 'Two episodes from the life of Niels Lyhne in eleven pictures after the novel by J.P. Jacobsen' and in *An Arabesque* (1911) Delius again turned to Jacobsen's words. *The Song of the High Hills* (1911) was inspired by the Norwegian mountains while *North Country Sketches* (1913-14) is associated with Yorkshire. *Life's Dance*, of which the final version was made and first performed in 1912,[13] was based originally on Helge Rode's play, although, according to Jelka, the original programme had vanished by the time of the final version. *On hearing the first Cuckoo in Spring* (1912)[14] uses a Norwegian folksong, probably borrowed from Grieg's setting of it. And the ballad for orchestra *Eventyr* (*Once upon a time*), inspired by the Norwegian P.C. Asbjörnsen's folk-tales, stands as an epilogue in this group, as it was not composed until 1915-17. Lionel Carley and Robert Threlfall have observed that 'a note of cool and spare astringency is introduced into his music'[15] at the time of *North Country Sketches*, and this cooler quality can also be felt in *An Arabesque* and *Eventyr*. Both the Jacobsen inspired works can be said to have similarieties in mood and imagery to works of Munch. The words of *An Arabesque*, with their association of love, death and flowers, use images which we find in such Munch works as the Baudelaire *Fleurs du Mal* drawings (1896) or the lithograph *The Flower of Love*,[16] and Delius's brilliantly appropriate setting is full of this aspect of *fin-de-siècle* exotic pessimism. *Fennimore and Gerda*, Delius's last opera, carries to a conclusion tendencies in his stage works apparent since the nineties, a compression of the drama into mood pictures, 'Short, strong emotional impressions given in a series of terse scenes', as the composer put it.[17] He now declared that 'realism on the stage is nonsense, and all the scenery necessary is an impressionistic painted curtain at the back with the fewest accessories possible'.[18] The work has some similarities with Munch, although one should not try to press parallels too closely. Fennimore's hopeless and doomed affair with Niels has a Munchian flavour and Delius's 'Ninth Picture', where she rejects him after Erik's death has much of the mood of a painting like *Ashes* (1894, Nasjonalgalleriet). Again, the acting out of the tragedy against the background of fjord and trees recalls so many of the artist's *Life Frieze* subjects. It could be claimed that Delius's happy ending, so unlike Jacobsen's, is much more sweetly lyrical than Munch, but then Munch at fifty could also paint pictures of relatively genial optimism, as in the *Alma Mater* wall of the University murals.

It is understandable that with this impressive stream of compositions to his credit Delius spent most of his time at Grez composing and he seems to have been visited there by Norwegian friends, Oda Krohg and her son Per.[19] He also had to make a considerable number of visits to England and Germany in connection with performances of his works. But in 1910 there started to appear a marked decline in his health, which seriously concerned his wife and friends.[20] Jelka took him to a sanatorium in Dresden, which did no good, and then to one in Wiesbaden which yielded better results, and by the end of that year he had picked up again, at least for the time being. During the summer of 1911 the Deliuses visited Norway in July and August, as we know from letters he wrote to Nina Grieg, but we know little of his movements there. One letter, dated 26th July 1911 is addressed from Lanvaasen Høifjeld Sanatorium, saying that he has spent a week there.[21] He wrote to her again from Golaa Høifjeld Sanatorium, telling her that he probably will not be able to come and see her at Troldhaugen after all.[22] It would seem, from the addresses, that Delius's health had been troubling him again and that this had occasioned his stays at the two sanatoria. But we know nothing of whether he met Munch anywhere,

a) *Ibsen and Nietzsche surrounded by genius.* *c.1909.*
    Oil on canvas, OKK. M.917. Munch-Museet.
b) *Self-portrait with Wine Bottle.* *1906.*
    Oil on canvas, OKK. M.543. Munch-Museet.

a) **Death of Marat.** *1907.*
   Oil on canvas, OKK. M.4. Munch-Museet.

b) **Landscape from the Reinhardt Frieze.** *1906-7.*
   Tempera on canvas, OKK. M.833. Munch-Museet.

a) ***Towards the Light*** *or* ***Mountain of Mankind with Zarathustra's Sun.*** *c.1909-10. Oil on canvas, OKK. M.778. Munch-Museet.*

b) ***The Sun.*** *1909-16.*
Oil on canvas. University of Oslo, Assembly Hall.

Self-portrait with Spanish 'flu'. *1919.*
Oil on canvas. Oslo, Nasjonalgalleriet.

Frederick Delius. *c.1920.*
Lithograph, OKK. G/1. 407; Sch.473.

a) **Delius at Wiesbaden.** *1922.*
     Black crayon, OKK. T. 639. Munch-Museet.

b) **Delius at Wiesbaden.** *1922.*
     Lithograph. OKK. G/1. 427; Sch.498.

a)   *Sketch of mural design for Oslo City Hall. 1929. Black crayon, OKK. T. 2351. Munch-Museet.*

b)   **Dr Lucien Dedichen and Japp Nilssen (seated).**
    1925-6. Oil on canvas, OKK. M. 370. Munch-Museet.

or other Norwegian friends.

In 1913 Delius visited Norway again, and he wrote to Munch proposing a meeting. The postcard makes it clear that Munch had written to him fairly recently.

Delius to Munch.
(35, D.22)
Postcard addressed to:
Herrn Edvard Munch
Kunstmaler
Grimsrød[23]
pr. Moss, Norvège.

postmarked GREZ 30-6 13

Dear Friend —
— I have received your card —
  I leave Antwerp next Saturday 5th and arrive in Kristiania on Tuesday evening. I will be staying at the Hotel Westminster — and would be very pleased if you could collect me on Wednesday at 12 or 1 o'clock so that we can be together. I am staying until Thursday or Friday and then an going on to the Jotunheim.[24]
Best wishes
Frederick Delius

I would think it rather likely that they met. Munch's postcard which Delius mentioned may well also have referred to the composer's forthcoming visit to Norway. Munch did not exhibit at *L'Indépendants* that year, so his card cannot have been one of his customary requests for help over that. Grimsrød is no great distance down the fjord from Oslo, so no considerable travelling would have been involved.

There is also a possibility that Delius visited Munch at Grimsrød on either this or a subsequent visit to Norway. Mrs Inger Alver Gløersen, who with her family knew Munch for many years and who has written a charming account of the artist's life,[25] has told me that she has recollections (albeit rather faint ones) of Delius going to see the artist there about a picture. Unfortunately she was unable to remember in what year this visit took place.

On this Norwegian visit Delius travelled in advance leaving Jelka at home working, to follow him later. A postcard which he sent her in July[26] suggests that he has been in Christiania before going on to the mountains; 'You must either on the way up or on our way home stop at Kristiania to see the Munchs in the National Gallery — all the best ones — of years ago.[27] They are wonderful — Also the Viking Queen Ship. Perfectly marvellous . . . .'.[28] He says that he has been to see Milly Bergh,[29] but there is no mention of his having seen Munch, despite his

113

enthusiasm over the pictures in Nasjonalgalleriet, so it seems unlikely that he did at this stage.

Sir Thomas Beecham has claimed that: 'The outbreak of war in 1914, with the exception of the fatal malady that finally overcame him ten years later, was the greatest single blow he suffered during his long and troubled career'.[30] In the first place performance of Delius's works in Germany stopped. Whereas before the war he had probably been regarded in that country almost as a German composer (particularly with his original name of Fritz Delius), but now his British nationality ensured his exclusion from concert programmes there. Consequently German income from royalties on his works (most of which had been published in Germany) dried up, a severe financial loss. The result was naturally to make him even more part of the English musical world.

During the autumn of 1914, fearing the rapid German advance into France, the Deliuses left Grez, but hearing of the result of the Battle of the Marne, they soon returned there again. However, the feeling of insecurity remained and in November they decided to go to England. Friends there were quick to help them and on arrival they went to stay at a house in London, owned by Thomas Beecham, 8a Hobart Place. In December they moved to another house owned by Beecham near Watford and this remained their base until the end of April 1915. Delius's health had been troubling him again, as they now returned to Hobart Place while he underwent three weeks physiotherapy. In June he consulted Harley Street specialist Byres Moir, who prescribed a trip to Norway, so in July he and Jelka made their way there again, from Newcastle to Bergen. Records of his movements in Norway that summer are scanty, but letters to friends like Philip Heseltine and Percy Grainger tell us that in mid August he was at Gloppenfjord, Nordfjord and in September at Geilo.[31] These locations are all either in western or central areas and we do not know whether he visited Christiania or not. Likewise we have no record of any meeting with Munch, although the artist also did some travelling that year, visiting Trondheim in August and Copenhagen in the autumn, both times in connection with exhibitions. In October the Deliuses went to Denmark, ending their stay with nearly a week in Copenhagen at the beginning of November. Here they probably met their old friend Helge Rode, as there was an exchange of letters between them proposing such a reunion. (Delius to Helge Rode 20 October 1915, letter in possession of the Rode family). As Munch's Copenhagen exhibition opened in November there a meeting between the three men might have been just possible, but there is no documentary evidence of one. After leaving Copenhagen, the Deliuses travelled back to Grez by way of Bergen, Newcastle and London.

Despite the kindness of friends and the fact that he was now securely part of the English musical world, Delius was not really happy living in England. In a letter to Percy Grainger, written from Denmark in October 1915, he refers to the depression he had experienced while living at Watford.[32] Consequently they decided to return to Grez, which they reached on 20 November, 1915, and they remained there until the war was nearing its end. An important new and increasingly deep friendship in France was that of a wealthy American couple domiciled there, the sculptor Henry Clews and his wife Marie. Unfortunately Delius's health was still giving conern,[33] and in the summer of 1918 they went for several months to Biarritz, hoping that the sun and bathing would do him good.

Health problems made no slowing up in Delius's production of music and the war years saw many new compositions. These include a Requiem, attacking the folly of war, to words from the Old Testament and Nietzsche (1914), *Eventyr* (1915-17), the *Poem of Life and Love* (1918) and some songs. But there were also five more works of a purely abstract character: two concerti, one for violin and cello (1915) and one for violin (1916), a violin sonata (1914-15), a cello sonata and a string quartet (1916). This was doubtless as a result of interest shown in his work by English instrumentalists, such as the violinists Albert Sammons and May Harrison, and May's sister, the cellist Beatrice Harrison, to whom most of these works are dedicated.[34] As concerts in wartime England were somewhat restricted, the larger orchestral works had to wait for peformance until peace returned, whereas most of the chamber works received their first performances during the war years.

115

Chapter IX

1918–1925

DURING THE FOUR YEARS AFTER THE END OF THE WAR THERE IS MUCH evidence of contact between the artist and the composer. The actual correspondence is often brief and rather scrappy, but it implies more positive contact than it actually states. It is also during these years that Munch made his two lithographic portraits of Delius.

For Delius the period was one of steadily declining health, with frequent travelling in search of cures. By the end of it he was incapacitated at Grez, blind and paralyzed. Fortunately he was sustained by the truly selfless devotion of Jelka and supported by a number of faithful friends who visited and helped him. Mostly these were musicians, men like Percy Grainger, Balfour Gardiner and Philip Heseltine, and they were invaluable in enabling him to hear his music or, together with Jelka, helping him to write it down. Jelka also assumed the responsibility of writing all his letters, by dictation. During the first half of this period Delius still produced a fair number of compositions, but by its end he had almost ceased to write music.

Munch, however, continued to lead an active life. His health was generally robust and even his contraction in 1919 of Spanish influenza he turned to good account in his painting, as in the splended *Self-portrait with Spanish 'flu'*, (Nasjonalgalleriet). His output of paintings and prints maintained itself steadily, while he continued to exhibit regularly. Although now firmly based at Ekely, he had not yet turned into the hermit he was later to become and he continued to make trips abroad.

Extant correspondence opens up again with a postcard from Delius in Biarritz.

Munch to Delius
(36, D.23)
Postcard, written in French[1], addressed to:
Monsieur Edv. Munch (Maler)
pr adr Hr Blomqvist
Kristiania
Norvége
(re-addressed to 'Ekely' pr Sköien.)   postmarked BIARRITZ 9-8-18

Dear friend,
    I hope that all goes well with you. We have been here for 2 months for sea baths.[2] I
hope to see you in Norway next year
                 A thousand good wishes from both of us
                            Frederick Delius

Munch exhibited pictures from his *Life Frieze* at Blomqvist's premises, Christiania, in 1918,[3] and the fact that Delius addressed his postcard there suggests that they had been in touch earlier in the year.

The Deliuses returned from Biarritz to Grez to find that their house had been occupied and ruined by French troops. They consequently went to England where they stayed until the following summer, mostly in London, but with two months in Cornwall during the spring of 1919. Delius was warmly greeted by the English musical world and a number of first performances were given of his work written during the war years.[4]

In the summer of 1919 he and Jelka went to Norway, but before this Jelka had re-visited Grez to see about having their house there made habitable again. Munch remained in Norway that year. Apart from his attack of Spanish influenza it was a busy period. His important new paintings included the *Bathing Man* (1918), *Self-portrait with the Spanish 'flu* and *Horses Ploughing* (both 1919), all in Nasjonalgalleriet. That year he again had an exhibition at Blomqvist's, while 57 of his prints were shown in New York. Although no record remains of contact between him and Delius during the summer, I think that the tone of the next letter from Delius (37, D.24) makes it most likely that they saw something of each other.

According to Sir Thomas Beecham[5] it was while the Deliuses were in Norway that they heard the good news that *Fennimore and Gerda* was to be produced at the Frankfurt Opera House that autumn. Consequently at the end of their Norwegian stay they went on to Germany, travelling through Denmark and arriving in Frankfurt somewhere about the end of September.[6] There they stayed for about a month, assisting in the rehearsals and attending the first performance.

The production, which seems to have been a conscientious and careful one, was an honourable attempt to re-establish Delius's pre-war reputation in Germany. The conductor was Gustav Brecher and the opera was generally well received, although not uncritically so, and both the principal singers and Delius's writing for the voice received some adverse comment.[7] But although performances of other Delius works in Germany were to follow, his acceptance there was never again so complete as it had been prior to 1914.

An interesting (if perhaps partly unconscious) tribute to Munch

117

appears in a drawing lithographed on the cover of the original vocal score, published by Universal Edition in 1919. It shows Fennimore and Erik embracing by the fjord, while Niels sits dejectedly under a tree some little distance off. The design is rather Munch-like, although less strong, and it is almost certainly by Jelka Delius. In a letter to the publisher, dated 13.11.1920, she states that she has received the cover sheet and thinks that 'the reproduction is fairly good', but proposes certain modification of tone values in the printing; 'I would like the red background to be somewhat darker, grayer, subdued, also the hands of the sitting figure a bit darker'.[8] Although Jelka does not actually state that she is the artist, the tone of the letter imples that she is. Apart from similarities to Munch in the general design, the embracing couple on the cover seem to be loosely derived from his famous motif *The Kiss* and Jelka, great admirer of the artist that she was, would surely have known this picture, at any rate in the woodcut version (OKK G/t.580, Sch.102).

It would also be interesting to know if Jelka had ever made any designs for the scenery of *Fennimore and Gerda*, as it would seem quite

Illustration by Jelka Delius [almost certainly] from cover design of vocal score of Fennimore and Gerda.
Universal Edition 6305, 6308, published 1919.
(Reproduction by courtesy of Dr Lionel Carley.)

The Kiss. Woodcut, OKK. G/t. 580-28; Sch.102.
There are a number of variants of this woodcut between 1897 and 1902.

likely. Delius had asked for 'an impressionistic painted curtain (see p.104), and Jelka's paintings were certainly impressionistic. The scenery for the Frankfurt production was by Walter Brügmann, but this would not preclude Jelka from having painted some idea sketches, either at the time of a hoped-for, but frustrated, production in 1914 at Cologne,[9] or later for Frankfurt. In a later letter to Universal Edition (5.6.1932) Delius asks the publisher 'if you are safely keeping the sketches for the stage paintings of *Fennimore and Gerda*', as he wanted them to show to Sir Thomas Beecham; '. . . the sketches were painted in oil and were in a thick, relatively large tube'.[10] But he does not mention who they were by and we do not know if Universal Edition ever sent them to him.[11]

From Frankfurt, Delius wrote to Munch.

Delius to Munch
(37, D.24)

Untermain Kai 3
c/o Dr H. Simon
Frankfurt a/M 10 Oct 1919

Dear Friend —
We arrived here safely and find everything very interesting and stimulating — plenty of enterprize — a much more interesting spirit than before the war. I am often together with Swarzenski.[12] A fine new museum for Modern Art has been built here and Swarzenski would very much like that you especially should be represented with 2 or 3 of your best pictures. He has asked me to write to you and put the matter near to your heart — Can you not send 4, 5 pictures so that he can choose. Of course he will pay all the expenses. There are wonderful things among the modern pictures. e.g. Dr Gachet by Van Gogh — One of the most beautiful Renoirs and several Manets etc. Have you seen my Gauguin yet? Tell Jappe[13] I would like to hear what is happening about it. Write soon

Your old friend
Frederick Delius

The first performance of my opera will take place on the 18th and I am in the middle of rehearsals —[14]

Delius's letter seems to have achieved its purpose with regard to the Munch pictures. Swarenski purchased two paintings directly from the artist in 1920 or 1921,[15] *Man with Duck* (1912) and *Seated Woman* (1916).[16]

In August 1918, Delius had written from Grez to Henry and Marie Clews: 'We are taking the Gauguin (*Nevermore*) to London in order to try and sell it — If we don't suceed I shall have to try and make a loan'.[17] (This was a time of financial difficulty for the Deliuses, due to the cessation of royalty payments from Germany.) They took it with them, but it looks as if no sale was effected in London and that they took it on to Norway with them in 1919, hoping no doubt that they might have better success through some of their Norwegian contacts. Jappe Nilssen as a leading art critic must have had some hopeful ideas about possible buyers, so presumably they left the painting with him to try and sell when they left Norway. This is also positive evidence that Delius was in touch with the Munch circle in Norway that year.

Jappe Nilssen's efforts were unsuccessful and Delius must have been in correspondence with him about this, although the only letter which has survived is the one from Delius in December 1920 (quoted below), by which time the painting had been returned to London. All this clearly took some time, as in autumn 1920 Delius wrote to Munch about it.

Delius to Munch
(38, D.25)
Written in Norwegian, in Jelka Delius's handwriting.

Grez sur Loing
Seine et Marne
23.9.1920

Dear Munch,

I wrote to Jappe Nilssen and asked him, if he could not get 28000 Kroner for my Gauguin, to send the picture to Hr Marchant[18] Goupil Gallery 5 Lower Regent Str London.

It is about a month or six weeks since I wrote and so I sent a telegram and received no reply. I am therefore afraid that he has not received my letter.

Will you be so kind, dear Munch, and look into the matter and write to me what is happening.

When are you coming down to visit us here?

We both send you our warmest greetings.

Your friend
Frederick Delius

Jappe Nilssen now sent Delius's *Nevermore* to London, whether after prodding by Munch or not we do not know. A letter from Delius in Frankfurt, where he had gone at the end of November,[19] to him clears the matter up, and it seems pertinent to quote it here.[20]

Written in Norwegian, in Jelka Delius's handwriting.
1 Dec. 1920

Carlton Hotel
Frankfurt a/M
Tyskland

Dear Friend

Your letter has been forwarded to me here, and I am quite astonished that you are still without your money.

The same day as I got your letter of 27 October I sent instructions to my Bank in London (National Provincial and Union Bank of England 208-209 Piccadilly[21]) to send you 180 Kroner 90 ore, the sum you had been so kind to lay out for me. I have written again to have the sum sent to you *immediately*; and to ask what happened to my first letter.

Marchant wrote to tell me that the picture has now arrived, but was so badly packed that it got 2 "skratches"[22] on the varnish and that it would be up to the insurance company to pay for it. But I do not know the insurance company's name and must therefore ask you to make the claim for me. The company must then send a representative to Goupils, 5 Lower Regent Str London and assess the damage, and then pay for it. Of course it was a great shame that the case disappeared. It was specially made and cost £3 and was *"tin lined"*[23]

We are both very sorry to hear that you are so poorly, and we sincerely hope that there will soon be an improvement!

We plan to stay here for two months and then travel to London.

Please tell me immediately whether you have now received the money.

Yours sincerely,
Frederick Delius

Gauguin's *Nevermore* was then sold (presumably after the scratches had been eradicated), for 'almost £3,000'.[24] After passing through several hands it was finally purchased by Samuel Courtauld and now hangs in the Courtauld Collection, London.[25]

Letters like those about the Gauguin make it clear how much contact between Munch, Delius and mutual friends has not been recorded or correspondence survived. This applies equally to the next letter from Delius to Munch, written only a few weeks after the last one (38, D.25).

Delius to Munch
(39, D.26)
Written in Norwegian in Jelka Delius's handwriting.

Grez sur Loing
Seine et Marne 13.10.20

Dear Munch,

Won't you come and stay with us out here for a few days? It is so lovely here now with the autumn atmosphere, so we could chat together a little and drink some of the wonderful bottles of wine which we buried during the Battle of the Marne.[26] There are 2 good trains a day 10.50 a.m. and 5.45 p.m. from the Gare de Lyon to Bourron station.[27] Couldn't you come on Saturday, you must not dash off without us having seen you. We would both be so happy to see you again.

Please send us a telegram about your arrival because we must book a driver to fetch you at Bourron.

Best wishes from us both
Your old friend
Frederick Delius.

Unfortunately we do not know to where this letter was addressed, but it seems clear that Munch was staying in or near Paris and that he had informed Delius of this. Although there has been some uncertainty about Munch's movements abroad in 1920,[28] this letter looks like positive evidence of a visit to France during the autumn.[29] However we cannot say whether he visited Delius at Grez, although the first of the portrait lithographs which Munch made of the composer points in that direction.

This portrait (OKK G/1.407-5, Sch.473) has usually been dated c.1920, from the figures written on the back of one of the prints in Munch-Museet. However there is nothing to indicate whether these apply to that particular print or to the original drawing. Another of these prints is owned by Dr Eric Fenby, who had it from Delius, and this one is signed and dated 1 January 1922. However it is unlikely that this refers to when the drawing was made, as at that time Munch was in Norway, while Delius was about to leave Grez for a sanatorium in Germany. More probably it refers to its dispatch to Delius or was added, incorrectly, by Munch at a subsequent meeting. Comparing the lithograph with photographs of Delius, it certainly appears to be a good likeness of the composer as he looked around 1920, although this can only be a guide to within a year or so. Delius looks younger and less frail here than in the portrait Munch made of him at Wiesbaden in 1922. So we can say that the drawing was probably made either on one of the visits Delius made to Norway in 1919 and 1921 or during Munch's visit to France in 1920. Thus the date can still stand as c.1920.

Munch continued to work vigorously. Now that the University Murals were behind him, he must have been hoping to receive other large public commissions. A project to build an imposing new city hall in Christiania was now afoot and he had made portraits of the lawyer Hieronymous Heyerdahl, the prime mover behind the scene, and Arnstein Arneberg, one of the two architects, in 1916 and 1917. Munch had always wanted to achieve a permanent home for his collected *Life Frieze* paintings, and it is likely that he had hopes in this direction, with the City Hall project, when he exhibited them in 1918. As many of the original *Life Frieze* pictures had been sold, the artist continued to re-work the motifs and about 1921-22 he started what Arne Eggum has called 'a shore frieze on a monumental scale',[30] starting with a new version of the *Dance of Life*. In fact these and later ideas for murals for the City Hall were all ultimately to be frustrated. However at the beginning of 1921 the Freia Chocolate Factory started to negotiate with Munch for the decoration of the factory's dining rooms. The artist produced sketches for both rooms, although he only carried out one. These were twelve paintings of figures engaged in outdoor occupations against the scenery of Aasgaardstrand, mostly developed from earlier *Life Frieze* and *Reinhardt Frieze* motifs. These were executed in 1922. The unrealized sketches for the other room were on the theme of working men and were Munch's first attempt on a new frieze with motifs from working-class life.[31]

Apart from large-scale decorative projects there are many important new individual paintings from these years. The theme of the artist and his model, for example *Model by a Wicker Chair* (1919-21); landscapes like *The Wave* (1921) and *Starry Night* (1923-24); scenes recalled from his past life, such as *The Bohemian's Wedding* (1924-5) and a new version of *The Bohemian's Death* (1925). And there were also a considerable number of new prints. About 1916 Munch had ceased to make etchings, but he continued making lithographs and woodcuts, both new subjects and re-workings of old ones.

Although Munch was gradually isolating himself with his work at Ekely, this did not happen all at once. During the first half of the nineteen-twenties he continued to make trips abroad, often in connection with the frequent exhibiting of his work in the Scandinavian and

Germanic countries. His connections with Germany remained particularly close. He became a member of the German Academy in 1923 and an honourary member of the Bavarian Academy, in Munich, in 1925, while continuing to support German artists both by buying large quantities of their prints and raising money for them by selling some of his own. Despite some recurring bronchial troubles, he was fortunate with his health which made possible his still vigorous programme.

But for Delius it was a different story, and much of the first half of the nineteen-twenties was spent in unsuccessfully searching for cures as his ailments increased. There was a consequent slowing down in his composing. Two important new works came from 1920-21, the Concerto for Violoncello and Orchestra and the incidental music for a production of James Elroy Flecker's play *Hassan*. This last was for a lavish production in London by Basil Dean, requiring a great deal of music, and although its presentation was delayed until 1923, its success was ultimately to earn the composer a substantial amount of money. Delius wrote additional music for the 1923 London production, assisted by Percy Grainger. After 1923 Delius was to achieve nothing more than a few sketches for the next five years.

Delius spent the first part of 1921 in London, composing the Cello Concerto and attending performances of his works, which were now taking place quite frequently in England. In the summer he and Jelka migrated once more to Norway. Here they were now able to make more permanent arrangements for their stays. They leased a site at Lesjaskog, in North Gudbrandsdal, in the centre of Norway, not so far from the mountainous districts of the Jotunheim and Dovre-fjell which had appealed so much to Delius. They designed a chalet to be built there, which they called *Høifagerli*, and building was completed by the time they came to Norway the following year. We do not know whether there was any meeting with Munch on this visit.

After Norway they returned to Grez, to remain there for the rest of the year. It was now that the really serious decline in Delius's health began to show. Sir Thomas Beecham writes: "Growing weakness, accompanied by pains in both arms and legs increased rapidly, and Jelka took him off in January 1922 to a sanatorium in Wiesbaden'.[32] Delius remained at German spas for most of the first half of the year. In April Munch came south, on his way to Berlin and Zurich, where he was to have a major exhibition. On the way he stopped at Wiesbaden and he was able to meet Delius there. It was on this occasion that he made another lithographic portrait, *Delius at Wiesbaden*, (OKK G/1.427, Sch. 498).

The portrait shows the composer seated (probably) in a wheelchair, which he was now increasingly obliged to use. The sensitive, intelligent face looks rather frail, and he wears a hat. He appears to be seated in a park or public gardens, and in the background people sit and listen to a concert which is being provided by a band on a covered stage. Munch also made another, probably preliminary, drawing in connection with this, given the same title by Munch-Museet (OKK T.639). The setting is the same, but the likeness of the composer, shown this time without hat or spectacles, is less close.[33]

At Wiesbaden Munch may also have given Delius greetings from another old friend, Jappe Nilssen, who wrote to the artist: 'If you meet Delius and his wife, do give them my regards; it was sad to hear that things are not well with him'.[34]

Shortly afterwards the Deliuses left Wiesbaden, going on to another spa, this time Wildbad. From there he sent Munch a postcard, which missed him and so had to be sent after to him in Zurich.

Delius to Munch
(40, D.27)
Written in Norwegian, in Jelka Delius's hand.
Postcard addressed to:
Herrn Edvard Munch
Hotel Kaiserhof
Wiesbaden
(re-addressed to Kunsthaus *Zürich*)

Hotel zur Post
Wildbad
Scharzwald 17.5.1922

Dear Friend,

We have arrived here in this delightful place; it is almost like Norway. Everything is very cosy, a nice old hotel with excellent food, one can also inhale here and I will do that and get rid of my cold. It is sheltered and warm here, a much better place than Wiesbaden, lovely smell of pine trees. I took my first bath[35] today. We will stay here for perhaps a month or six weeks.

Thanks for the last time![36]

Your old friend
Frederick Delius

Greetings from Jelka

Delius and Jelka left Germany for Norway late in June. They wrote to Munch informing him of when they arrived and proposing a meeting.

Delius to Munch
(41, D.28)
Written in Jelka Delius's hand.
Postcard addressed to:
Hrn Edvard Munch
Villa Ekely

125

Sköien
Kristiania, Norwegen
Re-addressed to Zürich, Berlin and then back to Sköien. Kristiania.

Karlsruhe. 23.6.22

Dear Friend,
    We are leaving tomorrow the 24th from Hamburg and arrive at the Victoria Hotel
(Christiania) on Monday evening. Please telephone me there to say if you have time
to come into town.

Sincerely yours
Frederick Delius

But it seems unlikely that such a meeting could have been arranged.
Munch returned home at the end of June.[37] Delius's postcard can
hardly have reached Ekely before about 25th June, and as it was
forwarded from there to Zurich, Munch's imminent arrival can hardly
have been expected. Even if he had returned home within a few days,
the postcard can hardly have made its north European tour and
returned to Ekely in time to catch him before Delius left for Lesjaskog,
which he had reached by the beginning of July.[38]

The building of the chalet *Høifagerli* was now completed and Delius
and Jelka were able to spend the summer up there. By early September
they were ready to move south again and Jelka wrote to Munch:

Jelka Delius to Munch
(42, D.29)
Postcard addressed to:
Edvard Munch
Villa Ekely,
Sköien
pr Kristiania
Dear Friend,
    We are leaving here tomorrow, Thursday for Kristiania Victoria Hotel, where we
shall be on Friday and we shall be going on at about noon on Saturday by Condor[39]
to Hamburg. Should you come into town we should be *so very* glad to see you. I shall of
course have to go to the Consulate etc but Delius will probably remain in the hotel,
please telephone first!
    Thanks for the last time![40]

Sincerely yours
Jelka Delius

Lesjaskog 5 Sept 1922

Delius's stay in Christiania was so brief on this occasion that it did
not leave much time for a meeting with Munch. However it would
certainly have been possible, and I should like to think that Munch
cared for his friend sufficiently to have arranged it.

For the winter of 1922-23 Delius settled in Frankfurt, where quite a number of performances of his music were to take place. He celebrated his sixtieth birthday (actually his 61st[41]) there at the home of a close friend, Dr Heinrich Simon, proprietor of the *Frankfurter Zeitung*. Jelka writes of them being 'surrounded here by delightful and friendly musicians and poets and also Beckmann, a great German painter:[42] 'They are giving a chamber-music concert[43] at the house of a great friend. Percy Grainger is here and will play some of his things'.[44]

In April Delius was again taking the waters for his health, this time at Oeynhausen, near Hanover. On 1st June *Hassan* received its first performance, in a German translation, at Darmstadt, with the original version of Delius's music, less some cuts.

In May, Munch had come to Berlin, where he had an exhibition that month, and afterwards he went on to Zurich and Stuttgart before returning home again. But there is no evidence that his path crossed with that of Delius on this trip.

And in the summer of 1923 Delius went back to Norway, probably fairly soon after the Darmstadt performance of *Hassan*. It was to be his last visit to that country.

Hassan was now scheduled for production in London in September, and Delius was called on for modifications and additions to his music for the play. He worked on these while at Lesjaskog, dictating the music to Jelka, as he was unable to write himself. On this trip he was joined for a time by Percy Grainger, who wrote one of the pieces for him, the 'General Dance'.[45] The athletic Grainger contributed to what must have been Delius's last sight of a Norwegian sunset from the mountains. Dr Eric Fenby has told the story how Delius, seated in a chair lashed to poles, was carried a seven hours' ascent up a nearby mountain to see the sunset, Grainger bearing one end and Jelka and two servants the other.[46] The event is remembered in Lesjaskog, where the chair still exists.

Munch returned to Norway from his foreign travels during the summer, but we have no evidence to say whether he met the composer or not.

On leaving Norway, the Deliuses returned to Grez, and from thence they went to London for the final rehearsals of *Hassan*. The revised version (of both play and music) received its first performance at His Majesty's Theatre on 20th September. The production was by Basil Dean and the conductor on the first night was Eugene Goossens. *Hassan* was a great success, both artistically and financially. 1923 also saw the appearance of the first English book on Delius, by his friend and admirer Philip Heseltine (Peter Warlock[47]). This financial success enabled Delius and Jelka to winter on the Mediterranean. They stayed about three months at Rapallo, where they leased Gordon Craig's villa[48] and then spent a month near Cannes, where their friends Henry and Marie Clews were now living. On the whole the sunshine did Delius's health good, and the month near Cannes was a particularly happy one; Delius actually made some sketches for new compositions.[49] The rest of 1924 and 1925 were to be painful and dispiriting.

Delius and Jelka returned to Grez at the turn of April/May. His sister Clare, who visited them there that year noted the great deterioration of his health, and by midsummer Jelka took him again to Germany in search of cures. At the health resort of Wilhemshöhe they found a doctor who was convinced that Delius could be cured. Back at Grez in August, he seemed better in walking and in his sight, and in November they returned to Germany (Cassel) to continue under the same doctor's treatment. Up till Christmas improvement seemed to continue, Delius even being able to write a short letter to Henry Clews in his own hand. But with the beginning of 1925, a relapse set in and the doctors were unable to hinder its rapid progress. By the middle of the year they were back in Grez, with Delius paralyzed and blind.

In August Jelka wrote to Marie Clews:

'I have thought of you often, but I thought that all the world knew of Fred's sad state: he cannot see at all. We have passed a terrible winter at Cassel, trying to save his eyes and seeing them get worse and worse, trying all specialists etc. At last we came back here end of May and since then his general state is *slightly* improved, but not the eyes. He therefore cannot walk at all. We have a man who carries him up and down, and he lies most of the day in the garden on his chaise-longue. That lovely garden all full of flowers and he cannot see it! His mind is lucid and as active as ever and of course to keep him from depression I read to him a tremendous lot'.[50]

With one notable exception, his visit to London in 1929, he was now to stay immobilized at Grez for the remainder of his life.

Chapter X

1926–1934

DESPITE DELIUS'S IMMOBILITY DURING THE LAST NINE YEARS OF HIS LIFE, what has survived of the correspondence with Munch is some of the most revealing. The actual letters which Munch sent to his friend have disappeared, but he retained drafts for five letters and they are now preserved in Munch-Museet. The letters from Delius and Jelka sent to Munch show that a number of letters from the artist did continue to arrive at Grez.

Several of the draft letters are comparatively long and touch a note of considerateness and affection rather new to Munch's side of the correspondence and he relates news about old friends. No doubt he was touched by Delius's plight and some of his remarks are clearly meant to be kindly and encouraging. But as the artist's life at Ekely became increasingly withdrawn and solitary he became more dependent on memories from his past life. Less and less could he bring himself to part with any of his paintings, which became like a family to him,[1] and among these his portraits of old friends occupied a special place.[2] And with equal assiduousness he stored written material, notes and jottings, his own attempts at literary compositions, letters from friends and drafts of his letters to them. So it is hardly surprising to find expression in his draft letters of affection towards old friends, such as Delius, who he felt had never betrayed him.

Although now in his sixties, Munch's life was still organized entirely round his work. A number of his paintings continued to be re-workings of earlier motifs, for example during the twenties he painted a fifth and sixth version of *The Sick Child* (OKK M.52 and M.51). Others are new themes, such as the fine double-portrait Dr Lucien Dedichen and Jappe Nilssen (1925-6, OKK M.370) and landscapes, *The Red House* (1926, Private Collection) and *P.A. Munch's Grave, Rome* (1927, OKK M.1018). But probably his greatest preoccupation was with working out ideas for decorating the new Oslo[3] City Hall which was still being planned, and he left a great number of sketches from the nineteen-twenties connected with this. When interviewed in 1928, he declared: 'I am greatly interested in the plans to make a frieze on the subject of

129

working life in Oslo'.[4] He was helped over material for this by the construction of a new indoor winter studio at Ekely (previously he had relied on his open-air studios, where paintings hung winter and summer), which gave him ample opportunity of making studies of building workers in action. But unfortunately, despite the serious efforts he put into the project, he was never able to bring it to completion. A final commission was never agreed on, and by 1931, when the foundation stone of the City Hall was eventually laid, Munch was almost seventy and temporarily prevented from painting by an eye complaint.

This eye complaint occurred in 1930, when a blood vessel burst in his right eye, and as his left eye was weak he could paint little for about a year. However he did manage to complete some lithographs and woodcuts.

Munch's work continued to be widely exhibited in northern Europe. Outstanding were major retrospective exhibitions in Berlin and Oslo in 1927, and important shows in Oslo, Stockholm and Chemnitz in 1930. An interesting exhibition in Zurich in 1932 combined Munch's work with that of Paul Gauguin. But in fact not a year went by without his representation in many galleries. He also started to attract a little attention in Britain and the United States. London saw his work in 1928 and 1936, and his paintings were exhibited in Edinburgh in 1931.[5] In America his works were included in exhibitions in Pittsburgh, Detroit and San Francisco.

Munch travelled abroad fairly extensively in both 1926 and 1927, making two excursions in each year. In both years he visited Germany, Italy and Paris and it was probably on the 1926 visit to Paris that he met Delius for the last time. After 1927 he did not leave Norway again, except for a visit to Gothenburg in 1937. His health troubles and growing older must have been important contributors to his increasingly hermetic life in Norway. In 1933 he celebrated his seventieth birthday. Numerous greetings and tributes streamed in from Scandinavia and Germany and he was made a knight Grand Cross of the Order of St. Olav. Jens Thiis and Pola Gauguin both published biographies of him,[6] while the press was full of articles. But although he could hardly fail to be gratified by at least some of these acclamations, Munch took care to keep himself inaccessible. 'He managed to have cancelled plans for a torchlight procession in his honour, and he spent the whole of his birthday driving round in a taxi so that nobody should be able to get hold of him'.[7]

' During 1926 and 27 Delius continued to lead an uneventful existence at Grez. Although blind and paralyzed his mind retained its full keenness, but his incapacities made it impossible for him to communicate compositional ideas to the point of getting them written down and worked out. Through his strength of will he managed to achieve a stoical resignation, but Beecham has told us that 'laughter was just as frequently on his lips and his sense of sardonic humour remained unblunted'.[8] Friends faithfully continued to come and visit him, many of them musicians like Balfour Gardiner and Percy Grainger, who were able to play some of his own music for him, and acquisition of a radio enabled him to hear broadcasts of his music which continued to be performed, especially in England and Germany.

In the summer of 1928 a young musician from Delius's native county of Yorkshire became moved by the composer's plight and offered to come and live with the Deliuses at Grez and become his amanuensis. This was Eric Fenby. The offer was accepted and Fenby arrived in October. After initial difficulties in establishing communication, he and the composer evolved a method of taking down compositions and getting them into a playable form. Fenby remained with Delius on and off for five years and the stimulation of their collaboration brought forth a rich and un-hoped for Indian summer of compositions. Some of these, like *A Song of Summer* (1929-30) and *Idyll* (1932), used material from earlier Delius compositions,[9] others were works which the composer had drafted earlier, but had been unable to complete, such as *Cynara* (1907-27), *A Late Lark* (1924/5-29) and *Songs of Farewell* (1920/21-30). Others were either entirely new: *Caprice and Elegy*, for violoncello and orchestra (1930), or new works using some material from slight sketches earlier in the nineteen-twenties, such as the Violin Sonata No.3 (1930). While some of these works are rather slight ones, others like *Songs of Farewell* and *Idyll* are extended compositions, using voices and orchestra.[10]

In addition to the new lease of life provided by Eric Fenby, 1929 proved to be a year of outstanding importance. In the spring Delius was created a Companion of Honour. News of new compositions boosted interest in his music in England and this culminated in the Delius Festival in London in the autumn, organized by Sir Thomas Beecham. This was the largest concentration of Delius's music yet presented together and consisted of four orchestral and vocal concerts and two chamber ones.[11] The paralyzed composer was transported to London for the festival, the last time he was to leave Grez during his lifetime. The festival was successful in arousing considerable public interest and 'Delius was both moved and impressed by the warmth of his welcome in London'.[12]

Back in Grez, the last four years of Delius's life passed quietly. New compositions were still to come from his collaboration with Fenby; old

131

friends continued to visit him, and there was a notable visit from Elgar, in the year before both composers were to die. He continued very interested in Norway and Dr Eric Fenby has told me that he would more often discuss his memories of Norwegian personalities and places than German ones. Every Thursday lunchtime a Norwegian provincial newspaper, which was somehow regularly procured, was read aloud to him by Jelka, a ritual which delighted Percy Grainger.

Munch visited Paris during the autumns of both 1926 and 1927. It seems probable that he came to see Delius on the earlier of these occasions, because of a letter which Jelka sent him and a letter which he drafted to the composer.

While in Paris on the 1926 visit, Munch had written to Delius, although the letter has not survived. Jelka replied immediately.

Jelka Delius to Munch.
(43, D.30)
Gare Bourron   Grez
depart Gare de Lyon

Sunday 31.11.1926
(in fact 31.*10*.1926)

Dear Munch,

Delius was so indescribably glad to hear from you from Paris! But both your letters arrived together only this morning and I sent a telegram immediately to see if you would not visit us. Please, please do so, we would so much love to see you again, and you know how badly things have been going for my husband, although he has been better again during the last few months, but he can hardly see at all.

You have a good train 10.43 and could be here for lunch, a car is in Bourron.[13] There is also a train about 4 o'clock in the afternoon. If you cannot come tomorrow, please come, *whenever you like* we are of course always here and it would make us very happy.

Yours ever
Jelka Delius

P.S. You can also get here directly from Paris by car, just take a taxi, 69 kilometres, via Fontainbleau

A query is caused by the date on Jelka's letter. Munch was in Paris on 21st October, as we know from a letter which he sent to Karen Bjølstad for her birthday.[14] He was still in Paris on 4th November, as he wrote from there to Jappe Nilssen on that date.[15] But it is most unlikely that he was still there at the end of November as he travelled home through Mannheim, where an important exhibition of his work was being held at the Kunsthalle from 7th November, 1926-9th January 1927.[16] He even gave Jappe Nilssen a Mannheim address in his letter, implying that he was about to leave Paris. I am sure, therefore, that Jelka wrote November when she meant October. This seems substantiated by the facts that 31st October was on a Sunday in 1926 and that anyway November has only thirty days.

In any case Munch drafted a letter to Delius, after his return to Norway,[17] which confirms that they had met, and although we have no proof that some such letter was sent, I think it likely that it was.

Munch to Delius.
(43a, Md.6)

Undated but probably late 1926

Dear Friend Delius

I am so glad that I have seen you and your wife again — And it makes me especially glad to see that you looked so well and that you have kept your fine cheerful voice — That you [have kept] your optimistic good humour which I have so often envied you — He who has this strong inner self is happier than so many others — This year I saw many old friends again in Paris too — I went and visited old haunts — I thought of the poor but beautiful time when I had my studio in the rue de la Sante — I remember the times when I wanted to sell old wine bottles in order to get something to eat — And I could not even get 10 centimes for them. Then you remember, at that time I would often dine at your place — would drink fine wine and you would cheer me with your good humour — At that time you took me to Mollard where they were so kind to me. All our acquaintances had certainly become very old — Molard was an old man — I also met Ouvrés (isn't that his name?) the printmaker[18] — But he looked just the same as before — Jappe Nilssen is very poorly and ailing. My good friend also complained a good deal about life — I think it cheers him up a bit to lash the young painters — He does that pretty well too — But quite a number are dead — But I do meet old friends of yours — I cannot understand why one does not hear more of your music[19] — Everyone talks of how in other countries and especially in England you are reckoned one of the greatest — I and Jappe Nilssen believe that it comes from the fact that you were always too modest about your own things — and that you always took an interest in the rest of us —.[20]

I would suggest that Jelka wrote her letter to Munch on the 31st October and that Munch did in fact visit Delius on one of the first days in November. On returning to Paris he then saw William Molard in time to be able to write to Jappe Nilssen on 4th November: 'I have been to see Mollard, who is very old and has a couple of old friends'.[21] Then, after returning to Norway and seeing Jappe Nilssen again, he drafted the letter to Delius telling him of old mutual friends seen in Paris after he had visited the composer at Grez.[22]

The next letters come from late 1928. Eric Fenby was now in Grez and with his assistance Delius was starting to compose again. Although Jelka had helped take down his music earlier in the nineteen-twenties there was a limit to what she could do as she was not a professional musician. But Fenby was, and he was therefore able to take down scores for the full orchestra, which Delius so much loved.

Delius had heard from Munch, although the letter has not survived,[23] and both he and Jelka replied.

133

Delius to Munch.
(44, D.31)
Written in Jelka Delius's handwriting.

Delius dictates: (station) Bourron 19.11.1928
Dear Friend,
 Your kind letter gave me great pleasure, and I hear also from Jappe[24] that you are getting on so well and that also pleases me very much.
 My health is generally a little better and I am less weak and can eat a little more. I should always be pleased if you could visit me; your room here is always ready.
 Although it is quite autumnal I go out daily in my wheel-chair. We have had a wonderful summer and for months I have always been out of doors.
 Sadly my Jotunheim days are over, something I miss very much.
 I am very happy to hear that you continue to have such great success with your art.[25] You know how I love and understand your work —
 Please write to me again soon, everything that concerns you interests me. And please, do not miss visiting me when you next come to Paris.
Your old friend
Frederick Delius

Jelka Delius to Munch.
(45, D.32)

GREZ
(station) Bourron
19.11.28

Dear Munch,
 You gave Delius great pleasure with your kind letter. When I look at him, I always have to think of *you* because I always feel that *nobody* could make a picture of him as *you* could. He is now so beautiful, so expressive; particularly when he listens to music he is fantastically absorbed, serene, quite unique. You could paint or draw this so splendidly.[26]
 Please, please, when you are anywhere near us again do come and paint him.
 Here you would have peace, a studio, and good red wine and the two of us, your loyal friends.
 We have a new gramophone, a work of art, not mass-produced, but hand-made. We have a number of Delius's orchestral works[27] which sound really magnificent on it; much better than on the big famous gramophones, which are much more expensive.
 But *you must paint* the picture of the sick Delius. You will make a masterpiece of it.
Yours ever
Jelka Delius

Jelka wrote again in February 1929.

Jelka Delius to Munch.
(46, D.33)
Postcard addressed to:
Mons. Edvard Munch
Skøyen
Oslo
Norvège

postmarked GREZ
2.2.29

134

Dear Friend,

Just in case you now have a radio please listen to a Delius Concert on the London Radio Friday 8th Febr 9.35 p.m. English time. It is conducted by Sir Thomas Beecham, the best conductor in England and a very fine programme the last item: "Eventyr" ballad for orchestra after Ashbjornson.[28] We now have a new radio-set and hear splendidly, it is a Ducretet and is French. Delius is not too bad. We have had a real winter with snow.

Yours ever
Jelka Delius

Three attempts by Munch to answer this letter survive in draft form. The first also contains a short note from Jappe Nilssen.

Munch to Delius.
(46a, Md.7)
Written in Norwegian.   No date, but probably February
(or March) 1929.

Dear old friend Delius

It delighted me to have a letter from you — and above all that things go well with you — you have indeed rare ability to look life bravely in the face.

— It was not possible for me to make a connection with London[29] — I spoke to the Radio office here but was told that a connection could not be made —

On the other hand he was interested in the possibility of a concert on the Radio here — How should one set about it?[30]

A note from Jappe Nilssen to Delius is appended, written in French.

Dear friend!

I shall be writing a letter to you in a few days.[31] Munch is here at home with me and wants me to improvise a letter, while he is seated by me chattering away at the top of his voice. So this is only a short greeting which I am sending you.

With greetings to your wife I give you a firm handshake.

Yours Jappe Nilssen

A little later, Munch made another attempt to write the letter.

Munch to Delius.
(46b, Md.8)
No date, but probably February or March 1929.
Dear Delius

Already some time ago I wrote a letter to you including a few words from Jappe — but when I see that I wrote it in Norwegian[32] — Now it always takes me a fortnight to write a letter — then the time passes — I thank your wife for the letter — Unfortunately it was not possible here to hear London.

Couldn't one hear something of yours here on the Radio — I would like to go to Paris this summer and then I would spend a couple of days with you — I could perhaps paint you — Now I don't know how it goes[33] — I am overstrained by the exhibitions[34] — I shall perhaps have a rest by the sea in Holland[35] — For I have become so absent-minded that everything happens to me on my travels — When I have to take a train to Leipzig I arrive in Breslau and so on —[36]

Munch then went on to draft the letter a third time.[37]

Munch to Delius.
(46c, Md.9)

Undated, but probably March or even April 1929.

Dear Friend Delius

I had already written to you a month ago but then I see that I wrote in Norwegian — and so I did not send it[38] — I usually need 3 weeks to write a letter so it is delayed.

I thank your wife very much for her letter. Unfortunately it was not possible to hear anything from London here —

Perhaps it could be arranged some time that we hear something of yours on the Radio here

I have been thinking of making a short trip to Paris — but not until summer But it is not certain —

— It was to visit you and other friends —

I would have painted you then It would have been a very beautiful picture. I was very glad that you are fairly well. You have what I envy you for very much a wonderful optimism and you are strong minded — I am convinced that you can also see — One certainly does not see with the eyes alone but with the whole body

Do you remember how we — you, Helge Rode and I talked about things to come over 30 years ago in Aasgaardstrand We talked about the transparency of the body and telepathy — It was what we have now X-rays and Radio and the wonderful waves which connect the whole world and the whole stellar system with us[39] —

(Do you know that Helge Rode has become quite religious and writes books on religious subjects?[40]

Have you ever thought about writing your memoirs —? I have myself written a kind of spiritual diary for 40 years and am now at work arranging it.[41]

It is very interesting —

All best wishes to you and your wife
Your old friend
Edvard Munch

In view of the trouble which Munch took over the various drafts of this letter, it would seem probable that he eventually got something written and posted, but nothing has survived. In fact no further correspondence has come to light until 1934.

I find this rather surprising. It is true that Munch did not go to France again and that the beginning of the nineteen-thirties was a period which brought him troubles; there was, for example, the eye complaint, which afflicted him in 1930-31, and the deaths of his aunt Karen Bjølstad and of Jappe Nilssen, both people who meant a lot to him. But on the other hand as Munch became increasingly isolated and lonely, he lived more of his life in the company of the past through his old letters and notes, so one would expect to find him inclined to be in touch with such old friends as remained. Moreover there were events during those years where one would have expected to find the composer and the artist in communication. After Jelka's troubling to inform Munch about the performance of *Eventyr* in 1929, one would think it unlikely that she and Delius should not have told him about the extremely important Delius Festival in London during the autumn of that year. Again one might have expected to find some congratulatory exchange on the occasion of their seventieth birthdays, Delius's in 1932 and Munch's the following year, particularly as Munch's was made much of in Norway and drew numerous tributes from home and abroad.

Knowing the amount of correspondence between them which was sent, received and has since disappeared, one would be inclined to think that there had been letters between 1929 and 1934. A few passages in Munch's next, and final, draft letter (47a, Md.10) could, however, seem to suggest the opposite. Moreover, Delius's letters to Munch have been better preserved than the other way round; most of the letters demonstrably missing were those from Munch.[42] And if Delius had heard from Munch it is almost unthinkable that at this stage he would not have replied, in which case one would have expected Munch-Museet to have any such letter. So we finally have to accept that we just do not know whether there was contact during those years or not.

At the beginning of 1934 Delius was unwell for some time. Nevertheless in January he sent Munch a postcard.

Delius to Munch.
(47, D.34)
Written in Norwegian in Jelka's handwriting.
Postcard addressed to:
Herr Edvard Munch
Store Kunstmaler (Great Painter)
Skoyen
pr. Oslo
Norvège   postmarked GREZ
                                                              5.1.1934
Dear Friend,
    We both send you our heartiest New Year greetings and hope all is well with you.
Won't you come and visit us in the spring?
                        Your faithful friend
                        Frederick Delius.

It could be argued either that there is no implication of this being a continuation of recent correspondence, or that it is unlikely that such a brief note would be written after a four year gap from some very cordial

137

exchanges. In any case it seems particularly poignant in view of the composer's death following relatively shortly.

And Munch drafted a reply.

Munch to Delius.

(47a, Md.10)   The first page of this draft is reproduced opposite.
Written in Norwegian   The printed drawing is of Munch's cottage at
                                                              Aasgaardstrand.)

Dear Delius

It was an enormous pleasure for me to receive your card and New Year greetings —
And I am delighted that you are going on all right[43] —

I have often thought about writing to you. I recently met Sinding — he was looking well[44] —

Jappe our old friend is dead[45] — Helge Rode is very well He recently wrote in Politikken[46] about a book by Gaugin about me[47]

In it he talks about you and that summer we were together in Aasgaardstrand[48] —

I hear that you are a member of the academy of music in London. Hearty congratulations[49]

The drawing is of my cottage in Aasgaardstrand. I am often there painting[50]

I live completely like a hermit — Should I come to Paris at all I shall certainly paint you — We spoke about this last time[51]

Hearty greetings and wishes for a good year to you both.

Your devoted friend
Edvard Munch

Skoien pr Oslo 10/1 34

There seems no way of knowing whether Munch actually sent a letter like this but, in the circumstances, one certainly hopes that he did, as it would have given Delius very much pleasure.

By May, Delius's health had deteriorated and the same month Jelka had to go into hospital for a major operation. She was only released just in time to be with Delius when he died on 10th June. But her health never really recovered, and within a year she had followed him.

There is no record of how or when Munch heard of the death of Delius, or of his reaction to it. He himself was to continue living for nearly another ten years. During these years he lived a hermit-like existence at Ekely. Nevertheless he maintained contact with a few friends and continued to have his work exhibited at home and abroad. The most remarkable thing is that he continued working hard. He recovered from his eye complaint and, although he was not able to carry out the hoped-for decorations for the new City Hall, he produced a remarkable number of new works. His paintings were now painted in strong and brilliant colours; often they were re-workings of old themes, but there were also a number of new motifs. Some of these, painted late in life are a series of remarkable self-portraits.[52] His last work of all was

Kjære Delius!

Det var mig en overordentlig
glæde at få Dit kort og
nyaars hilsen – Og det glæder mig at
frøste Du lever ~~fortræffelig~~ . bra –

Jeg har ofte tænkt på at
skrive til Dig. Jeg traf Sunding
nylig . Han så kjæk ud .

Jappe vor gamle ven er død –
Helge Rode har det vist bra
Han skrev nyle i Politikken. ~~en~~
en bok om mig af Gauguin

a new version of the lithographic portrait of Hans Jaeger, his mentor from the old bohemian days, and long-since dead.[53] When one thinks of Munch's pessimistic concern throughout his life about his health, his determination and vigour as an old man is astonishing.

A shadow was cast over his later days by the policy of the Nazi government in Germany. His works were among those by so-called 'degenerate' modern artists which were confiscated from German museums in 1937. As Germany had been the first country to recognize his importance, and the home of his principal patron-friends, this must have given him great sorrow. However he kept in touch with such a good old friend as Max Linde, until the doctor's death in 1940, and he gave financial support to the young German painter Ernst Wilhelm Nay to enable him to stay in Norway. Munch never had any sympathy with the Nazis and when the Germans occupied Norway in 1940 he would have nothing to do with them, unlike some of his contemporaries such as the writer Knut Hamsun. Naturally he had anxieties during the occupation — at one time there was a possibility that the Germans would requisition Ekely, although fortunately this came to nothing — and he was not molested. On December 12th 1943 he was able to celebrate his eightieth birthday. A week later a large munitions store exploded on the Filipstad Quay; windows of his house were blown in and Munch, walking nervously about in the garden, caught a cold which turned to bronchitis. This he failed to shake off, and he died in his home on 23rd January. In his will he left all his works to the City of Oslo, where they are now cared for in Munch-Museet, part of the municipal art collections.

Epilogue

HAVING EXAMINED THE EVIDENCE, WHAT CONCLUSIONS CAN BE DRAWN AS to the relationship towards the two men?

We can see from the correspondence that there were other letters which have not survived and also there were many meetings over the years not specifically recorded. About twenty of the extant letters or drafts make it clear that other letters were also sent and received. In most cases these were communications from Munch to the composer. Munch was a jackdaw and hoarded letters, as well as his own notes, drafts and literary sketches. It is highly likely therefore that a good proportion of the communications from Delius or Jelka to him were saved, and consequently went to Oslo Kommunes Kunstsamlinger on his death, where they have been faithfully preserved in Munch-Museet. The Deliuses, on the other hand, were either less careful in preserving letters, or else more things must have disappeared in the somewhat confused situation caused by Delius's death and Jelka's illness and death relatively soon after,[1] before the setting up of the Delius Trust. This would explain why many fewer letters have survived from Munch than from Delius. It would also suggest gaps in contact between the two men are more likely when no letter survives in Munch-Museet than when nothing is preserved in the Delius Trust Archive. Thus for example the apparent lack of communication between 1929 and 1934 seems quite probable, even if one would have expected there to be some correspondence.

The letters suggest a firm, reliable friendship with full acceptance of each other, although each had friends with whom they were even more intimate. In the letters they do not address each other by Christian names and, even allowing for the greater formality of the period they lived in, both employed Christian names when corresponding with some of their most intimate friends. Both men were capable of long-term loyalty to those they liked and trusted and the relationship was a well-established one. Although the letters are short, they are consistently warm, respectful and frank and their tone is that of two equals. Munch's letters perhaps seem rather to take Delius for granted in the years between 1903 and 1908. But these were not easy years for him; a peripatetic existence, brooding over the Tulla Larsen affair, too much drinking coupled with demands of a growing success probably left him little time for great consideration of friends, unless he were actually in their company. In his later draft letters, when he was leading a more solitary life, he had time to think with affection of old loyal friends. In Paris, before his nervous breakdown, Munch had a valuable ally in Delius, and the composer did more to help him in a concrete way than vice versa. Sir Thomas Beecham has told us that helping friends was habitual with Delius.[2]

Delius was good at making friends in the earlier part of his life, before illness and suffering produced the more formidable character of his later years. He was good company and seems to have had a quiet assurance which impressed others. Munch recalls this in his late draft letters: 'Then, you remember, at that time I would often dine at your place — would drink fine wine and you would cheer me with your good humour —'.[3] And again: 'You have what I envy you for very much a wonderful optimism and you are strong-minded —'.[4] Clearly the touchy, hyper-sensitive Munch found Delius entertaining, emotionally reliable and reassuring. Moreover they had a great number of mutual friends and acquaintances in the nordic arts world which so strongly attracted the composer.

Munch could also be an attractive man, of interesting and thoughtful ideas. He was more withdrawn than Delius, and his insecurities and overdependence in alcohol made him at times difficult to handle. But Delius could be good with touchy people if he found them interesting. Both men were sensitive and also rather fastidious, probably a common bond contrasting with the bohemian milieu in which both spent much time in their earlier lives. Being involved in different arts, personal interests would never have clashed, while although both men were attractive to women there is no evidence of any rivalries occurring.

To what extent can one find similarities in the work of the two men? I would suggest to a limited extent. Being exact contemporaries and sharing much of the same background, Norwegian and cosmopolitan, one naturally finds a number of common sources of inspiration, the writings of Nietzsche and Ibsen for example, and perhaps J.P. Jacobsen, Vilhelm Krag and Helge Rode. Certainly the northern landscape played an important part in the works by both of them.

In fact it is as nature poets that Delius and Munch come closest together. Both can evoke the mood of the northern scene, with its long summer twilights, evocative yet crisply delineated, in that stylistic borderland between Impressionism, Symbolism and Expressionism.

Man can enter into it, in Delius's case usually the lonely voice singing with a poignancy which harmonizes with the mood of sunset afterglow and twilight that so often saturates his nature music. The solitary figure brooding by the twilight shore is a major theme for Munch too, but the painter also frequently sees man relating to nature in a more robust and positive way as in the scenes of agricultural workers and animals, which accompanied and followed the University murals.

With Delius nature worship is expressed in terms of a beauty-saturated Arcadia, which man must always yearn after, but which will always fade away from him. When he writes of love between humans it is nearly always the same; man is left with his visions, the love lost, unattainable or only possible of realization in death. (When he tries to conclude with a happy ending, as in *Fennimore and Gerda*, he is less convincing.)

If one compares two of their largest works, Delius's *Mass of Life* and Munch's University murals, both have connection with Nietzsche's *Also sprach Zarathustra*, Delius's work completely and Munch's in part. Similarities of mood may be felt between the bursting energy of Delius's opening chorus and the centrepiece of Munch's mural, *The Sun*, but there are considerable differences if the works are taken as a whole. Delius's *Mass* is really a great nature poem, fluctuating, as Christopher Palmer well describes it, 'constantly between the twin polarities represented by Teutonic romanticism on the one hand, and by Impressionist faery fantasy on the other'.[5] Although Munch described his University murals as representing the great eternal forces, they are essentially about the theme of man playing his part in relation to nature. In style they could be said to blend a kind of Fauvism with Scandinavian Vitalism and also something decidedly neo-classical.

Man for Munch is the prime subject, whether seen largely tragically, as in the *Life Frieze*, more in tune with nature, as in the University murals and the paintings of men working, or simply in the many portraits which he painted throughout his life. Thus his subject and emotional range is more varied than with Delius. It is impossible to imagine the composer wanting to achieve either the horrific tension of *The Scream*, or the almost socialistic themes inspired by working men, or the objective perception of the best portraits. Munch has a sharpness which can at times be very savage, as in the *Death of Marat*, and on other occasions comes out as mordant wit or irony, both qualities which I have not found in the works of Delius. Yet at times, when Munch's mood is more lyrical or more resignedly melancholy, he and Delius come closer together and produce works of individual genius which seem to inhabit very much the same world, as in *Evening* or in *Melancholy:*

the Yellow Boat and passages from *Fennimore and Gerda*.

There remains their feelings about each other's work, and for both of them their art was the biggest thing in their lives. One would like to be able to record discussion of mutual artistic interests, even of influence and collaboration between them. But although Delius was able to offer practical advice about exhibitions, Munch's letters only refer to music in relation to Delius twice, once in the case of the hinted at Jacobsen project in 1899[6] and more generally in a late draft letter[7]. But knowing their common interests in Nietzsche, Ibsen, the moods of the northern landscape, as well as numerous mutual Scandinavian friends and acquaintances in the arts, it is inconceivable, in a friendship of more than forty years, that artistic matters were never discussed. Despite the lack of direct written evidence, it is possible to deduce something from their attitudes to art and music respectively.

Delius was keenly appreciative of the visual arts and he was married to a painter. Their collection included work by Gauguin, Munch, Rodin, Daniel de Monfreid, Ida Gerhardi and, of course, Jelka's own work. He became close friends with the American sculptor Henry Clews, who portrayed him in alabaster (in 1916), while the Italian sculptor, Eleuterio Riccardi executed a fine bronze portrait bust (in 1921) on the commission of Lady Cunard. Towards the end of his life he was portrayed by James Gunn, Augustus John and Ernest Proctor, but as Delius was by then blind these late portraits came rather through his being a celebrity than through a deliberate selection on his part[8].

Delius owned a number of prints by Munch. After Jelka Delius's death in May 1935 an inventory was made of the pictures in the house at Grez-sur-Loing and it lists twelve Munch prints. These are described as 'etchings', but the inventory was probably not made by an art expert so, in view of other evidence, I am sure that we can take this to mean prints in various media. Although the list gives subjects for five of the prints, these are not orthodox titles and are only of slight help in identification, except in the case of one self-portrait. However if the list is taken in conjunction with recollections of Eric Fenby it is possible to go a little further. Dr Fenby has described how the pictures impressed him when he arrived at Grez in 1928: 'A full-sized face of mad Strindberg by Munch frowned down at me from over the foot of the bed, and over the head was a framed photograph of Nietzsche. More fantastic creatures of Munch, dark with suicide, hung high up on the walls, which were covered by a coarse brown material . . .'[9]. Dr Fenby has tried to identify these prints for me although, as he pointed out, his stay at Grez was over fifty years ago, when he was unfamiliar with Munch's work. He thinks that these included portraits of Delius, Munch and Strindberg and at least six *Life Frieze* type subjects, although he feels that there may have been others as well, and the existence of three more is confirmed by the inventory. I would personally have expected Delius to own a copy of the lithographic portrait of Nietzsche (OKK G/1.268-2; Sch.247), which Munch refers to in letter 25 (p. 84), in view of his admiration for the philosopher. I have attempted to put together what evidence there is of the identity of the various prints in Appendix B (pp. 175-6).

After the deaths of Delius and Jelka the portrait of Delius passed to Eric Fenby. The remaining eleven prints were auctioned in Paris, together with other effects from the house at Grez[10]. Probably some of the prints had been given by Munch to Delius, as suggested in his draft letter 30a (p. 89) and Delius may well have bought others. Certainly he appreciated the work of his friend sufficiently to collect it and he could honestly write to Munch: 'You know how I love and understand your work' (letter 44, p. 134).

One can be a lot less certain about Munch's reaction to the music of Delius, indeed one is not really sure how much music as a whole meant to him[11]. I think, however, that the answer would probably be quite a lot. Eva Mudocci said of him: 'I think he liked good music, but I don't think he had any particular abilities or interests in that direction. He often came to our concerts'[12]. And during the nineties, the wife of his friend the critic Richard Mengelberg asked him to supper to hear her sister-in-law sing '. . . since you are also interested in music'[13]. On a later occasion, Gustav Schiefler recalled walking over the German mountains with Munch, who 'walked with springy steps through the forest singing Norwegian songs'[14]. As a boy Munch sang in a choir, and in later years he owned a piano[15]. After the accident to his finger, he could write to Jappe Nilssen: 'Do you think I can forget a shattered hand which hurts me each time I take up the palette — prevents me from sailing, which was my pleasure and from playing the piano which was often my consolation'[16]. His sister Inger played well enough to be able to earn money by giving piano lessons.

Munch had a number of musical friends apart from Delius, some of whom were also known to the composer. In his youth he was in love with the singer Milly Bergh, and during the nineties he was closely involved with Dagny Juell and her sister Ragnhild, both of whom had studied music professionally, and he painted them in 1892 as *Two music-making sisters* (Private Collection). In the early nineteen-hundreds he was closely attached to another musician, Eva Mudocci. Munch's many portraits of musicians range from the late eighteen eighties to at least 1922. They include the composers Hjalmar Borgström, Christian Sinding, Richard Strauss and, of course, Delius; the violinists Arve Arvesen and Eva Mudocci; the pianist Bella Edwards and the singer Cally Monrad Reimers. Munch also knew Busoni. William Molard was a keen amateur composer and the artist very likely met other musicians in his circle. Apart from portraits Munch on a number of occasions depicted musicians in performance[17], apart from many paintings which use the theme of dancing. In general background, then, Munch had plenty of contact with the musical world.

During the nineties, however, it goes rather deeper than this. In the Black Piglet circle in Berlin and the Molard circle in Paris music was cultivated as a powerful emotive and expressive force, while a desire to fuse it with the other arts into a total artistic experience is characteristic both of these particular groups and of the period in general. Munch, indeed, later referred to the *Life Frieze* in terms of musical analogy: 'When they (the paintings) were placed together, suddenly a single musical note went through them and they became completely different than they had been. A symphony resulted'.[18] The fact that much of the music-making within the two groups was of an improvisatory or amateur kind did not lessen the strength of its emotive appeal. Recollecting these days as late as 1928, Munch could still describe the vividness of Przybyszewski's piano playing: '. . . he could suddenly leap up in ecstasy and rush to the piano in such haste as if following inner voices which called him. And during the deathly silence which followed, the immortal music of Chopin resounded through the narrow room and transformed it suddenly into a radiant festival hall, a shrine of art. And he was so completely carried away and he interpreted the wonderful paintings of his great compatriot with such mastery, that he made us listen, breathless, fascinated, oblivious of time and place, until the last chord died away'.[19]

And one could instance many other examples, Holger Drachmann improvising poetry while accompanying himself on piano or guitar, Strindberg playing a few chords on the guitar when feeling particularly sad, or Munch's close friend the poet Sigbjørn Obstfelder improvising plaintive melodies on the violin in the dark.

The atmospheric and emotive possibilities of music were its features most esteemed in these circles and it is hardly surprising that in the circumstances the music of Chopin and Wagner particularly appealed to men like Munch. It was the same with Delius. 'Only Chopin and the later Wagner enjoyed his complete favour . . .' wrote Sir Thomas Beecham.[20] So to their common admiration of so much literature of the period can be added their liking for much of the same sort of music.

And to this could be added that both of them inclined towards partly improvisatory art, art which flowed and evolved to express feeling rather than one which meticulously structured or neatly tailored. And yet, despite so much common background, there is so little to tell us what Munch thought of his friend's, or for that matter any other, music. I am inclined to think that through family background and through the tastes of his circles in the nineties Munch liked music in a romantic, probably rather general way, and that later, in retrospect, he probably still liked this kind of music. I think such liking was probably often linked to associations with people and places rather than any continuing critical appreciation. He must almost certainly have heard some of Delius's music at one time or another, and one would imagine probably liked rather than disliked it, or he would hardly have considered the projected Jacobsen scheme. But none of his letters mention any Delius composition by name, nor do they suggest any strong personal appreciation of his merits. One of his late draft letters (p. 133, 43a, Md.6) perhaps supplies a clue to his attitude:

'I cannot understand why one does not hear more of your music (i.e. in Norway) — Everyone talks of how in other countries and especially in England you are reckoned one of the greatest — I and Jappe Nilssen believe that it comes from the fact that you were always too modest about your own things — and that you always took an interest in the rest of us —'.

The note of slight surprise is surely indicative, as is the way he writes 'Everyone talks of . . .'. One would rather have expected him to say something like 'I have always thought you were one of the greatest'. It is almost as though earlier Munch had accepted Delius's 'interest in the rest of us', together with the practical help which this implied, without investigating his work too deeply, and is only in reflective old age awakening to the fact of how great his friend's achievement has really been.[21] (In fact, considering the number of Delius's good friends in Norway, especially some distinguished musical ones, it really is surprising that his music never made as big an impact there as it did in Germany or England. Possibly the scandal over the *Folkeraadet* music had a lasting effect, although one would have thought that his continuing friendships in the Norwegian musical world would have outweighed this. Perhaps Delius was a victim of the fact that, until comparatively recently, opportunities for the performance of new large-scale orchestral works was rather limited in Norway, and that what new works were performed would have mostly been those of Norwegian composers.)

To sum up the evidence of this correspondence, we can surely say that in the case of Delius, his liking for Munch as a person was augmented by an appreciation of his art. With Munch, however, it would seem that it was Delius's personality which particularly attracted him. With the composer's sensitive and reliable character ·Munch must have felt reassured that here was one of his relatively early friends in the world of arts who had remained consistently loyal and helpful, and who, unlike a number of others had never betrayed him.

Notes to Text

Chapter I. Early lives

1 Delius appears to have started to use the English form of his name rather than the German one about 1903. See p.68, letter 7, D.4.

2 In 1624 the name of the city was changed from Oslo to Christiania. This name was used, with some variation in spelling, until 1925 when it was changed back to Oslo.

3 Ragna Stang: *Edvard Munch. The Man and the Artist*, London 1979, p.31.

4 Ibid. p.67. As with most Norwegian artists of this period, Munch associates Impressionism with realistic naturalism, not with the 'rainbow palette' which French Impressionists like Monet and Renoir had achieved by that date. Munch did not use the latter until a year or two later.

Chapter II. 1889-1891

1 See Rachel Lowe-Dugmore: *Delius's First Performance, Musical Times*, March 1965, pp.190-2.

2 Lionel Carley and Robert Threlfall: *Delius. A Life in Pictures*, Oxford 1977, p.20.

3 A very friendly letter, written in English, from Stenersen in Norway to Delius in France, dated 12.7.90, is preserved in the Delius Trust Archive. It discusses Stenersen's reaction to the Norwegian mountains, but makes no mention of Munch.

4 *Edvard Munchs brev. Familien*, Oslo 1949, p.92, no.85.

Chapter III. 1892-1895

1 Alf Bøe: Introduction to catalogue of exhibition *Frederick Delius og Edvard Munch*, Munch-Museet, Oslo 1979, p.7.

2 Published in *Festskrift til Francis Bull paa 50 Årsdagen*, Oslo 1937, p.301 ff.

3 Ibid. p.307.

4 Ibid.

5 Edvard Munch: *Livsfrisen tilblivelse* (Genesis of the Life Frieze), probably dated 1929. Quoted in Ragna Stang op. cit, p.116, quotation 37.

6 But, in contrast, see also Lionel Carley: *Delius, the Paris Years*, London 1975, p.56: 'Florent Schmitt, incidentally, is on record as saying that Molard's musical theories had had a considerable effect on both Ravel and himself. How interesting it might prove to be if the manuscript of Molard's only known work, *Hamlet*, were one day to come to light.'

7 Ibid. p.54.

8 Ibid.

9 Ibid. p.49. Greig had sent Delius a book of Krag's poems for Christmas in 1891. The Krag poem which Delius set to music c.1892-93 was *Jeg Havde en Nyskaaren Seljefløjte*.

10 There seems to be some doubt about the exact date. Evert Sprinchorn, in his introduction to Strindberg, *Inferno, alone and other writings*, New York 1968, p.58, gives December. On the other hand, Bente Torjusen writes '. . . in the fall . . .'. Bente Torjusen: *The Mirror*, in *Edvard Munch; Symbols and Images*, catalogue of exhibition at the National Gallery of Art, Washington, 1978, p.198.

11 Several years later Christian Krohg interviewed Madame Charlotte and the resulting article, *Maecenaten*, appeared in *Verdens Gang* on 29th November 1898. In it Madame Charlotte contributes considerable reminiscences of Gauguin and Strindberg and a shorter one of Munch.

12 Johan H. Langaard and Reidar Revold: *A year by year record of Edvard Munch's life*, Oslo 1961, p.25.

13 Bente Torjusen, op. cit, p.198.

14 Karen Bjølstadt to Edvard Munch. *Edvard Munchs brev Familien*, Oslo 1949, p.152, no.175.

15 Letter from Paul Gauguin to William Molard, from Auckland, dated 'end June, 1895'. Paul Gauguin: *Letters to his wife and friends*, ed. M. Malingue (Paris 1946), London n.d, p.202, no.159.

Chapter IV. 1896-1898

1 Lionel Carley, op. cit, p.62.

2 Sir Thomas Beecham: *Frederick Delius*, London 1959, p.72.

3 Natanson, Thadée: *Correspondance de Christiania: Edvard Munch*, in *La Revue Blanche*, no.59, Nov. 1895, pp.477-78.

4 *La Revue Blanche*, no.60, Dec. 1895.

5 Japanese prints he could have seen in various places in Paris, notably at Bing's shop. When Gauguin left finally for Tahiti he left a number of his prints and wood blocks with the Molards, where Munch would have been able to see them.

6 Bente Torjusen, op. cit, p.196.

7 August Strindberg: *L'exposition d'Edvard Munch*, in *La Revue Blanche*, no.72, June 1896. Reproduced in Ingrid Langaard: *Edvard Munch: Modningsår*, Oslo 1960, p.366.

8 *Le Peintre Ed. Munch*, in *La Presse*, May 1897. Munch reprinted the article (in translation) in the catalogue for his Christiania exhibition at Dioramalokalet in 1897 and in the pamphlet *Livs-frisen* which he issued in connection with his 1918 exhibition at Blomquist's, also in Christiania.

9 *Edvard Munchs brev Familien*, op. cit, p.156, no.80.

10 and 11 Lionel Carley: *Delius, the Paris years*, op. cit. p.66.

12 Frederick Delius to Mrs Blehr, dated 8 December 1896, Riksarkivet (State Archives), Oslo. Original in German. Randi Blehr was married to Otto Albert Blehr, the Norwegian prime minister, who was painted by Munch in 1927-8. There are nine known letters from Delius to Mrs Blehr, dating between 1892 and 1896, but this is the only one to mention Munch.

13 Published in *The Sackbut*, December 1920, Volume I, no.8, pp.353-54. *The Sackbut* was a musical periodical, edited by Delius's admirer, the young composer Philip Heseltine ('Peter Warlock'). In 1923 he published his biography of Delius and in it he included a version of the article, substantially the same but with a few small alterations; Peter Warlock (Philip Heseltine): *Frederick Delius*, revised edition, London 1952, pp.49-52.

14 In Peter Warlock, op. cit, p.51, a further sentence is interpolated here: 'He was constantly imagining that attempts were being made to assasinate him by occult or other means.'

15 August Strindberg to Edvard Munch, postmarked 19/7/96. Written in Swedish. Transcript in Munch-Museet, Oslo. Also published in *Strindbergs Brev. XI, Maj 1895-November 1896*, ed. Torsten Eklund, Stockholm 1969, p.277.

16 Max von Pettenkofer (1818-1901), German chemist. His publications include *Beziehungen der Luft zu Kleidung, Wohnung und Boden* (Movement of air through clothing, rooms and floors), 4th edition 1877.

17 August Strindberg: *Inferno*, translated by Mary Sandbach, London 1962, p.86.

18 Evert Sprinchorn, op. cit, p.78.

19 Frederick Delius to Jutta Bell-Ranske, dated 15 July 1896. Delius Trust Archive. Sir Thomas Beecham, op. cit, p.83, claims that Delius made a concert tour in Norway that summer with the violinist Halfdan Jebe and the author Knut Hamsun, the latter well known to Munch. But I have found no supporting evidence of any contact between Delius and Hamsun.

20 See Lionel Carley: *Carl Larsson and Grez-sur-Loing in the 1880s*, The Delius Society Journal, no.45, October 1974, pp.8-25.

21 Full accounts of the *Folkeraadet* episodes can be found in: Rachel Lowe-Dugmore: *Frederick Delius 1862-1934. A catalogue of the Music Archive of the Delius Trust, London*, London 1974, pp.60-65 and 172-6.
Lionel Carley: *Delius's 'Norwegian Suite'*, in *Anglo-Norse Review*, Dec. 1978, pp.12-14.

22 Two letters from Gunnar Heiberg to Frederick Delius. Delius Trust Archive. Both written in Norwegian.
Letter 1. Undated, but probably September 1897. Heiberg writes that the play will probably be put on in the very near future and outlines some of the scenes.
Letter 2. Dated 27/9/97. Heiberg sends a message from the conductor of the Christiania Theatre, Per Winge, giving the limitations of the orchestra's brass section. He goes on: 'Within the next few days the 400 frcs will be sent to you from the Gyldendalske boghandel in Copenhagen. . . . I am looking forward very much to seeing you again . . . But Christiania is no fun as a town and I am longing to get back to Paris.'

23 The years at the turn of the century were particularly beset by bad feeling over Norway's union with Sweden. Most Norwegians wished this to be abolished and patriotic pride ran high. Ultimately the Union was dissolved in 1905, when Norway became completely independent.

24 Christian Krohg: *Fritz Delius*, in *Verdens Gang*, October 1897. Reproduced in Rachel Lowe-Dugmore: *Frederick Delius 1862-1934*, op. cit, in facsimile pp.63-64 and translated by Lionel Carley pp.172-74. Two other contemporary accounts are translated on pp.174-76.

25 Milly Bergh to Frederick Delius, dated 31 December 1907. Delius Trust Archive.

26 By this time they possessed a number of friends and acquaintances in common, who were all members of Christiania's bohemian set. These included Christian Krohg and his painter-wife Oda, who carried on a triangular relationship with her husband and Gunnar Heiberg (Heiberg dedicated his play *Folkeraadet* to her); her sister, Bokken Lasson, and close friend Milly Bergh, together with her husband the actor Ludvig Bergh; (Milly Bergh had inspired Munch's early love and he refers to her in a number of early writings as 'Mrs Heiberg'); the critics Sigurd Bødtker and Jappe Nilssen, the last one of Munch's loyalest champions.

27 William Molard to Edvard Munch, dated 7.3.97. Munch-Museet. Written in Norwegian. The year's date is clearly a slip, as Molard mentions Norwegian reactions to the *Folkeraadet* music, and should read 98.

28 Julien Leclercq had many Scandinavian interests and was friend and helper of Strindberg. In the autumn of 1897 he lectured in Scandinavia in connection with an exhibition of French art.

29 The important influence of Nietzsche on the arts world of the period can hardly be overrated, (note for example the Nietzschean sentiments expressed by William Molard in his letter to Munch, see p.45). Shortly before Delius wrote his *Mitternachtslied Zarathustras*, Gustav Mahler had used some of the same words in his Third Symphony (1895-96), and Richard Strauss had written his tone poem *Also Sprach Zarathustra* (1896).

30 Bente Torjusen (op. cit, p.206) thinks that this was the same Edouard Gerard who wrote the favourable review of Munch's work in *La Presse* in 1897. But there is some considerable doubt here as the author of the review wrote his name (in his own handwriting) as 'Gerard', without any accent.

31 Paul Gauguin to Daniel de Monfreid, 12 January 1899. Quoted in Lionel Carley: *Delius, the Paris years*, op. cit, p.71.

32 In her article *The Mirror*, op. cit, Bente Torjusen has discussed the composition of the series very thoroughly. She considers that 25 prints from the series were exhibited at Dioramalokalet, but that three of them were not included in the catalogue, pp.186-89.

33 Nasjonalgalleriet had previously purchased two paintings by Munch, *Night in Nice* in 1891 and *Self-portrait with a Cigarette* in 1895.

34 Munch offered two reasons for his determination not to marry: 'I have always put my art before anything else. Often I felt that women would stand in the way of my art. I decided at an early age never to marry. Because of the tendency towards insanity inherited from my mother and father I have always felt that it would be a crime for me to embark on marriage.' Quoted in Ragna Stang, op. cit, p.174.

35 When Christian Krohg published his article on Madame Charlotte's *crémerie, Maecenaten*, in November 1898 (op. cit) he gives the concluding words to Madame Charlotte: 'Also greet Munch and tell him to send me a little sketch; it will be hung upstairs in my own room in a place of honour.' But in its context it does not sound as if Munch had visited the *crémerie* as recently as earlier that year. It is not known if he ever sent her a sketch.

Chapter V. 1899-1902

1 Peter Warlock, op. cit, p. 57. See also pp.58-62 for extracts from contemporary reviews.

2 Two letters from Gunnar Heiberg to Frederick Delius. Delius Trust Archive. 1) Dated May 1899. 2) No date, but the context makes it clear that it was written at about the same time, possibly slightly later.

3 Alfred Hauge to Edvard Munch, from Marlotte, dated 7 July 1899. Munch-Museet.

4 'paa Hardanger Viddern' (Hardanger Plateau) is written in Norwegian. This and the Jotunheim are two of the most famous mountain areas in Norway and Delius had visited both on previous occasions in company with other Norwegian friends.

5 *The Sick Child* is one of Munch's two best known subjects (the other is *The Scream*). There are six versions of the oil painting and a number of graphic ones, for example a drypoint of 1894 and an etching and a colour lithograph of 1896. In a draft letter in Munch-Museet, dated 26/6/97, Munch promised his friend the art historian and print dealer Meier-Graefe fifty new prints of *The Sick Child*, although he does not specify the medium (see Bente Torjusen, op. cit, p.191). Munch had been very active with prints for the past few years, for example *The Mirror* scheme, and clearly Delius knew something of this. But we cannot say certainly to what version(s) Delius was referring and the fact that he uses the word *Radierungen* (etchings) does not help us precisely (see note 8, below). Gerd Woll thinks it possible that it may have been a re-working of an earlier plate, as was a frequent practice of Munch.

6 Aasgaardstrand is a village on the Oslo fjord, some sixty-five kilometres south of the capital. Munch started going there in 1888 and from then until about 1905 it remained his favourite summer resort in Norway. It was to become something of an artists' colony. The cottage which Munch bought there in 1897 is today preserved as a museum.

The coast in and around Aasgaardstrand provided the setting for countless Munch pictures and he was later to reminisce to Rolf Stenersen: 'Have you ever walked along that shore and listened to the sea? . . . Have you ever noticed how the evening light dissolves itself into night? I know no place that has such a beautiful lingering twilight . . . To walk about in the village is like walking among my own pictures. I always get such a strong urge to paint when I go for a walk in Aasgaardstrand.' (Rolf Stenersen: *Edvard Munch. Close-up of a Genius*, Oslo 1969, p.53).

The low-lying shore with its trees appealed to Munch far more than mountainous country, as he suffered from agoraphobia, unlike Delius who loved walking in the Norwegian mountains.

7 William Molard and his family.

8 Munch has used the Norwegian word *raderinger* which normally means 'etchings'. However, I think that neither he nor Delius use the word absolutely precisely and that in it they include the various intaglio printing techniques, i.e. drypoint, engraving on metal, aquatint and mezzotint. This would of course considerably broaden the field as to which prints they might have been referring to. (See also p. 53).

9 The Danish writer Jens Peter Jacobsen.

10 John Boulton Smith: *Portrait of a friendship. Edvard Munch and Frederick Delius*, in *Apollo*, London, Jan. 1966, pp.39-40. (Also in Norwegian, in *Kunst og Kultur*, Oslo 1965.) John Boulton Smith: *Frederick Delius and Edvard Munch*, in catalogue of exhibition at Munch-Museet, April 1979, pp.14-16. Lionel Carley: *Delius, the Paris years*, op.cit, p. 47. Bente Torjusen: *The Mirror*, op. cit, pp.200-01.

11 Christian Krohg in *Verdens Gang*, 27 Nov. 1891. English translation in Ragna Stang, op. cit, pp.73 and 96.

12 August Strindberg: *L'exposition d'Edvard Munch*, op. cit.

13 Paul Gauguin to William Molard, 16 March 1902. Lionel Carley: *Delius, the Paris years*, op. cit, p.47.

14 Ibid, p.70. Dr Carley states that this was in the autumn and implies that the year was 1897 or 1898.

15 Richard Hove: *Frederick Delius*, in *Nordisk Tidskrift*, 1964, no.2.

16 Arne Eggum: *Munch and music*, in catalogue of exhibition *Frederick Delius og Edvard Munch*, op. cit, p.42

17 Roy A. Boe: *Edvard Munch og J.P. Jacobsen's 'Niels Lyhne'*, Oslo Kommunes Kunstsamlinger *Arbok 1952-59*, Oslo 1960, pp.9-12.

18 Reinhold Heller: *Love as a series of paintings*, in *Edvard Munch. Symbols and Images*, op. cit, p.107, fig.8.

19 William Molard to Edvard Munch, op. cit, Munch-Museet.

20 Rachel Lowe-Dugmore: *Frederick Delius 1862-1934*, op. cit, p.69.

21 Helge Rode to Frederick Delius, dated 14-9-98. Delius Trust Archive. Both this and the next letter are written in English and Rode's rather faulty use of the language has been retained.

22 Helge Rode to Frederick Delius, dated 28-2-99. Delius Trust Archive.

23 There is still some doubt as to the exact date of the painting in Nasjonalgalleriet. Munch has signed it twice, in one place putting the date 1899 against his signature and in another, 1900.

24 Arne Eggum in catalogue of exhibition *Edvard Munch 1863-1944*, Stockholm 1977, p.82.

25 Ibid. Munch clearly means Italian painters before Raphael, not the Pre-Raphaelite Brotherhood.

26 Ibid. Ragna Stang, op. cit, p.111, gives another quotation from Munch's notes (OKK T.2800): 'I have begun a new picture, *The Dance of Life*. One light summer's night, in the middle of a meadow, a young priest is dancing with a woman with flowing hair. They stare into each other's eyes and her hair wraps itself round his head. The background is a mass of whirling people — fat men biting women on the neck. Caricatures and strong men entwining women.'

27 Jelka Delius to Eric Fenby, 27 October 1933. Quoted in Rachel Lowe-Dugmore: *Frederick Delius 1862-1934*, op. cit, p.72.

28 Helge Rode to Edvard Munch, postmarked 26.10.95. Munch-Museet. Written in Danish.

29 Quoted in Ragna Stang, op. cit, p.138.

30 Frederick Delius to Jappe Nilssen. Dated 16 October, but postmarked 15 October, 1900. Written in French. Copy in Delius Trust Archive.

31 Composed in 1895.

32 Jappe Nilssen to Frederick Delius. Undated, but Rachel Lowe-Dugmore suggests c.1900. Written in Norwegian. Delius Trust Archive.

33 Lionel Carley writes that Delius certainly knew a number of Paris brothels and that he probably contracted syphilis, which was to have such severe consequences for his health later in life, between 1896 and the end of the century. *Delius, the Paris years*, op. cit, p.68.

34 La Revue Blanche no.24, 188, April 1907 In Lionel Carley, ibid, p.74.

35 Delius had probably become friendly with Schmitt and Ravel through the Molard circle. Schmitt was to make a piano score of *A Village Romeo and Juliet* and Ravel of *Margot le Rouge*.

36 19 July 1903. Lionel Carley and Robert Threlfall, op. cit, p.47.
37 Now incorporated in Hagen's Stadtisches Karl-Ernst Osthaus Museum.
38 See Lionel Carley: *Jelka Rosen Delius: Artist, Admirer and Friend of Rodin. The Correspondence 1900-1914*, part II. Nottingham French Studies, Vol. IX, no.2, 1970, pp.88-92. Osthaus appears to have been quite a sharp business-man.
39 Munch drafts of literary works. Munch-Museet.
40 At Dioramalokalet.
41 At Hollaendergården.
42 The Berlin Secession was founded in 1896 and held its first exhibition in 1898. Although the group represented the progressive German artists, at the beginning some members still considered Munch too wild. By 1902, however, its leaders were men who had sympathized with Munch at the time of his notorious Berlin exhibition of 1892, Max Liebermann, Ludvig von Hofmann and especially Walter Leistikow.
43 Interestingly, Jelka Delius submitted 2 paintings for this exhibition, but they were rejected. However, her friend Ida Gerhardi exhibited a portrait of Busoni there and, according to Busoni, Munch admired it very much. (Postcard from Ida Gerhardi to her sister, Lilli, postmarked 16 April 1902.) Ida Gerhardi felt that at the exhibition 'Only the things by Munk were interesting'. (Letter from Ida Gerhardi to her sister, Lilli, dated 20 April 1902.) I am indebted to Dr Lionel Carley for the information and quotations.
44 Gustav Schiefler: *Verzeichnis des graphischen Werks Edvard Munchs bis 1906*, Berlin 1907.
45 Quoted in Nic Stang: *Edvard Munch*, Oslo 1972, p.186.
46 Arne Eggum in Stockholm exhibition catalogue 1977, op. cit, p.84. Arne Eggum considers that Munch probably planned an autobiographical novel about their relationship.
47 Edvard Munch to Jens Thiis, dated 10/11/04. Quoted in Ragna Stang, op. cit, p.187.

Chapter VI. 1903-1904

1 Munch is still apprehensive about Tulla Larsen, now in Paris with Arne Kavli. Her 'allies' will have been those of the Christiania bohemian circles who had taken her side against Munch, many of whom visited Paris regularly. For many years his finger, with its wound from the revolver accident of 1902, was to forcibly remind him of the whole Tulla Larsen affair.
2 Delius must have informed Munch about a visit to Düsseldorf, presumably in connection with a performance of his symphonic poem *Paris* there, which took place on 12 February 1903 under Julius Buths. Delius arrived there on 9 February.
3 *Edvard Munchs brev. Familien*, op. cit, p.174, no.209.
4 Max Linde to Edvard Munch, 18/III 03, from Lübeck. *Edvard Munchs brev. Fra Dr Max Linde*, Oslo 1954, p.16, no.437. Original in German.
5 Jelka Delius to Auguste Rodin, from Grez, 12.3.03. Lionel Carley: *Jelka Rosen Delius: Artist*, op.. cit, p.92.
6 Ibid.
   There is a gap in Jelka's correspondence with Rodin from mid-March to mid-September 1903 and we hear no more of her dealings with Hr. Osthaus. However, Osthaus did ultimately purchase two Rodin bronzes, *Eve* and *The Age of Bronze*, and a marble *Minotaur*.
   In 1904 Rodin was to present Jelka with one of his bronzes, a small cast of Pierre de Wiessant, one of the *Burghers of Calais*.
   Surviving correspondence between Jelka and Rodin continues up to 1914.
7 R.S. Berend. Apart from the one letter from him to Munch (see p.69) and the mention in Delius letters to the artist at this time, I have been unable to find any reference to Berend outside this correspondence.
8 Probably Edouard Charles Albert Robin.

9   The titles of the paintings are given in the catalogue of the 1903 *Salon des Indépendants* as:
    Portrait.
    Une forêt.
    Une nuit claire.
    La pluie.
    L'été.
    Une nuit chaude.
    La mère.
    Une femme.
    As these titles are quite different from the two titles given in German by Delius (*Der Baum* and *Das melankolische Frau*), and as they are mainly different from the titles by which these paintings are known today, identifications of the pictures mentioned in the letter are by no means certain.
    The Tree is presumably the painting catalogued as *Le forêt*, and this could possibly be *The Forest*, of 1903, in Munch-Museet (OKK M.301). Although Munch-Museet considers it unlikely that Munch would refer to this picture as *Der Baum*, I feel that the possibility is still there, as Munch confuses singular and plural when using French and German on other occasions. (See 25, M.9 and 26, M.10, p.84.)
    The Melancholy Woman (probably catalogued as *Une femme*) is most likely *Melancholy (Laura)*, 1899, (OKK M.12), although it might just possibly be *Heritage (La mère)*, 1897-99 (OKK M.11). But *Heritage* could also be the one Delius refers to as 'the large picture', as its size (141 x 120 cm.) is larger than the other paintings in the exhibition which are positively identifiable.
    One of 'the small pictures' was the 1902 version of *Girls on the Jetty* (Pushkin Museum, Moscow). Its size, 83 x 73 cm, is a modest one for Munch at this period, and it was purchased from the exhibition by the Russian collector Ivan Morosov for 500 francs, the price suggested by Delius.

10 If Delius posted his letter in Grez on Monday 23rd March, Munch might well have received it on the 24th March and replied the same day.

11 Again the use of the words for prints. Munch wishes to wait until his '*Radierungen*' arrive before taking his '*Gravüren*' to Dr Robin. 'Etchings' for the former and 'engravings' for the latter seems reasonable, although Dr Jan Askeland tells me that he suspects that Munch's '*Gravüren*' in this case referred to woodcuts.

12 Munch had previously rented a studio in Paris, from 1896-98, at rue de la Santé, 32. On this later occasion he finally took one at boulevard Arago 65.

13 To Dr Robin.

14 Delius actually uses the word '*ein Amateur*'. This was Ivan Morosov.

15 i.e. to Paris.

16 It is interesting to see that Delius has started to use the English version of his name, 'Frederick'.

17 Max Linde to Edvard Munch, 14.4.03, from Lübeck. Linde wrote that he would not be able to come to Paris himself and asks Munch whether Herr Osthaus has shown up there yet. (*Edvard Munchs brev. Fra Dr Max Linde*, op. cit, p.19, no.442.)

18 *Edvard Munchs brev. Familien*, op. cit, p.175, no.210. The picture was another reference to the version of *Girls on the Jetty* purchased by Morosov.

19 R.S. Berend to Edvard Munch, Thursday, no date but probably during the first half of April, 1903, from 110 Bd. Malesherbes, Paris. Written in French. Munch-Museet. This is the only communication from R.S. Berend to either Munch or Delius to have been discovered, although it seems as if Delius was quite well-acquainted with him at this stage.

20 The German word '*verbummelt*' suggests both drinking and wasting time.

21 Eccentric spelling, addresses in mixed languages and frequent forwarding round Europe are common features of this correspondence and reflect considerable credit on the postal services of those days.

22 Compare Delius writing on the same occasion to an even older friend, Edvard Grieg (28th September 1903):
'On the 25th I married my friend Jelka Rosen here in Grez (civilement of course). I have got away even further from God and Jesus. We lived together in 'unrecognized' marriage for 6 years but we found it really more practical to legalize our relationship — one gets everything cheaper and receives gratis and without further ado a certificate of honesty and good morals — she is a painter and very gifted . . .'
Yours
Frederick Delius
(new name!)
(Quoted in Carley and Threlfall, op. cit, p.50.)
With regard to the 'new name', see letter 7, D.4, p.68.
See also Jelka to Rodin, 14.9.1903: '. . . I am with my friend Delius; and now we are to be married on the 25th of this month. I am a little apprehensive of this ceremony at the town hall at Grez; but one must no doubt learn to be ridiculous with grace!'
(Lionel Carley: *Jelka Rosen Delius, Artist*, op. cit, p.94, no.39.
In fact according to the marriage register at Grez the wedding took place on 23 September 1903.
23 In 1896 and 1897 Munch had produced two lithographs for Lugné-Poë's productions at Théâtre de l'Oeuvre. See p.31.
24 Delius's tone poem *Life's Dance* was to be performed at Düsseldorf on 21st January 1904, under Julius Buths. His opera *Koanga* received its first complete performance at Elberfeld on 30th March 1904, conducted by Fritz Cassirer.
25 A letter sent by Dr Max Linde to Munch in Berlin (*Edvard Munchs brev. Fra Dr Max Linde*, op. cit, p.30, no.459) is postmarked 'Lübeck 17/12 03'. He writes: 'As I shall be pleased to see you at Christmas, I would suggest that you go first via Hamburg and arrive here on the 28th.' (Original in German.) This would fit with Munch's remarks on his movements at the close of this letter to Delius.
26 See p.31.
27 Presumably Bing's shop, *L'Art Nouveau*, see p.31.
28 The Berlin Secession exhibition showed 47 prints by Munch. The artist exhibited his prints twice in Hamburg during 1903, once in January with Cassirer and later in the year with the Gesellschaft Hamburgischer Kunstfreunde, at which last he showed 45 prints. He also exhibited his painting in Hamburg during the spring with Commeter. (Johan H. Langaard and Reidar Revold, op. cit, p.34). (For further reference to Cassirer and Commeter, see pp.76-7.)
29 The important art patron and author Count Harry Kessler had known Munch since the eighteen-nineties. From 1895-1900 he was an associate editor of the periodical *Pan*. Munch made several portraits of Count Kessler, including a lithograph of 1894-95 (OKK G/1.190, Sch.29) and an oil portrait in 1904 (Collection of S. Bergesen jnr.). At the time of Munch's reference here, the Count had been named as director of the local museum at Weimar by the Grand Duke, who also planned to start an art centre there. In fact Munch did not go to Weimar in January 1904, but later in March-April.
30 The exhibition with the Vienna Secession opened on 6th January 1904 and continued until March. The initial invitation had been sent to Munch, via Dr Linde, in May 1903 by the President, F. Myrbach.
31 Presumably Bing's shop, *L'Art Nouveau*.
32 See n.28 and n.30, above.
33 Tulla Larsen.
34 The mysterious reference to 'the white cat' has been discussed by Bente Torjusen in her article The Mirror (op. cit, p.204 ff). She is inclined to consider identifying the appelation with Judith, the daughter of Ida Ericson and stepdaughter of William Molard. This does not seem to me very likely, particularly as Judith had been engaged to marry Édouard Gérard since 1897 and finally married him in 1902.
Munch may not have been referring to a woman at all, but if he were, Tulla Larsen could be a possibility, as Delius could well have conveyed some news of her from Paris,

which would have been bound to stir Munch.

35 Eva Mudocci thought that she first met Munch in a cafe in Paris in 1903. She was in the company of Bella Edwards and a Norwegian, Rulle Rasmussen. (Interview with W. Stabell, BBC Norwegian Service 18/5/50.)

36 Eva Mudocci's daughter, Mrs Isobel Weber, says that she, her twin brother and their mother met Munch together somewhere around 1914-16, either in Copenhagen or Germany. Mrs Weber claims that Munch later made a portrait from memory of her and her brother, but I have been unable to trace this. There is also a letter from Munch to Eva and Bella, thanking them for sending greetings on his seventieth birthday. In her BBC interview (op. cit.) Eva Mudocci said that her last meeting with Munch was in Paris 'some years before the last (i.e. second) world war. This must have been not later than 1927, his last visit to that city.

37 The important French art dealer, who had earlier been associated with some of the Impressionists.

38 See p.72, n.31.

39 The home of Lugné-Poë's Théâtre de l'Oeuvre, see p.71, 12, D.8.

40 Ludvig Peter Karsten was one of the best Norwegian painters in the generation following Munch. He and Munch admired each other's work and Munch painted his portrait in 1905 (Thielska Gallery, Stockholm). Karsten also knew Grez well and on the occasion to which Delius refers he had probably seen the composer, or at least mutual acquaintances. In a letter to Munch written on 20th January (quoted on pp.74-5), Karsten mentions that he is short of money.

41 *Edvard Munchs brev. Fra Dr Max Linde*, op. cit, p.30, no.460. Original in German.

42 Ibid. p.30, no.461. Original in German.

43 Metres.

44 Paul Durand-Ruel. The important French art dealer who had been the first to handle the work of the Impressionists on a large scale. To some extent Georges Petit was his rival.

45 A comment on the hanging procedure at the *Salon des Indépendants* is provided by C.R.W. Nevison in his autobiography *Paint and Prejudice*, (London 1937, p.49). He is writing of the time a few years prior to the first world war, therefore not long after the date of Munch's letter. He writes: 'At the Salon des Indépendants' I was unlucky. Although there was no hanging committee I was always badly placed, but what could I say when all the positions were drawn by ballot. In my cynical old age I am not surprised that the artists with the biggest names invariably drew the best positions.'

46 See letter 13, M.5, p.71.

47 This anticipated complaint seems in answer to Delius's remark about Ludvig Karsten. Of course, since the debâcle of the Tulla Larsen affair Munch regarded Heiberg as an enemy, of whom bad things could be expected, but the comment also reveals Munch's strong streak of Protestant family honour.

48 Ludvig Karsten to Edvard Munch. Original in Norwegian. Munch-Museet.

49 The printer in Paris who had printed much of Munch's work since the eighteen-nineties. Munch had left some of his lithographic stones in his keeping. (See also p.75, letter 16, D.10.)

50 Ambroise Vollard was the French art dealer particularly noted at this time for handling the work of Cézanne and Post-Impressionist artists.

51 The artists Hans Heyerdahl and Christian and Oda Krohg have all been mentioned earlier in this study. Karl Edvard Diriks was another Norwegian painter.

52 Ludvig von Hofmann had formed the *Gruppe XI* in Berlin in 1892, together with Max Liebermann, Curt Herrmann and Walter Leistikow. (See *Post-Impressionism*, catalogue of exhibition at the Royal Academy, London 1979, p.159.) Leistikow also contributed an article, *Die Affaire Munch*, to the *Freie Bühne* on that occasion, one of the very few to show understanding of the artist.

53 From 1898-1901 Paul and Bruno Cassirer operated their art gallery on the Unter den Linden, Berlin, jointly. In 1901 Bruno Cassirer withdrew to go in for publishing,

although he still continued to deal in graphic art.

54 These letters demonstrate the amount of trouble which Munch's friends and patrons were prepared to take in order to help him. Nos.462-465 go into particular detail about the contract (*Edvard Munchs brev. Fra Dr Max Linde*, op. cit. pp.31-5), no.463 having attached to it a proposed contract drafted by Gustav Schiefler.

Chapter VII. 1905-1908

1 *Societé des Artistes Indépendants.*

2 Delius's German leaves it ambiguous as to whether the 'overcrowding' applies to people or pictures 'who will not get in'. I think he is referring to pictures; in other words many artists who are not members of the Society would not get their pictures hung. It was not obligatory to belong to *L'Indépendants* in order to exhibit but in fact most exhibitors were members.

3 The Prague exhibition opened on 5th February and Delius replied from Grez to this letter on 11th February, so it looks as if Munch returned to Berlin immediately after the exhibition had opened and wrote to Delius from there between 7th and 9th.

4 Munch's exhibition at Galleri Manes, Prague, included 75 paintings and 50 prints.

5 Munch went to Aasgaardstrand during the spring of 1905, but Delius did not visit Norway again until the following year.

6 Presumably Norwegian enemies who Delius might encounter in Paris (like Tulla Larsen or Gunnar Heiberg) and French friends (like William Molard or Achille Ouvré).

7 See letter from Eva Mudocci to Munch, p.83.

8 The text of the postcard together with the following notes were taken from a typed copy in Munch-Museet. The face of the postcard shows a picture of a building, with the caption: 'EXPOSITION DU STATUE RE A. RODIN, PRAGUE. KINSKEHO ZAHRADA 10.V — 15 VII. 1902'

9 Presumably the enclosure was some form of receipt from *L'Indépendants*, but it does not seem to have survived.

10 Delius uses the word *Blätter*. The sheets of prints will have been those referred to in letter 22, M.8.

11 Delius has made a slip in writing the month. He means March; (See p.79, letter 18, D.12).

12 At this time Munch wrote to Karen Bjølstad: '— In Prague there was a lot of glory but little money — here in Hamburg money plays a more important role'. (*Edvard Munchs brev. Familien*, op. cit, p.203, no.248). The portrait was of a Fraulein Warburg.

13 There is also a printed address on this letter, reading '*Koppel 9*'. Munch has mis-spelt the word.

14 Presumably Bruno Cassirer.

15 No doubt Munch sent prints to the *Salon des Indépendants* on this occasion because most of his important paintings would have been in the Prague exhibition, which did not close until 12th March. Most of the titles are easily identifiable from the entries in the exhibition catalogue and from Munch's letters:

Wampyr (Vampire). Lithograph and woodcut. OKK G/t.567, Sch.34.

Mater Dolorosa(Madonna). Lithograph. OKK G/1.194, Sch.33

Strindberg. Lithograph. OKK G/1.219a, Sch.77.

L'onde (The Wave). 'Litho', possibly *Lovers in the Waves*. Lithograph. OKK G/1.213, Sch.71.

Le Soir (Evening; Melancholy). 'Woodcut in 3 colours'. OKK G/t.571, Sch.82.

Clair de lune (Moonlight). 'Woodcut in 3 colours'. OKK G/t.570, Sch.81.

Mallarmé. Either the lithograph OKK G/1.221, Sch.79, or the etching OKK G/r.164. I would think the lithograph to be more likely as the other prints exhibited were either lithographs or woodcuts. Moreover, by 1905 etching was generally less important to Munch than the other two media.

Le baiser. (The Kiss) Woodcut. OKK G/t.580, Sch.102.

All these prints came originally from the eighteen-nineties but a number of them also have later variants, as Munch reworked them over a number of years. Although in these cases it is impossible to say which variations he exihibited here, it seems likely that they would have been the more recent versions.

16 There is no knowing whether Delius received this card or not, as it has not survived.

17 During the years between 1896 and 1912 when Munch exhibited at the *Salon des Indépendants*, it was most common for the exhibitions to close in May. However in 1905 it closed on 30th April.

18 It looks as if Delius thinks that Munch should have a Paris dealer who would stock and sell his prints, and perhaps handle his exhibiting arrangements. But he may just have wanted to know of someone who would be responsible for packing and returning the works to Germany.

19 It was in 1905 that Norway finally became completely independent from Sweden. May and June were crucial months and events reached a climax on 6th-7th June when the Storting (Norwegian Parliament) presented Oscar II, King of Sweden and Norway, with a resolution dissolving the union. Sweden at first refused to accept this and for some time there was hostile and threatening reaction there, but diplomacy triumphed and King Oscar finally renounced the Norwegian throne on 26th October 1905.

20 The soup recipe is intriguing, as it suggests a degree of homely friendliness rather different from much of the correspondence, and certainly suggests a more domestic Munch than the usual picture of him. As a matter of fact Munch was for a considerable period a vegetarian and was always interested in health foods, especially if cheap. It also suggests that Munch had had the opportunity of tasting Jelka's cooking rather more recently than March 1903, the last date definitely established when he stayed with the Deliuses.

21 Hermann Esche, a wealthy stocking manufacturer of Chemnitz, and his wife were close friends as well as patrons of Munch and like Kollmann, Schiefler and Dr Linde, frequently helped him. Ragna Stang writes of this visit: 'When Munch finally settled down to a frenzy of painting in the last week of October 1905, he first painted the portraits of the children and then six other portraits of the family in the course of four days.' (Ragna Stang, op. cit, p.299, n259).

22 Munch wrote to Thiel accepting the commission on 25/7/1905. Letter at Thielska Galleriet.

23 This would fit in with Delius's letter of 20th February (20, D.13, p.80) where he says that he has not seen her for a long time.

24 In the manuscript of an unpublished biography of Eva Mudocci and Bella Edwards by Lucy de Knupfer, called *Music and Friendship*, the author says the following: 'Delius's own compositions, with their great delicacy of feeling, interested the artists very much. He wrote a 'Serenade' for Eva, whose playing he greatly admired. A frequent visitor at their studio, he showed a constant interest in their work and successes.' (Manuscript, Chapter IX, p.61). Eva Mudocci has queried the passage about the 'Serenade' in the margin. In fact the biography contains many questionable statements and I would not care to trust it except where the information can be checked against reliable sources.

I am sure that Eva Mudocci's letter reveals her feelings more correctly. Her daughter, Mrs Isobel Weber, has told me that Eva Mudocci showed little interest in Delius's music and attributes this to her mother's great love for the modern French school, especially Debussy, who had shown himself decidedly critical of some compositions by Delius.

25 Actually the work performed was not a symphony, but the variations for orchestra and chorus, *Appalachia*. The performance was by the Berlin Philharmonic Orchestra conducted by Oskar Fried, who had now joined the list of Delius supporters. Fried's letters to Delius are in the Delius Trust Archive; in one of them (4 January 1906) he asks Delius to come and help him through the score, which he considers 'damned difficult'. (Robert Threlfall: *A Catalogue of the Compositions of Frederick Delius. Sources and References*, London 1977, p.59)

26 Exactly what 'the matter' was is not known, but it was clearly something to do with exhibiting Munch's works at *L'Indépendants*, possibly paying his membership subscription to the Society.

27 To this someone, probably a postal official, has added:
'Grez sur loing
Seine et marne'.

28 For identification of these pictures see notes to letter 26, M.10.

29 Munch's uncertainty about the quality of the lithographic portrait of Nietzsche (OKK G/1.268-2) and his leaving the final decision to Delius is interesting. It may be simply that he was unsure about this particular work, which is drawn boldly and surely although one might argue that the line is a little coarse for Munch. But the whole commission, of having to make a posthumous portrait of a philosopher who he had never seen, was an unusual one for Munch. The artist had been an admirer of Nietzsche's work for many years and scholars have connected such works as the lithograph *Funeral March* (1897) with *Also Sprach Zarathustra*. (For the relationship between Munch and Nietzsche see the writings of Gösta Svenaeus, notably *Idé och innehåll i Edvard Munchs Konst*, Oslo 1953 and *Trädet på berget*, in (OKK Arbok 1963, pp.24-46) As a result of the portrait commission, Munch spent the winter of 1905-06 in and around Weimar studying the philosopher's writings and the surroundings in which he had lived. He intended the resulting oil paintings (Munch-Museet, Oslo and Thielska Galleriet, Stockholm) to be decorative and symbolic — 'not using the photographic technique that most painters use in their portraits' (Munch to Thiel, 21/6/1908, quoted in Ragna Stang, op. cit, p.185). Both versions are therefore to some extent experimental works, as was his oil sketch *Ibsen and Nietzsche surrounded by Genius* (OKK M.917) and the sketches for a related but unfulfilled project, a series of portraits of different writers. Although Munch often used photographs as an aid in his portrait painting, he usually had actual visual experience of the sitter to back this up, whereas the Nietzsche portraits were entirely a matter of reconstruction and imagination. It seems to me, therefore, that there is a certain tentative quality about the results of the Nietzsche project, which may have been why Munch was not quite sure about the lithograph.

30 Although on this postcard Munch has given titles and prices in French, in the postscript he slips back into the German currency, 'Marks'.

31 It is interesting that Munch had now made a portrait of van de Velde. Their contact at Chemnitz the previous year has already been mentioned, but their paths had crossed on a number of earlier occasion. By 1895 van de Velde had been a leader of *Art Nouveau* in Belgium. He decorated the interior of Bing's *L'Art Nouveau* shop in Paris, where Munch held his 1896 exhibition, and was well known to Munch's friend Meier-Graefe. He designed interiors and furniture for the Folkwang Museum at Hagen in 1901-02, only shortly before the Museum's director, Osthaus, began buying work by Munch. In 1904, van de Velde was appointed to a professorship at Weimar, then noted as a centre of progressive art ideas, at about the same time as Count Harry Kessler was named as director of the museum there. Count Kessler had wished to attract Munch to Weimar, and the artist had painted his portrait there in 1904. Thiel's commission for the Nietzsche portrait drew Munch to Weimar again, where Munch made the portrait of van de Velde in 1906, the year in which the designer became head of the new Weimar School of Arts and Crafts.

32 On the previous postcard Munch gave the titles in French. Here he gives them in German.
The catalogue of the *Salon des Indépendants* lists Munch's pictures as follows (attempts at identification have been added):
Les buveurs (*peinture à l'huile*). Whereas in 25, M.9, Munch gave the title in the plural (as the catalogue entry), he now gives it in the singular — *der Betrunkene* (The Drunkard). Pål Hougen has suggested that this painting might well have been *Self-portrait with Wine Bottle*, OKK M.543 (sometimes titled *Self-portrait in Weimar*).

The subject of this self-portrait is really loneliness, as the painter sits alone in the restaurant of the Artists' Society in Weimar, isolated from the other seated figure and the two waiters in the background, all of whom are also isolated from each other. The picture was painted in 1906, which would fit the pattern that all the pictures he sent to Paris were new ones. A title of either 'Drinker' or 'Drinkers' could be applied to this painting, although I feel that the singular one would be more appropriate.

Paysage de Thuringerwald (peinture à l'huile).

Paysage de Thuringerwald (peinture à l'huile). Munch painted a number of Thuringian landscapes while staying in that part of Germany during 1905-06, so these titles might refer to several pictures. Three possible candidates are:

German Landscape, c. 1905-06. OKK M.688

German Landscape, Elgersburg, 1906. OKK M.568

Thuringian Landscape (Melting Snow near Elgersburg), 1906. Von der Heydt Museum, Wuppertal.

Monsieur K . . . (lithographie). Almost certainly the lithographic portrait of Albert Kollmann, 1906. OKK G/1.260, Sch. 244.

M. Henry van de Velde (lithographie), 1906. OKK G/1.262, Sch. 246

Nietzsche. The lithographic portrait of 1906. OKK G/1.268-2, Sch.247.

33 Munch appears to have raised the prices of the paintings and now gives the prices of the lithographs in francs.

34 The word issuing from the monster's mouth is not entirely clear, but Arne Eggum thinks it expresses the noise the monster is making — 'Ugh'. He points out that the expression 'Ugh' is frequently used by Norwegian children when playing Red Indians, a subject which had attracted Munch as a child.

35 Presumably written on one of his short trips from Weimar to Berlin.

36 Presumably the papers were forms connected with collection of the pictures.

37 By now nearer to four years ago.

38 Munch had gone to Jena to paint a portrait.

39 Munch refers here ironically to the denouement of his affairs with Tulla Larsen, which both inflicted a 'hellish wound' on his nerves and also literally, through the revolver accident, on his finger. The 'dear friends' are those like Gunnar Heiberg and Sigurd Bødtker who have become enemies through taking Tulla Larsen's side. As quite often, the drafts are fuller and more personal than the letters sent.

40 Clearly Delius had not received any letter corresponding to the one Munch drafted (28a, Md4).

41 He did. See 31, D.19 and 32, D.20.

42 In view of Munch's peripatetic existence and his inaccurate way of addressing his communications, it is surprising that he and Delius were able to keep in touch so well, and it reflects considerable credit on the French and German postal systems. For example, Munch writes on 15th April from Berlin (27, M.11); Delius replies to this on 19th April (28, D.17). He writes again to Berlin on 1st May (29, D.18) and this letter is re-addressed to Munch at Bad Kösen ((near Weimar). On the same day Munch writes from Jena, but puts the address of his Kösen hotel on the back, presumably because he intended returning there.

43 Another reference to the Tulla Larsen affair.

44 Munch is referring to the name of the hotel, literally 'Courageous Knight'.

45 Mrs Mitchell. Presumably a member of the firm Mitchell and Kimbell referred to by Munch in 28a, Md.4.

46 The name is not quite clear. No doubt the writer was an official of *L'Indépendants*. The original of notice and postscript is in French.

47 Probably May, as the postcard seems to fit into the sequence of the correspondence here, although April would also be possible. 1906 was the year in which Munch spent much time in spas near Weimar, such as Bad Kösen and Bad Ilmenau, and we know that he was in Kösen in both April and May.

48 It is not clear why the French should have been angry with Munch's paintings again. It sounds as if he may have had some unfavourable reviews. A cutting from *Liberté*, sent by the *Lynx* press cutting bureau, is preserved in Munch-Museet. The date marked on it by the *Lynx* bureau is not quite clear, but looks like '23 Mars 1906'. The review only contains a one line reference to Munch and describes his work as 'dazzling without being clear'. Allowing for the fact that the French critics did not usually give much favourable attention to Munch's work after the turn of the century, this criticism hardly seems very relevant to the pictures which he probably exhibited at *L'Indépendants* in 1906. (See also p.97). Alternatively Munch may merely have felt that *L'Indépendants* had hung his pictures badly again (see 15, M.6, p.74), for the reason that they did not like them.

49 According to Munch-Museet, Munch quite frequently gave prints to friends, particularly those friends who had done him services. Dr Eric Fenby recalls that there were Munch prints hanging in the house at Grez, and has tried to identify some of them for me. (See p.144-5).

50 For an account of Delius attending rehearsals of *Sea Drift* at Essen, see Eric Fenby: *Delius as I knew him*, London 1937, pp.203-04.

51 Ingse Vibe (Müller) was an actress who married Titus Vibe Müller. Munch painted a full-length portrait of her in 1903 (OKK M.272).

52 Postcard, postmarked AASGAARDSTRAND I VII 06 (Munch-Museet) Jelka Delius contribution is in German, Inge Vibe's in Norwegian.

53 There is no such word as 'palmefest' in Norwegian. However, some kind of celebration is meant. As it was summer I am tempted to suspect something in the open air, perhaps a bonfire or a barbecue.

54 Munch here uses the Norwegian word for Germany, rather than German or French, no doubt because he was in Norway.

55 Inger Munch and Karen Bjølstad. They were using Munch's cottage for the summer as he was away in Germany.

56 There is no record of Munch visiting France that year.

57 Quoted in Sir Thomas Beecham: *Frederick Delius*, op. cit, p.141.

58 In common with Munch, Gordon Craig enjoyed the patronage of Count Kessler, and Reinhardt was trying (unsuccessfully) to get Craig to produce plays by Shakespeare and Shaw for him. In view of the enthusiasm for Ibsen shared by Munch and Craig the fact that the latter was now deeply interested in making woodcuts in a pioneering manner not so far removed from Munch's own, one might have expected to find some signs of sympathetic rapport, but this does not seem to have been the case. Reinhardt's collaborator Arthur Kahane, who sat between Munch and Craig at the party, recalls that 'Gordon Craig would not let the foreign language prevent him from remarking in his rather aggressive and imperious English manner, "I saw an exhibition of your best painters in Stockholm. All the pictures by your best painters were very bad. The best of the paintings were by Strindberg." To which Munch laconically replied, "Pleased to hear it! Because if Strindberg is our best painter, then I am our best writer." ' (Arthur Kahane: *Edvard Munch*, in *Berlin Tageblatt*, 28th October 1926. (Translated from the German by Dr Carla Lathe.) Presumably the Stockholm exhibition was a large and general selection of Scandinavian painting and there is no other evidence that the two men were familiar with each other's work, although one would have expected Craig to have seen the Ibsen sketches which Munch made for Reinhardt.

59 The industrialist, author and radical politician, Walther Rathenau, had purchased Munch's painting *A Rainy Day in Christiania* in 1893. He was a friend of Count Harry Kessler, who wrote a book on him, *Walther Rathenau*, New York 1930.

60 *DIE MUSIK*, VI, 12, Jahr 1906/1907. Quoted in Lionel Carley and Robert Threlfall, op. cit, p.58.

61 Max Reinhardt to Edvard Munch, 1906. Quoted in Carla Lathe: *Edvard Munch and his Literary Associates*, catalogue of exhibition at University of East Anglia, Norwich 1979, p.34.

162

62 Letter from Engelbert Humperdinck to Frederick Delius, 12th March 1907. Delius Trust Archive. Original in German.
63 Max Chop: *Frederick Delius*, Berlin 1907.
64 *Appalachia, Brigg Fair, In a Summer Garden* (first version), *Life's Dance, Over the Hills and Far Away, Paris* and *Sea Drift*.
65 As Delius wrote to Granville Bantock: 'I conducted without a catastrophe and that is about all — I don't think I shall try any more —'. (17th December 1908. Quoted in Lionel Carley and Robert Threfall, op. cit, p.65.)
66 Sir Thomas Beecham, op. cit, p.146.
67 A list of the original officers and committee members can be found in Lionel Carley and Robert Threlfall, op. cit, p.63.
68 Frederick Delius to Granville Bantock, from Grez, 11th April 1911. Quoted in Lionel Carley and Robert Threlfall, op. cit, p.69.
69 Although the MS full score give 1909-11 for the date of composition of *Fennimore and Gerda*, most authorities give 1908-10. See Robert Threlfall: op. cit. London 1977, p47.
70 Munch did not return to Norway that year.
71 Grieg had written to Grainger, less than a month before his death: 'You have become a dear young friend who has made more rich for me the evening of my life.' He goes on to discuss Grainger's folk-song settings, something which deeply interested him. Quoted in Sir Thomas Beecham, op. cit, p.137.
72 Ibid.
73 Milly Bergh to Frederick Delius, dated 31st December 1907. Delius Trust Archive.
74 Edvard Munch to Jens Thiis, 1907. Quoted in Ragna Stang, op. cit, p.16.
75 See p.160, n.32.
76 In *Edvard Munch, Symbols and Images*, op. cit, p.26.
77 When Jens Thiis and Pola Gauguin were writing their biographies of Munch for his seventieth birthday, he wrote letters to them both which included the following statement: 'At the beginning of the century I felt a need to break the surface and the line — I felt they could become a mannerism (.) I followed three paths: I painted some realistic pictures (of) children in Warnemünde then I took up the technique again in "Sick Child". On that occasion I copied this picture from Olaf Schou; later it came to our gallery, and also to Gothenburg. As one can see from "Sick Child" in the gallery, it is built up of horizontal and vertical lines — and penetrating diagonal strokes. After this I painted a number of pictures with very broad, often yard long lines or strokes that run vertically, horizontally and diagonally — the surface was broken and a sort of pre-Cubism found utterance.
This was the order: "Cupid and Psyche", "Consolation" and "Murder", ...' (otherwise called *Death of Marat*.) Quoted in Arne Eggum: *The Green Room*, Stockholm catalogue 1977, op. cit, p.92.
It is worth also considering the likelihood that Munch's long strokes were at least partly derived from the effect of the gouged striations which he had been using in his woodcuts for some years.
78 This series of works has been analyzed in some detail by Arne Eggum in *The Green Room*, Stockholm catalogue 1977, op. cit, pp.82-103.
79 Munch's remarks about hanging imply that the letter was written during the course of the exhibition, and his interest in reviews suggest a time fairly near the beginning.
80 '*Le Lynx* Ex-Artistic Correspondence; E. Bonneau, 38. Rue Fontaine', with branches in Berlin, London, Brussels etc. The office still exists, but under new auspices. (see also p.162, n.48.)
81 *Death of Marat II* (OKK M.4). Munch would surely have wished to show a painting completed in his new technique and he refers to it as 'an experiment'.
82 Munch showed four paintings in the *Salon des Indépendants* in 1908, listed in the catalogue as:
La mort de Marat
Etude de Femme

Soir
Nuit claire (tableau decoratif)
The 'decorative picture' will have been a sketch for the frieze in Max Reinhardt's *Kammerspieltheater*, which Munch painted in 1906-07. In these paintings Munch reworked and varied themes of people in outdoor life which had mostly originated from Aasgaardstrand. Interestingly they are painted in tempera rather than the artist's more usual oils. Eight of these *Reinhardt Frieze* paintings are now in the Berlin Nationalgalerie (catalogue nos.242-9). Munch-Museet has a number of paintings designated as sketches for this series.

83 Molard's last extant letter to the composer is dated 23rd December 1908, but it is quite likely that they still kept in touch later than this.

84 At the time Munch wrote to his friend Christian Gierløff: 'My and my beloved's child, the *Death of Marat*, which I carried within me for nine years, is not an easy painting. Nor, for that matter, is it a masterpiece — it is more of an experiment. If you like, tell my enemy that the child has now been born and christened and hangs on the wall of L'Indépendents.' Edvard Munch to Christian Gierløff, 13/3/08. Quoted in Ragna Stang, op. cit, p.206.

85 '... tout ce bataillon de fumistes ...' Press cutting from a French paper in Munch-Museet, without date or title of the paper. However the review states that it is of the 1908 *Salon des Indépendants*. There is no means of knowing whether it was sent to Munch by *Le Lynx*.

86 The exhibition opened on 23rd November.

87 Edvard Munch to Jappe Nilssen, 17/10/1908. Quoted in Ragna Stang, op. cit, p.210.

Chapter VIII, 1909-1918

1 Edvard Munch to Ernest Thiel, 28/10/08. Quoted in Ragna Stang, op. cit, p.209.

2 Edvard Munch to Sigurd Høst, 1909. Quoted in Ragna Stang, op. cit, p.18.

3 *Alpha and Omega*. Gustav Schiefler has stated that it was he who advised Munch, shortly before his breakdown, to compose a series of drawing about his experiences of love, and Munch responded with a fable about a kind of first man and woman placed together on a desert island. He wrote that the fable deals 'in jest and earnest, with the age-old story, which must be repeated once more, of man, who since time immemorial has allowed himself to be beguiled by the faithless breed of women.' (Edvard Munch to Jappe Nilssen 1/3/1909. Quoted in Ragna Stang, op. p.211.) Munch wrote the fable himself and illustrated it with eighteen lithographs together with a title page and vignettes (OKK G/1.301-327, Sch. 306-327).

4 The closing date for the competition was 15 May 1909. The work of twenty-two painters (including Munch) was submitted. From these, four artists were chosen to submit full designs, Gerhard Munthe, Eilif Peterssen, Emanuel Vigeland (painter brother of the more famous sculptor, Gustav) and Munch. By the summer of 1911 the jury had, with some division, decided in favour of Munch, and a fund-raising committee was formed with a view to buying the works for the University.

5 '*The Frieze of Life* deals with the individual's joys and sorrows seen from close quarters — the University murals portray the powerful forces of eternity.' Edvard Munch: *Livfrisens Tilblivelse* (Origin of the Life Frieze), quoted in Ragna Stang, op. cit, p.235.

6 Christopher Palmer has suggested that the opening of Richard Strauss's symphonic poem *Also sprach Zarathustra* (written in 1896) provides an even closer parallel, with its 'cosmic, all-embracing but static energy', to the irradiation from Munch's *Sun*. *(Delius, Portrait of a Cosmopolitan*, London 1976, p.100.) This is probably true, and the similarity was to strike Richard Strauss. When he took part in a concert in the University assembly hall during or shortly after the first world war, he was very impressed with Munch's paintings and stayed behind after the concert, walking up and down looking at them. Next morning he insisted on meeting Munch, and they went together to Nasjonalgalleriet to see the artist's pictures. Strauss is said to have remarked: 'These paintings give me exactly what I try to give expression to in my compositions'. (Johs.

Roede: *Spredte erindringer om Edvard Munch*, in *Edvard Munch som vi kjente ham. Vennene forteller*, Oslo 1946, pp.47-8.) It is not recorded what Munch thought about Strauss's works. Delius admired some of them, but considered his *Also sprach Zarathustra* 'a complete failure'. (Letter from Delius to Edvard Grieg, 28th September 1903. Quoted in Lionel Carley and Robert Threlfall, op. cit, p.50.)

7 Letter from Delius to Philip Heseltine, 23rd June 1912. Quoted in Lionel Carley and Robert Threlfall, op. cit, p.57.

8 A revised edition appeared five years later. Curt Glaser: *Edvard Munch*, Berlin 1922.

9 Munch was in fact invited to send paintings to the Armory Show, so it is surprising to find him only represented by eight prints.

10 Munch's representation in the *Salon des Indépendants* was: 1910. *L'enfant malade*. Perhaps the version of *The Sick Child* now in the Tate Gallery, London, probably painted c. 1907.

Four prints from *Alpha and Omega* (There is no indication in the catalogue of which ones.

1912. *Les trois femmes* (lithograph). Perhaps a version of *Three stages of Woman*, (OKK G/1.238, Sch.122)

Homme et femme (woodcut in two colours).

Nuit d'hiver. Possibly one of the number of landscapes which Munch painted at Kragerø during the winter of 1911-12.

11 *Westminster Abbey*, (Sch.381). Schiefler dates this lithograph as 1912, but it must be 1913. Doubts have been raised in some quarters as to whether Munch in fact ever went to London. But it seems most likely that he did. Apart from the lithograph, Munch expressed his intention of going there in a letter to his aunt (*Edvard Munchs brev. Familien*, op. cit, p.234, no.303) and she replied on 27th April (in an unpublished letter in Munch-Museet) saying 'How nice that you are going to England, it must be very interesting'. (Munch-Museet).

12 1909 *Paris* (Boston, conducted by Max Fiedler). 1910 *Brigg Fair* (New York, conducted by Walter Damrosch). 1912 *In a Summer Garden* (Boston, conducted by Max Fiedler). Significantly two of these were introduced by a German conductor, while Walter Damrosch, who conducted the third, was born in Germany although coming to New York at the age of nine.

13 By the Berlin Philharmonic Orchestra under Oskar Fried.

14 No.1 of the *Two Pieces for Small Orchestra*. The Grieg setting was 1 *Ola-dalom, i Ola-kjønn*, op.66, no.14.

15 Lionel Carley and Robert Threlfall, op. cit, p.68,

16 Or the lithographs *The Flower of Love* (1896), *Flight* (1908), *The Poison Flower* (1908), *Omega and the Flowers* (1909), and one could find more examples.

17 Quoted by Eric Fenby in introduction to the gramophone recording of *Fennimore and Gerda*, EMI, London 1976, p.3.

18 Ibid.

19 Oda Krohg wrote to Delius from Paris on 22nd February 1909, asking him for information about a hotel in Grez where she and her son could stay for a week or so. Letter in Delius Trust Archive.

20 Beecham says that this illness took 'the form of chronic nervous indigestion coupled with pains in the back.' (Sir Thomas Beecham, op. cit, p.159), while Norman O'Neill (another close friend of the composer) stated that the signs of his oncoming illness showed first in 1911. (Peter Warlock, op. cit, p.153.)

21 Frederick Delius to Nina Grieg. 26th July 1926. Bergen Library.

22 Frederick Delius to Nina Grieg. Undated, but almost certainly written on the same trip. Bergen Library.

23 Munch rented Grimsrød manor house in 1913.

24 The Jotunheim mountains, in Oppland.

25 Inger Alver Gløersen: *Den Munch Jeg møtte* (The Munch I met), Oslo 1956. Mrs Gløerson does not mention Delius's visit to Grimsrød in her book.

26 Frederick Delius to Jelka Delius, 10.7.13. Delius Trust Archive.

27 Thanks to the Olaf Schou gift and Jens Thiis's purchases of 109-10, Nasjonalgalleriet now owned a number of Munch's most important paintings from the nineties, including *The Scream, Puberty, The Day After, Death in the Sick Room, Madonna, Mother and Daughter* and *The Dance of Life*.

28 The Oseberg ship and treasure, which had been excavated in 1904.

29 Two letters in the Delius Trust Archive from Milly Bergh to Delius (written in Norwegian) give the day and month, but not the year. They cannot have been written earlier than 1908 — her previous letter was 31st December 1907. One, dated 17th April, says 'what fun it will be to see you here in the summer', while the other, dated 3rd September, suggests that the Deliuses should come and see her at Slemdal. But as neither of them give the year, we cannot be sure whether they connect with this visit or not, although it would seem quite possible.

30 Sir Thomas Beecham, op. cit, p.170.

31 These movements have been established by Rachel Lowe-Dugmore, who gives a chronology for Delius from November 1914 until November 1915 in *Documenting Delius*, published in the *Delius Society Journal*, Oct. 1976, no.65. This has been of great value as previous accounts made conflicting statements and left considerable doubts. For example, Sir Thomas Beecham (op. cit, pp.171-2) claims that Delius stayed for nearly a year at Watford, whereas Sir Henry Wood, in his *My Life of Music* (London 1938, pp.387-8) states that the Deliuses spent a month at his London house in Elsworthy Road.
(Sir Henry Wood had received his knighthood in 1911 and Sir Thomas Beecham was to be similarly honoured in 1916.)

32 See Rachel Lowe-Dugmore, ibid. pp.12-14.

33 Jelka Delius wrote to Marie Clews on 23rd July 1917: 'I have been very troubled about him. He was really not at all well lately . . . He always forbids me to say that anything is the matter with him . . . He felt so very weak and low and depressed —'. Quoted in Lionel Carley and Robert Threlfall, op. cit, p.73.

34 The dedications were as follows: Violin Concerto — Albert Sammons; Violin and Cello Concerto — May and Beatrice Harrison; Cello Sonata — Beatrice Harrision.

Chapter IX. 1918-1925

1 This is the only occasion in the extant correspondence where either Delius or Munch used French. Munch was much more at home in Norwegian or German, while Delius did not very much like using French. Even here he uses the German (or Norwegian) word 'Maler', rather than the French equivalent.

2 The sea baths were presumably curative, as Jelka could write from Biarritz to Marie Clews: '— Oh, how I wish you could see him so well, his eyes so *entirely* alright again. It is the greatest blessing.' 30 July 1918. Quoted in Lionel Carley and Robert Threlfall, op. cit, p.23.

3 Munch exhibited twice at Blomqvist's during 1918. At the first exhibition which opened 16th February, he showed 20 paintings from the *Life Frieze*, c. 100 drawings and watercolours, 5 studies for *Ghosts* and 2 supplementary designs for the University paintings. At the second, which opened 15th October, he showed 57 paintings. Arne Eggum writes (Stockholm exhibition catalogue 1977, op. cit, p.33): 'The designation "Frieze of Life" was first used by Munch himself in a lengthy article in the newspaper *Tidens Tegn* on October 15th 1918. On the same day an exhibition of 20 paintings from the "Frieze of Life" in was opened at the Blomqvist Art Exhibition in Kristinia. The article *Tidens Tegn*, also published in the exhibition catalogue, was a long explanatory introduction.'

4 1918 (November), Cello Sonata. 1919, Violin Concerto, *Eventyr* and the revised version of the String Quartet.

5 Sir Thomas Beecham, op. cit, p.184.

6 On 19th September they were on the point of leaving Christiania. On 6th October they were in Frankfurt.

7 *Frankfurter Zeitung*, 21st October 1919. Extracts from the long critical notice are quoted in Lionel Carley and Robert Threlfall, op. cit, p.75, and Sir Thomas Beecham, op. cit, pp.186-7.

8 I am indebted to Dr Lionel Carley for supplying me with copies of this and the next letter, from the Delius Trust Archive.

9 A production of *Fennimore and Gerda* in Cologne had been proposed in 1914, but the project was abandoned because of the war. See Robert Threlfall, op. cit, p.49.

10 See note 8, above.

11 No such sketches have survived in the Delius Trust Archive.

12 Georg Swarenski was Director of the Stadelsches Kunstinstitut at Frankfurt and Professor at the University there. He emigrated to the United States in 1938.

13 Jappe Nilssen.

14 The fact that Delius does not give the name of his opera could suggest that he has already mentioned it to Munch earlier. This would mean that he and Munch had been in touch fairly recently, perhaps even seen each other, when he was in Norway that year. But as he has clearly seen Jappe Nilssen, the information could have passed to Munch through him. However, as noted earlier in this correspondence, Delius could be very casual in references to performances of his works, although once again he can always find time to be helpful for his friend.

15 1921 seems the more likely date as, according to J.H. Langaard and Reider Revold (op. cit, p.50), Munch visited Frankfurt during that year.

16 The Frankfurt museum no longer owns these paintings, which are in the possession of the family of Thomas Olsen. They were among eighty-two of Munch's pictures removed from German museums after his work had been classed as 'Degenerate Art' by the Nazi government in 1937, and sold to gain foreign currency for the Third Reich. A number of these paintings were bought by the Norwegian dealer Horst Halvorsen and found their way into Norwegian collections. See Ragna Stang, op. cit, p.304, n.411.

17 21st August 1918. Delius Trust Archive, quoted in Lionel Carley and Robert Threlfall, op. cit, p. 73.

18 William Marchant was the proprietor of the Goupil Gallery.

19 Beecham says that the visit to Frankfurt was in January 1921, 'for a few weeks' (Sir Thomas Beecham, op. cit, p.189), but the date on the letter to Jappe Nilssen would seen to establish an earlier date of arrival, although Delius intended to stay through January. Since the performance of *Fennimore and Gerda* there, Delius's music seems to have enjoyed some popularity in that city. Beecham (referring to 1922) writes of '. . . frequent performances of his music, both in Frankfurt and neighbouring towns.' (Ibid. p.191.) He further quotes a letter from Jelka to Marie Clews, dated 1st January 1923: 'We are now in Frankfurt . . . as there are quite a number of Delius performances coming on.' (Ibid. p.192.)

20 Delius Trust Archive.

21,22,23 The name of the Bank, and the words 'skratches' and 'tin lined' are written in English in the original, 'skratches' mis-spelt.

24 Sir Thomas Beecham, op. cit, p.189. '. . . it may be remembered that in 1898 he had acquired this picture for five hundred francs, or twenty pounds in English money at that time . . .'

25 See D. Cooper: *The Courtauld Collection. A Catalogue and Introduction*, London 1954, cat. no.30, pp.96-7.

26 When the Deliuses left Grez after the outbreak of war in 1914, they buried their wine and some other valuables in the garden.

27 The nearest station to Grez.

28 See J.H. Langaard and Reidar Revold, op. cit, p.50.

29 Delius's previous letter, written on 23rd September (38, D.25) was clearly sent to Munch in Christiania. Letter 39, D.26, written some three weeks later, was just as clearly sent to someone quite near, almost certainly in Paris. So Munch must have communicated with Delius in between, probably in answer to his earlier letter.

30 Arne Eggum has dealt with this in this Stockholm exhibition catalogue 1977, op. cit, pp.33-38. The actions of the characters are set against the Norwegian shoreline.

31 See Gerd Woll, ibid. pp.212-13.

32 Sir Thomas Beecham, op. cit, p.190.

33 At first glance this drawing does not look particularly like Delius. However on closer scrutiny features are quite consistent with photographs and other portraits of the composer at this time. Moreover, although even sketchier than the lithograph, the setting is the same and details like the wheelchair and the bow tie appear in both. A further drawing in Munch-Museet (OKK T. 2061) also uses a somewhat similarly shaped profile head, superimposed on a crowded landscape. Here though the head is less typically Delius, and the setting less obviously explicable. The profile head and a top-hatted head with its back to the spectator appear in the foreground as if engaged in conversation; they are drawn over a number of the crowd figures. The sketch looks like a preliminary idea for a composition. I am greatly indebted to Hr. Ole Petter Bjerkek for drawing my attention to these two drawings.

34 Letter from Jappe Nilssen to Edvard Munch, 10th May 1922. In Erna Holmboe Bang: *Edvard Munchs Kriseår*, Oslo 1963. J.H. Langaard and Reidar Revold (op. cit, p.51) state that Munch went on from Wiesbaden to Berlin in April and from there to Zurich in May. In that case Munch would probably not have had a chance to pass on Jappe's message.

35 Medicinal bath.

36 'Tak for sidst' (Takk for sist). There is no generally used colloquial equivalent in English for this Norwegian phrase. It really means 'thank you for the last occasion on which we met'. The phrase always refers to the last physical meeting, and so confirms that they met in Wiesbaden.

37 J.H. Langaard and Reidar Revold, op. cit, p.51.

38 A letter from Jelka to Adine O'Neill was sent from the Molmen Hotel, Lesjaskog, dated 2 July 1922. (Delius Trust Archive, quoted in Lionel Carley and Robert Threlfall, op. cit, p.77.) Presumably they were staying at the hotel prior to moving into 'Høifagerli'.

39 Neither I nor Dr Lionel Carley have been able to trace anyone named 'Condor' associated with Delius at this time. Dr Carley has suggested that 'Condor' might be the name of the ship on which the Deliuses were to travel to Hamburg, and this seems a reasonable probability unless other evidence should be uncovered.

40 'Tak for sidst', written in Norwegian although the rest of the letter is in German. The use of this phrase does suggest that there had been a meeting, but presumably this could still refer to the Wiesbaden meeting earlier in the year. A meeting in Gudbrandsdal seems most unlikely, and there is no evidence that the Deliuses returned to Christiania that summer until travelling back to Germany.

41 Philip Heseltine discovered that Delius had been born a year earlier than he, or anyone else, supposed. This discovery did not take place until after the sixtieth birthday party. See L. Carley and R. Threlfall, op. cit, p.78.

42 Max Beckmann who made a portrait drawing of Delius in that year. (Reproduced in L. Carley and R. Threfall, ibid.)

43 Percy Grainger's copy of the programme of this concert is reproduced in L. Carley and R. Threlfall, ibid.

44 Letter from Jelka Delius to Henry and Marie Clews, 23rd January 1923. (Delius Trust Archive, quoted in L. Carley and R. Threlfall, ibid.)

45 See Robert Threlfall, op. cit, pp.53-54; also Rachel Lowe-Dugmore: *Frederick Delius 1862-1934*, op. cit, p.168.

46 Eric Fenby: *Delius as I knew him*, London 1937, pp.74-75.

47 Peter Warlock: *Frederick Delius*, London 1923. (Revised ed. London 1952.)

48 There is no evidence that Delius and Craig were personally acquainted or knew each other's work.

49 Jelka Delius mentions an orchestral work in a letter from Rapallo to Marie Clews, 5

March 1924 (Delius Trust Archive. Quoted by L. Carley and R. Threlfall, op. cit, p. 83.) One wonders whether it might have been the *Fantastic Dance* completed in 1931 with the help of Eric Fenby, but apparently sketched a few years previously. (See R. Threfall, op. cit, p.159.)
Beecham states that he started a new violin sonata while at Cannes. (Sir Thomas Beecham, op. cit, p.193) This was also completed with the help of Eric Fenby, in 1930. (See also R. Threlfall, op. cit, p.182.)
50 Letter from Jelka Delius to Marie Clews, 31st August 1925. Delius Trust Archive. Quoted in Lionel Carley and Robert Threlfall, op. cit, p.84.

Chapter X. 1926-1934
1 'My pictures are the only children I have, and in order to be able to work I must have them around me.' Edvard Munch quoted in Ragna Stang, op. cit, p.272. See also ibid. p.227.
2 Munch referred to these pictures of his friends as 'the Lifeguards of my Art.' When Titus Vibe Müller offered him 50,000 Kroner for a portrait, Munch declined to sell, saying: 'I also must have some friends on the wall.' Ragna Stang, op. cit, p.222.
3 The name of the capital had been changed back from Christiania to Oslo on 1st January 1925.
4 Quoted by Gerd Woll in the Stockholm exhibition catalogue 1977, op. cit, p.216. The City Hall decorations are further discussed by Gerd Woll, ibid. pp.214-17.
5 1928, London. 5 paintings included in exhibition of Norwegian art, arranged by the Anglo-Norse Society at the Royal Society of British Artists galleries, 25th Sept. — 21st Oct.
  1931, Edinburgh. 12 paintings at the Society of Scottish Artists, 28th Nov. 1931 — 9th Jan. 1932.
  1936, London. Paintings and prints (number unknown) at the London Gallery.
6 Jens Thiis: *Edvard Munch og hans samtid.* Oslo 1933. Pola Gauguin: *Edvard Munch*, Oslo 1933.
7 Ragna Stang, op. cit, p.271.
8 Sir Thomas Beecham, op. cit, p.198.
9 *A song of Summer* was based on part of the *Poem of Life and Love* (1918-19), while the music of *Idyll* was extracted from the unperformed opera *Margot la Rouge* (1901-02).
10 Dr Eric Fenby's book, *Delius as I knew him* (First published London 1936) is indispensible reading. It gives a detailed account of his years with Delius, with full discussion of their musical collaboration.
11 Full programmes of the concerts are given in Sir Thomas Beecham, op. cit, p.201-04.
12 Ibid. p.205.
13 It is not quite clear whether she means that he can get a taxi at Bourron or that their own car will be waiting there. The German simply reads '. . . in Bourron ist Bil'. I would think the former, as she does not know when or if he will arrive, but it is a point of small importance.
14 *Edvard Munchs brev. Familien*, op. cit, p.253, no.346.
15 Edvard Munch, in Paris, to Jappe Nilssen, in Oslo. In Erna Holmboe Bang, op. cit, p.103-05.
16 J.H. Langaard and Reidar Revold, op. cit, p.53-54.
17 That Munch wrote this after his arrival home in Norway is substantiated by the facts that he has been with Jappe Nilssen again and that the draft was with his effects on his death.
18 Achille Ouvré.
19 i.e. in Norway.
20 In the original, these words come at the end of the last side of a double sheet of paper. It is likely therefore that the letter continued further, but that the concluding part has been lost.
21 In Erna Holmboe Bang, op. cit, p.105. One would have expected Munch to write 'I

have been to see Molard . . . and a couple of old friends', but 'and has a couple of old freinds' is a literal translation from the Norwegian.

22 The date of 1920 has also been proposed for this letter, but I think late 1926 or early 1927 much more probably for the following reasons: a.) Munch's letter to Jappe Nilssen, 4th Nov. 1926, from Paris also refers to Molard as being 'very old'. As Molard's dates were 1862-1936, this means that he would only have been 58 in 1920, and would thus have been more likely to have seemed 'very old' in 1926, at the age of 64. b.) I think that Munch saw Delius after the composer had become blind and paralyzed. The first paragraph so stresses the qualities which Delius had retained — 'beautiful lively voice', 'optimistic good humour', 'strong inner self' — as if he were encouraging the composer that he has many good things left, by implication despite the things which he has lost. Delius was not blind at the time of Munch's portraits of c. 1920 and 1922. c.) Jappe Nilssen was to die in 1931, and reference to his poor health suggest a later rather than earlier date.

23 This letter could have been similar to the one Munch drafted in 1926 (43a, Md.6), but as nearly two years have elapsed since then I think that the Deliuses are replying to another letter, received more recently.

24 Jappe Nilssen, who had also kept in touch with the composer.

25 We do not know if Munch had referred to any specific successes, or whether he had just generally remarked that things were going well. However 1928 was a good year for him. His work had been exhibited in Munich, San Francisco, Stockholm and London; he had sold the 1907 version of *The Sick Child* to the Gemäldegalerie, Dresden (the painting is now in the Tate Gallery, London); and he had been working on designs for the Central Hall of the new Oslo City Hall.

26 Although Munch was never able to make another portrait of Delius, portraits of the composer in the last few years of his life by James Gunn, Augustus John and Ernest Proctor, all bear out Jelka's description of him.

27 By the time this letter was written Sir Thomas Beecham had recorded several of Delius's orchestral works: *The Walk to the Paradise Garden* from *A Village Romeo and Juliet* and *On Hearing the First Cuckoo in Spring*, (both 1927), and *Summer Night on the River* (1928). Eric Fenby recalls hearing Beecham's recording of *On Hearing the First Cuckoo in Spring* with Delius on the day after his arrival in Grez in October: '. . . it is always a fascinating thing to observe the effect of a man's music on himself . . . A curious other-worldliness possessed him. With his head thrown back, and swaying slightly to the rhythm, he seemed to be seeing with those now wide-open yet unseeing eyes, and his spirit ebbed and flowed with the rise and fall of his music.' Eric Fenby, op. cit, p.23.)

28 The fact that Jelka has gone to the trouble of writing to Munch especially to advise him of a Delius broadcast, suggests that the artist may have showed a little more interest in his friend's music in the missing late letters than he had in the surviving earlier ones; cf. 43a, Md.6 and Chapter XI.

29 i.e. to hear Sir Thomas Beecham's broadcast concert.

30 I have not been able to find any record of such a concert having been arranged and think it most unlikely that it ever was.

31 No such letter has survived.

32 Here Munch seems rather forgetful. On several past occasions Jelka had written to Munch for Delius in Norwegian (nos. 38, 39, 40), so, although the composer was now blind, she would presumably have been able to translate anything written in Norwegian for him.

33 Munch must mean that he is unsure what his movements will be and therefore not certain if he will get to Paris.

34 Which exhibitions Munch is referring to is unclear. He had a large exhibition of prints in Stockholm in February 1929 and another in Oslo in May.

35 Munch actually writes 'Holland am See'. Arne Eggum suggests that Munch may have been thinking of health cures at some North Sea resort, (but fresh air rather than

bathing), as he had discussed such things with his friends some years before; he possessed a book about North Sea resorts. Munch-Museet has no record of any Munch exhibition in Holland at this time.

36 Munch must have been thinking generally about past journeys as J.H. Langaard and Reidar Revold (op. cit.) record no travels outside Scandinavia after 1927.

37 I have placed the letters in this order because it seems to me more natural for successive drafts to add fresh material rather than to delete it.

38 See letter 46b, n.32.

39 See p.58.

40 Delius remained a Nietzschean nature-worshipping atheist to the end. Munch could perhaps be described as a thoughtful agnostic who believed, a little vaguely, in man's soul and in great eternal forces. Hence his amusement that Helge Rode, who presumably in earlier days had held views near to those of friends like Munch and Delius, should now have 'gone religious'.

41 Although Munch made many notes of this kind, he never succeeded in making an orderly assembly of them. In a will dated 1930, he charged his friend and executor Professor Kristian Schreiner with the final reading of his 'literary sketches'. In an article published in 1946 Schreiner reminisced, quoting Munch: 'I have decided that you, after my death, are to go through all this. I believe that some of what I have written may be of literary interest and can throw light on my art.'
In his final will, written in 1940, Munch wrote: 'The drafts for my literary works are to go to the City of Oslo, which in accord with the judgement of experts will decide whether and to what degree they are to be published.' See Gerd Woll: *The Tree of Knowledge of Good and Evil*, in *Edvard Munch; Symbols and Images* op. cit, pp.229-255, where Munch's 'literary' and 'spiritual' notes are discussed thoroughly. The two quotations above are to be found on p.299 of the catalogue.

42 This point will be elaborated at the beginning of Chapter XI.

43 Ironically, by now Delius was not 'going on all right'. Jelka wrote to Eric Fenby on 23rd January 1934: 'Fred has been unwell for nearly a week and has given me great anxiety . . .'. Eric Fenby, op. cit, p.215.

44 The composer Christian Sinding was a friend of both Delius and Munch. The artist made a lithographic portrait of him in 1911, (OKK G/1.339-3, Sch.359).

45 Jappe Nilssen died in 1931. This suggests that Munch had not written to Delius since then, although he could be forgetful or repeat himself.

46 *Politikken* — the Danish newspaper.

47 Pola Gauguin: *Edvard Munch*, Oslo 1933.

48 Munch writes of Helge Rode speaking of 'that summer we were together in Aasgaard-strand'. This suggests that they were only together there once, although without actually stating it, and Munch's memory as an older man was not always reliable. Consequently it cannot be said to offer a definitive answer to the problems of when they all met, discussed on pp.23 and 58.

49 Delius never received such a title. In 1929 he was made a Companion of Honour and offered an Honorary Doctorate by Oxford, although he had to decline the latter as he was unable to travel to receive it; in 1932 he was given the Freedom of his native Bradford. Most likely Munch had heard news of one or other of the above honours in a garbled version.

50 During 1933 Munch had rather 'broken out' of Ekely and he spent a lot of time painting at his old haunts of Aasgaardstrand, Hvitsen and Kragerø.

51 This sounds as if Munch now thinks it rather unlikely that he will get to Paris again. The reference to painting Delius, 'We spoke about this last time', could follow on from Munch's two previous draft letters (46b, 46c). But he could of course have repeated the proposition in an intervening letter, if there were one.

52 *Self-portrait eating a 'truly magnificent cod's head'*. 1940, oil, OKK M.63.
Self-portrait between the Clock and the Bed. c. 1940-42, oil, OKK M.23.
Self-portrait by the Window. c. 1940, oil, OKK M.446.

Self-portrait with a Stick of Pastel. 1943, pastel, OKK M.749.
53 1943-44. OKK G/1.548.

Chapter XI. Epilogue.

1 See also pp.144-5.
2 Sir Thomas Beecham, op. cit, p.218. Sir Thomas is not very reliable in his specific
    reference to Munch here.
3 See p.133, no.43a, Md.6.
4 See p.136, no.46c, Md.9.
5 Christopher Palmer, op. cit, p.104.
6 See p.50, no.2, M.1.
7 See p.133, no.43a, Md.6.
8 A different view of Delius's appreciation of art is given by the sculptor, Sir Jacob
    Epstein: 'The composer of sweet and melancholy music was argumentative, cranky
    and bad-tempered, and we had many a set-to. . . . For one thing he (Delius) imagined
    himself a tremendous authority on Art. This was founded on the fact that in Paris,
    years ago, he had bought a picture of Gauguin's. Also Mrs Delius was a painter.
    Delius would lay down the lay on Art, and absurd laws they were too.' Epstein. *An
    Autobiography*, London 1955, pp.116-7.
    Epstein does not give date to when he met Delius, but I think it was probably in the
    early nineteen-twenties. As Delius did become more difficult and acerbic as his illness
    increased, and as Epstein himself had very positive views and could also be
    pugnacious, it is probably not surprising that their views clashed. But however
    suspect Delius's 'laws' about art might have been, this would not alter the fact that he
    liked and appreciated quite a lot of art.
    It is a great pity, though, that nothing came from Epstein's wish to make a portrait of
    the composer: 'I should have liked to do a bust of Delius, for I think all those
    drawings made of him are unbelievably sentimental, especially those made during his
    last illness. The artists imagined that a sick man must be a saint, and they drew him
    with a saint-like martyrs's expression on his face.' Ibid.
    Clearly Epstein had not seen the Munch lithographs.
9 Eric Fenby, op. cit, p.14.
10 The auction was held at the Hôtel des Ventes, Paris on 28 February 1936, the
    auctioneer a Monsieur Hubert Buzot. Among the many effects from the house at Grez
    were a great number of pictures by Jelka Delius.
11 For additional discussion see Arne Eggum, *Munch and Music*, op. cit, pp.35-49.
12 Translated from transcript of an interview with Eva Mudocci by Waldemar Stabell
    on the BBC Norwegian Service, 18/5/50.
13 I am greatly indebted to Dr Carla Lathe for providing me with this information, and
    also to drawing my attention to several other passages quoted in this section.
14 Gustav Schiefler: *Meine Graphiksammlung*, completed and edited by Gerhard Schock,
    Hamburg 1974, p.38. original in German.
15 A piano is show in *Self-portrait. The Night Wanderer*, 1920s. OKK M.589.
16 Munch to Jappe Nilssen, 20/4/09, in Erna Holmboe Bang, op. cit, p.77. Original in
    Norwegian.
17 a.) *Inger at the piano*, 1889. OKK M.1107.
    b.) *Military band on Karl Johan Street*, 1889, oil, Kunsthaus, Zurich.
    c.) *Two music-making sisters*, 1892, oil, Private Collection.
    d.) *Funeral March*, 1897. OKK T.392.
    e.) *The Violin Recital*, 1903. OKK G/1.254, Sch.211.
    f.) *Delius at Wiesbaden* (with a concert taking place in the background), 1922. OKK
         G/1.427, Sch.498.
18 Munch, draft letter, probably to Jens Thiis, c. 1933, Munch-Museet. Quoted in
    Reinhold Heller: *Edvard Munch's 'Life Frieze': Its Beginnings and Origins*, Indiana
    University Ph.D. thesis, 1969, p.36.

19 Munch: *Mein Freund Przybyszewski*, in *Pologne Litteraire*, 15th December, 1928. Translated by Carla Lathe in *Edvard Munch and his Literary Associates*, op. cit, p.21.

20 Sir Thomas Beecham, op. cit, p.195.

21 It would appear that Jappe Nilssen did appreciate Delius's merits earlier. See p.60, letter from Jappe Nilssen to Delius, probably written c. 1900.

Appendix A

RECOLLECTIONS OF STRINDBERG

By Frederick Delius

From *The Sackbut*, December 1920, Vol. I, No.8, pp.353-4.

(Remainder of the article, not printed in the main text, pp.32, 41.)

'. . . Or I would sometimes fetch Strindberg for a walk in the afternoon and we would go through the Luxembourg Gardens and around the Panthéon, again up the Boulevard Raspail, and down the Boulevard St Michel, turning down the Boulevard St Germain towards St Germain des Près, then up again through Rue de Tournon, the Galeries de l'Odéon and back, through the Luxembourg Gardens.

Another favourite walk of ours was the the Jardin des Plantes. Strindberg seemed extremely interested in monkeys at that time. He had a theory that the gorilla was descended from a shipwrecked sailor and an ordinary female monkey. One of his great proofs of this was the similarity between the inside of the paw of the gorilla and the palm of the hand of an old sailor. He showed by photos of both, and indeed there was a great resemblance.

Strindberg was then also greatly occupied with alchemy, and claimed to have extracted gold from earth which he had collected in the Cimetière Montparnasse, and he showed me pebbles entirely coated with the precious metal. He asked me once to have one of these samples analysed by an eminent chemist of my acquaintance. My friend examined it and found it to be covered with pure gold. He was hugely interested and expressed the desire to make Strindberg's acquaintance. So I arranged a meeting in my rooms for a certain Wednesday afternoon at three o'clock. My friend arrived quite punctually, but we waited an hour in vain for Strindberg. At a quarter past four a telegram arrived with these words: "I feel that the time has not yet come for me to disclose my discovery. — Strindberg." The scientist went away very disappointed, saying to me: "Je crains que votre ami est un farceur."

Strindberg also professed to have extracted pure carbon out of sulphur, and in fact I found him sometimes in his room stooping over an open coal fire stirring something in a retort. At the time he did not tell me what he was doing, but afterwards it dawned on me that the carbon probably came from the coal smoke of the open chimney.

Another day he told me that he had discovered a way of making iodine at half the usual cost, and that he had inspired an articles in the *Temps* about this new method. The article created an immense sensation, especially in Hamburg, where iodine seemed to be monopolised; for in one day iodine dropped forty per cent. on the Hamburg Exchange. Unfortunately, nothing further was ever heard of this affair.

He was very much interested in spiritism at that time. Paul Verlaine had just died and Strindberg had in his possession a rather large photo of the poet on his death-bed. He handed me the photo one day and asked me what I saw on it. I described it candidly, namely, Verlaine lying on his back covered with rather a thick eiderdown, only his head and beard visible; a pillow had dropped on the floor and lay there rather crunched up. Strindberg asked me did I not see the huge animal lying on Verlaine's stomach and the imp crouching on the floor? At the time I could never really make out whether he was quite sincere or trying to mystify me. However, I may say I believed implicitly in his chemical discoveries then. He had such a convincing way of explaining them and certainly was very ambitious to be an inventor. For instance, Röntgen rays had just been discovered, and he confided to me one afternoon over an absinthe at the Café Closerie des Lilas, that he himself had discovered them ten years ago.

His interest in spirits caused Leclerc and me to play off a joke on him. I asked them both to my rooms one evening, and after dinner we had a spiritistic séance in the form of table-rapping. The lights were turned down and we joined hands round a small table. After ten minutes' ominous silence the table began to rap and Leclerc asked it what message the spirits had for us. The first letter rapped out was "M," and with each letter Strindberg's and excitement seemed to increase, and slowly came the momentous letters "M E R D E." I do not think he ever quite forgave us for this.

(It was at this time Strindberg wrote his pamphlet "Sylva Sylvorum" . . . he confided to me that they had only come to kill him.)

'He was extremely touchy and often imagined he had been slighted without any cause whatever, as the following incident will show:

We would often gather at night at the studio of one of our mutual friends (Mollard), a very amusing and Bohemian interior. When we left our hosts would use the occasion to accompany us downstairs into the yard in order to empty their "boîte à ordures" and to give Bob, their little bastard dog, a chance of getting a little fresh air. Strindberg had been great friends with this couple and had been taking his meals with them for a couple of months at least. It appears Strindberg was there alone one night and it was getting late and they were evidently very tired, when the hostess suggested "si nous descendions la boîte à ordures," a ceremony which had become quite a known institution. Strindberg went down with them and said "good night" in the wonted friendly way, but never entered their house again, taking the allusion to the "boîte à ordures" as a personal insult to himself.

Shortly after Munch's supposed attempt to assassinate Strindberg I left for Norway and on returning heard that he had left for Sweden. I never saw him again.'

Appendix B

PRINTS BY EDVARD MUNCH AT ONE TIME IN THE POSSESSION OF FREDERICK DELIUS

After the death of Frederick Delius, on 10th June, 1934, all the pictures in the house at Grez-sur-Loing remained there in the possession of his widow, Jelka. Following her death, on 28th May, 1935, an inventory was made of them. This list remained with the papers of Sir Thomas Beecham and has recently been passed to the Delius Trust by his widow.

Naturally enough, most of the pictures are known or presumed to be by Jelka Delius herself, but twelve prints by Edvard Munch are listed, five hanging on the staircase and landing of the house, seven from a small bedroom. They are described as etchings, but it is most unlikely that many, if indeed any, were actually etchings. The one Munch print we know positively was owned by Delius (a portrait of the composer) and one that it is almost certain was in his possession (a portrait of Strindberg) only exist as lithographs, while all those which Eric Fenby has attempted to identify are either lithographs or woodcuts. On the list prepared for the auction sale in 1936, the eleven Munch prints are merely listed as engravings.

Of the twelve prints listed in the initial inventory, five only are described by subject: two are claimed to be 'of devils', one of a 'nude woman', one 'of Ed. Munck' (sic) and one of a 'woman's head'. This alone does not help us very far, but if this information is added to the memories of Eric Fenby, a little progress can be made.

Dr Fenby has been through many reproductions of Munch prints with me and thinks that the following were probably on the walls of the house at Grez:

1 *Delius*, lithograph. (OKK G/1.407-5; Sch.473).
The only absolutely positive identification. The print passed directly from Jelka Delius to Eric Fenby.

2 *Strindberg*, lithograph. (OKK G/1.219a; Sch.77).
As Dr Fenby mentions this portrait by name in *Delius as I knew him*, first published in 1936, when his memory of the household at Grez would still have been very fresh, I would regard this as reliable. Dr Fenby does not actually name any other Munch pictures at Grez in that book.

3 *Self-portrait with a Skeleton Arm*, lithograph. (OKK G/1.192; Sch.31).
Dr Fenby's memory seems to be confirmed by the listing of a self-portrait in the inventory.
4 *Madonna*, coloured lithograph. (OKK G/1.194; Sch.33).
This could perhaps be the 'nude woman' listed in the inventory. This print together
with the two next listed ones and the portrait of Strindberg were all among the
prints sent by Munch to Delius in February 1905 for him to place in the Salon des
Indépendants (see p.81). This might have given Delius the opportunity of
acquiring some or all of them.
5 *Lovers in the Waves*, lithograph. (OKK G/1.215; Sch.71)
Just possibly this might be the 'woman's head' referred to in the inventory, as the female
head is very prominent in the print. But it seems even more possible that this reference
in the inventory refers to a print not recollected by Dr Fenby.
6 *Vampire*, lithograph and woodcut. (OKK G/t.567; Sch.34).
7 *Puberty*, lithograph. (OKK G/1.189; Sch.8).
8 *The Scream*, Lithograph. (OKK G/1.193; Sch.32).
In *Delius as I knew him*, (op.cit. p.15), Eric Fenby writes: 'Over by the window to the garden
was a clever little sketch of a shrieking goblin'. The impersonal screaming head in 'The
Scream' could suggest this to someone new to Munch's work and the lithograph is
carried out in a bold, somewhat sketchy manner. As to my knowledge Munch never
actually portrayed devils, this subject might also suggest something diabolic to the
writer of the inventory, so this might be one of the subjects listed as 'of devils'.
9 *Fear*, either lithograph. (OKK G/1.512; Sch.61)
or coloured woodcut. (OKK G/t.568; Sch.62)
If my attribution of 'The Scream' is correct, I would suggest this as the other picture listed
as 'of devils'. It is closely related to 'The Scream' and the background is similar.
Moreover the coloured woodcut version has a special eeriness in its scratchy technique,
which could well suggest the diabolic to some viewers.
10 *Jealousy*, lithograph. (OKK G/1.202; Sch.58).
Dr Fenby was by no means certain about this print, but he thinks that it may possibly have
been among those at Grez.

It should be mentioned that a number of these subjects exist in various versions, but
understandably Dr Fenby could not identify specific variants.
This then is probably as far as we can go towards identifying the Munch prints which
Delius owned. Of the twelve prints inventoried one passed to Eric Fenby. The other eleven
were auctioned at the Hôtel des Ventes, in Paris, together with other effects from the house
at Grez, on 28th February 1936. The Munch prints together fetched 2,700 francs.

Geschrei

Ich fühlte das grosse Geschrei
durch die Natur

The Scream, 1895. Lithograph OKK G/l 193; Sch32.

Select Bibliography

Although this bibliography lists the principal works consulted and titles mentioned in the text it does not claim to be exhaustive. Readers requiring more extensive bibliographies are referred for Delius to Alan Jefferson's *Delius* or Lionel Carley's forthcoming *Delius: a Life in Letters*, and for Munch to Hanna B. Muller's *Edvard Munch. A Bibliography* or Ragna Stang's *Edvard Munch. The Man and the Artist*, all listed below. Where books from Norwegian sources have also appeared in English editions, I have referred to these, but in virtually all such cases there is also a Norwegian edition. I have only listed catalogues of museums and art galleries where they have some particular interest in relation to this study.

Ahlström, Stellan: *Strindbergs erövring av Paris. Strindberg och Frankrike 1884-1895.* Almqvist and Wicksell, Stockholm, 1956. Résumé en français.

Ahlström, Stellan: *Strindberg a Paris. Un aperçu.* In *La Revue d'Histoire du Théâtre,* Paris, 1978, no.3.

Arts Council: *Gauguin and the Pont-Aven Group.* Catalogue of exhibition at the Tate Gallery 1966. Introduction by Denys Sutton.

Askeland, Jan: *Angstmotivet: Edvard Munchs Kunst.* In *Kunsten idag,* Oslo, 1966, no.4. Norwegian and English text.

Bang, Erna Holmboe (ed. and introd.): *Edvard Munch og Jappe Nilssen. Efterlatte brev og kritikker.* Dreyer, Oslo, 1946.

Bang, Erna Holmboe (ed. and introd.): *Edvard Munchs Kriseår. Belyst i brever.* Gyldendal, Oslo, 1963.

Beecham, Sir Thomas: *Frederick Delius.* Hutchinson, London, 1959.

Beecham, Sir Thomas: *A Mingled Chime. Leaves from an Autobiography.* Hutchinson, London, n.d.

Boe, Roy A.: *Edvard Munch og J.P. Jacobsen's 'Niels Lyhne'.* In *Oslo Kommunes Kunstsamlinger Årbok 1952-59,* Oslo, 1960.

Carley, Lionel: *Carl Larsson and Grez-sur-Loing in the 1880s.* In *The Delius Society Journal,* no.45, October 1974, pp.8-25.

Carley, Lionel: *Delius, the Paris Years.* Triad Press, London, 1975.

Carley, Lionel: *Delius's 'Norwegian Suite'.* In *Anglo-Norse Review,* December 1978, pp.12-14.

Carley, Lionel: *An English-American Hardangervidde-Man.* In Munch-Museet exhibition catalogue, April-May 1979, pp.29-33.

Carley, Lionel: *Jelka Rosen Delius: Artist, Admirer and Friend of Rodin. The Correspondence 1900-1914.* Nottingham French Studies, Vol.IX nos. 1 and 2, 1970.

Carley, Lionel: *Delius: a Life in Letters*. Vol.I, 1862-1908. Scolar Press, London, 1983. (Vol.II is in preparation.)

Carley, Lionel and Threlfall, Robert: *Delius. A Life in Pictures*. Oxford University Press, 1977.

Chop, Max: *Frederick Delius*. Berlin, 1907.

Cooper, Douglas: *The Courtauld Collection. A Catalogue and Introduction*. Athlone Press, London, 1954.

Deknatel, Frederick B.: *Edvard Munch*. Chanticleer Press, New York, 1950.

Delius, Clare: *Memories of My Brother*. Ivor Nicholson and Watson, London, 1935.

Delius, Frederick: *Recollections of Strindberg*. In *The Sackbut*, December 1920, Volume I, no.8, pp.353-54.

Eggum, Arne: *The Green Room*. In Stockholm exhibition catalogue March-May 1977, pp.62-103.

Eggum, Arne: *Munch and Music*. In Munch-Museet exhibition catalogue April-May 1979, pp.35-49.

Eggum, Arne: *Munch's Late Frieze of Life*. In Stockholm exhibition catalogue March-May 1977, pp.33-39.

Epstein, Sir Jacob: *An Autobiography*. Hulton Press, London, 1955.

Fenby, Eric: *Delius as I knew him*. Bell, London, 1936, reprinted 1937.

Fenby, Eric: Introduction to recording of *Fennimore and Gerda* made by EMI Records Ltd. in association with Danmarks Radio, 1976. Issued as SLS 991.

Foreman, Lewis (ed.): *The Percy Grainger Companion*. Thames Publishing, London, 1981.

Gauguin, Paul: *Letters to his Wife and Friends*. Ed. Maurice Malingue. Trans Henry J. Stenning. Saturn Press, London, n.d.

Gauguin, Pola: *Edvard Munch*. Aschehoug, Oslo, 1933, new edition 1946.

Gerard, Edouard: *Le Peintre Ed. Munch*. In *La Presse*, May 1897.

Gérard-Arlberg, Gilles: *Nr. 6, rue Vercingétorix*. In *Konstrevy*, Stockholm, 35, 2, 1958, pp.64-8.

Glaser, Kurt: *Edvard Munch*. Berlin, 1917. New expanded edition 1922.

Gløersen, Inger Alver: *Den Munch jeg møtte*. Gyldendahl, Oslo, 1956 and 1962.

Heller, Reinhold: *Edvard Munch's 'Life Frieze': Its Beginnings and Origins*. Indiana University Ph.D thesis, MS, 1969. In Munch-Museet.

Heller, Reinhold: *Love as a Series of Paintings*. In National Gallery of Art, Washington, 1978 catalogue, pp.86-111.

Heller, Reinhold: *Edvard Munch: The Scream*. Allen Lane The Penguin Press, London, 1973.

Heseltine, Philip. See Warlock, Peter.

Hodin, J.P.: *Edvard Munch*. Thomas and Hudson, London, 1972.

Hougen, Pål: *Farge på trykk*. Munch-Museet catalogue, no.5, Oslo, 1968.

Hougen, Pål: *Edvard Munch. Tegninger, skisser og studier*. Munch-Museet catalogue A.3, Oslo, 1973.

Hougen, Pål: *Munch and Ibsen*. In *Edvard Munch and Henrik Ibsen*, catalogue to exhibition at St Olaf College, Northfield, Minnesota, 1978.

Hove, Richard: *Frederick Delius.* In *Nordisk Tidskrift,* 1964, no.2

Jaworska, Wladyslawa: *Gauguin and the Pont-Aven School.* Translated by Patrick Evans. Thames and Hudson, London, 1972.
Jefferson, Alan: *Delius.* Dent, London, 1972.

Kahane, Arthur: *Edvard Munch.* In *Berlin Tageblatt,* 28th October, 1926.
Kjellberg, Gerda: *Hänt och sant.* (Including memoirs of Judith Gérard.) Norstedts, Stockholm, 1951.
Knupfer, Lucy de: *Music and Friendship.* Manuscript.
Krieger, Peter: *Edvard Munch. Der Lebensfries für Max Reinhardts Kammerspiele.* Catalogue of exhibition at the Nationalgalerie, Berlin, 1978.
Krohg, Christian: *Fritz Delius.* In *Verdens Gang,* 23rd October, 1897.
Krohg, Christian: *Maecenaten.* In *Verdens Gang,* 29th November, 1898.

Langaard, Ingrid: *Edvard Munch: Modningsår.* Gyldendal, Oslo, 1960. Summary in English.
Langaard, Johan H. and Revold, Reidar: *A Year by Year Record of Edvard Munch's Life.* A Handbook. Aschehoug, Oslo. 1961.
Langaard, Johan H. and Revold, Reidar: *Edvard Munch. The University Murals.* Forlaget Norsk Kunstreproduksjon, Oslo, 1960.
Langaard, Johan H. and Revold, Reidar: *Edvard Munch. Masterpieces from the Artist's Collection in the Munch Museum, Oslo.* Forlaget Norsk Kunstreproduksjon, Stenersen, Oslo, 1964.
Langaard, Johan H. and Revold, Reidar: *The Drawings of Edvard Munch.* Kunsten idag, Oslo, 1958.
Lathe, Carla: *Edvard Munch and his Literary Associates.* Catalogue of exhibition at the University of East Anglia, Norwich, 1979.
Linde, Max: *Edvard Munch und die Kunst der Zukunft.* Gottheiner, Berlin, 1902.
Linde, Max: *Edvard Munchs brev. Fra dr. med. Max Linde.* Munch-Museets Skrifter 3, Dreyer, Oslo, 1954.
Lowe-Dugmore, Rachel: *Frederick Delius and Norway.* In *Studies in Music,* University of Western Australia Press, 1972, no.6.
Lowe (-Dugmore), Rachel: *Frederick Delius 1862-1934. A Catalogue of the Music Archive of the Delius Trust, London.* Delius Trust, London, 1974.
Lowe-Dugmore, Rachel: *Delius's First Performance.* In *The Musical Times,* March, 1965.
Lowe-Dugmore, Rachel: *Documenting Delius.* In *Delius Society Journal,* October, 1976, no.65.

Madsen, Stefan Tschudi: *Art Nouveau.* Translated by R.I. Christophersen. Weidenfeld and Nicolson, London, 1967.
Mitchell, P.M.: *A History of Danish Literature.* Gyldendal, Copenhagen, 1957.
Muller, Hanna B.: *Edvard Munch. A Bibliography.* In *Oslo Kommunes Kunstsamlinger Årbok 1946-1951,* Oslo, 1951. Supplement in *Oslo Kommunes Kunstsamlinger Årbok 1952-1959,* Oslo, 1960.
Edvard Munch: rammen av musikk og lyrikk. Centenary concert given by the Oslo Philharmonic Society, 12th December 1963. Programme notes by Ole Henrik Moe.
Edvard Munch som vi kjente ham. Vennene forteller. Dreyer, Oslo, 1946. Contributions from K.E. Schreiner, Johs Roede, Ingeborg Motzfelt Løchen, Titus Vibe

Müller, Birgit Prestøe, David Bergendal, Christian Gierløff, Pola Gauguin, L.O. Ravensberg and letters from Munch to Sigurd Høst.

Munch, Edvard: *Livsfrisen*. Pamphlet, probably published Oslo, 1918.

Munch, Edvard: *Livfrisen tilblivelse*. Pamphlet, probably published in Oslo, 1929.

Munch, Edvard: *Edvards Munchs brev. Familien*. Et utvalg ved Inger Munch. Forord av Johann H. Langaard. Munch-Museets Skrifter I. Johan Grundt Tanum, Oslo, 1949.

Munch, Edvard: *Mein Freund Przybyszewski*. In *Pologne Litteraire*, 15th December, 1928. 'Also in *Oslo Aftenavis* no. 25, 1929'.

Munch-Museet: *Frederick Delius og Edvard Munch*. Catalogue of exhibition, Oslo, April-May, 1979.

Munch-Museet: *Edvard Munch. Alpha and Omega*. Catalogue of exhibition March-August, 1981. Contributions by Alf Bøe, Arne Eggum and Gerd Woll.

Munch-Museet: *Oslo Kommunes Kunstsamlinger Årbok 1946-51*, Oslo, 1951.

Munch-Museet: *Oslo Kommunes Kunstsamlinger Årbok 1952-9*, Oslo, 1960.

Munch-Museet: *Oslo Kommunes Kunstsamlinger Årbok 1963*, Oslo, 1963.

Myers, Bernard S.: *Expressionism: a generation in revolt*. Thames and Hudson, London, 1957.

Natanson, Thadée: *Correspondence de Christiania: Edvard Munch*. In *La Revue Blanche*, no.59, Nov. 1895, pp.477-78.

National Gallery of Art, Washington: *Edvard Munch. Symbols and Images*. Catalogue of exhibition, Washington, 1978.

Nergaard, Trygve: *Refleksjon og visjon. Naturalismens dilemma; Edvard Munchs Kunst*. 1968. MS in Munch-Museet.

Nergaard, Trygve: *Despair*. In National Gallery of Art, Washington, 1978 catalogue, pp.112-141.

Nevinson, C.R.W.: *Paint and Prejudice*. Methuen, London, 1937.

Palmer, Christopher: *Delius. Portrait of a Cosmopolitan*. Duckworth, London, 1976.

Popperwell, Ronald C.: *Norway*. Benn, London, 1972.

Qvamme, Börre: *Norwegian Music and Composers*. Bond, London, 1949.

Redwood, Christopher (ed. and introd.): *A Delius Companion*. London, 1976. Revised edition, Calder, London, 1980.

Rewald, John: *Post-Impressionism from Van Gogh to Gauguin*. Museum of Modern Art, New York, n.d.

Royal Academy of Arts, London: *Post-Impressionism. Cross-currents in European Painting*. Catalogue of exhibition, London, 1979-80.

Schiefler, Gustav: *Verzeichnis des graphischen Werks Edvard Munchs*. Cassirer, Berlin, 1907. New edition Cappelen, Oslo, 1974. Vols I and II.

Schiefler, Gustav: *Meine Graphiksammlung*, completed and edited by Gerhard Schack. Hamburg, 1974.

Smith, John Boulton: *Frederick Delius and Edvard Munch*. In Munch-Museet exhibition catalogue, April-May 1979, pp.9-27.

Smith, John Boulton: *Portrait of a Friendship. Edvard Munch and Frederick Delius*. In *Apollo*, London, January, 1966. Also in *Kunst og Kultur*, Oslo, 1965.

Smith, John Boulton: *Munch*. Phaidon Press, Oxford and New York, 1977.

Smith, John Boulton: *Edvard Munch: European and Norwegian*. In *Apollo*, London, January 1974.

Smith, John Boulton: *Strindberg's Visual Imagination*. In *Apollo*, London, October 1970. Also in *Kunst og Kultur*, Oslo, 1970.

Söderström, Göran: *Strindberg och bildkonsten*. Forum, Sweden, 1972.

Sprigge, Elizabeth: *The Strange Life of August Strindberg*. Hamish Hamilton, London, 1949.

Stabell, Waldemar: *Edvard Munch og Eva Mudocci*. In *Kunst og Kultur*, Oslo, 1973, pp.209-30.

Stang, Nic: *Edvard Munch*. Grundt Tanum, Oslo, 1971. English edition Oslo, 1972.

Stang, Ragna: *Edvard Munch. Mennesket og Kunstneren*. Aschehoug, Oslo, 1977.

Stang, Ragna: *Edvard Munch. The Man and the Artist*. Translated by Geoffrey Culverwell and Anthony Martin, Edited by John Boulton Smith. Gordon Fraser, London, 1979.

Stenersen, Rolf: *Edvard Munch. Close-up of a Genuis*. Trans, and ed. by Reidar Dittman. Gyldendal, Oslo, 1969.

Stockholm: *Edvard Munch 1863-1944*. Catalogue of exhibition at Liljevalchs konstall and Kulturhuset, March-May 1977.

Strindberg, August: *L'exposition d'Edvard Munch*. In *La Revue Blanche*, no.72, June 1896. Reproduced in Ingird Langaard: *Edvard Munch: Modningsår*, Gyldendal, Oslo, 1960, p.366.

Strindberg, August: *Inferno, Alone and other writings*. Translated, edited and introduced by Evert Sprinchorn. Doubleday Anchor Books, New York, 1968.

Strindberg, August: *Inferno*. Translated by Mary Sandbach. Hutchinson, London, 1962.

Strindberg, Frida: *Marriage with Genius*. Cape, London, 1937.

Svenaeus, Gösta: *Idé och innehåll i Edvard Munchs Konst*. Gyldendal, Oslo, 1953.

Svenaeus, Gösta: *Trädet på berget*. In *Oslo Kommunes Kunstsamlinger Årbok*, 1963.

Svenaeus, Gosta: *Strindberg og Munch i Inferno*. In *Kunst og Kultur*, Oslo, 1969.

Svenaeus, Gösta: *Edvard Munch. Im männlichen Gehirn*. 2 vols. Vetenskap-societen, Lund, 1973.

Thiis, Jens: *Minneord om Helge Rode*. In *Festskrift till Francis Bull paa 50 Årsdagen*. Gyldendal, Oslo, 1937.

Thiis, Jens: *Edvard Munch og hans samtid. Slekten, livet og Kunsten, geniet*. Gyldendal, Oslo, 1933.

Threlfall, Robert (see also under Carley, Lionel): *A Catalogue of the Compositions of Frederick Delius. Sources and References*. Delius Trust, London, 1977.

Timm, Werner: *The Graphic Art of Edvard Munch*. Studio Vista, London, 1969.

Torjusen, Bente: *The Mirror*. In National Gallery of Art, Washington, 1978 catalogue, pp.184-227.

Warlock, Peter: *Frederick Delius*. Revised edition, ed. Hubert Foss. The Bodley Head, London, 1952.

Woll, Gerd: *Now the Time of the Workers Has Come*. In Stockholm exhibition catalogue, March-May 1977, pp.136-220.

Woll, Gerd: *The Tree of Knowledge of Good and Evil*. In National Gallery of Art, Washington, 1978 catalogue, pp.228-255.

Wood, Sir Henry J.: *My Life of Music*. Gollancz, London, 1938.

Index

Dates have been given, unless unavailable, for everyone mentioned in the correspondence and also for all those who were known to both Delius and Munch, either personally or through important influence. Where it has been felt that a name may not be familiar to many readers, and where this is not enlarged on in text or notes, a short biographical entry has been included. The letters 'ep' preceding a number indicate that the picture is illustrated on the end-papers, with that number.

Aasgaardstrand, Munch's cottage at: photograph, *34a,* 152 n6
Aasgaardstrand, Munch's cottage at: sketch by Munch on draft letter, 139
Académie Colarossi, 24, 29
Aguéli, Ivan, 25
Andersen, Hans Christian, 12, 13
Andray, Christianne, 60
Anglo-Norse Society, 169 n5
Antoine, André, 26, 27
Arbos, Enrique Fernandez, 93
Armory Show, The, 102, 165 n9
Arneberg, Arnstein, 123
l'Art Cosmopolite, 31
l'Art Nouveau, Galeries de and Salon de, 30, 31, 71, 73, 156 n27, n31, 160 n31
Arvesen, Arve (1869-1959), 14, 15, 20, 21, 22, 145, *ep6*
Asbjørnsen, Peter Christen (1812 -85), 103, 135
Association of Berlin Artists (See under Verein Berliner Künstler)
Augener Edition, 15
Autumn Exhibition, Christiania, 17, 22

Backström, Ragnhild, 145
Bantock, Sir Granville, 93, 163 n64, n68
Bastien-Lepage, Jules, 17
Baudelaire, Charles, 31
Bauerkeller, Mr., 11
Bavarian Academy, 124
Bax, Sir Arnold Edward Trevor, 93
Beckmann, Max, 127, 168 n42
Beecham, Sir Thomas (1879-1961), 29, 93, 94, 103, 114, 117, 119, 124, 131, 135, 142, 146, 150 n19, 165 n20, 166 n31, 167 n19, n24, 169 n11, 170 n27, n29, 172 n2, 175
Bell-Ranske, Jutta, 14, 42, 150 n19
Berend, R.S., 67, 68, 69, 154 n7, 155 n19
Bergh, Andrea Fredrikke Emilie (Milly) (1865-1937). Norwegian actress married to the actor Ludvig Bergh. Made her debut in Copenhagen in 1892 and became very well known in Christiania. She had inspired an early love in Munch, who refers to her in his early writings by the pseudonym of 'Mrs Heiberg'. She later maintained a long friendship with Delius. 44, 45, 94, 113, 145, 151 n25, n26, 163 n73, 166 n29
Bergh, Ludvig, 151 n26
Berlin Kammerspieltheater, 91, 97, 164 n82
Berlin, Komisches Oper, 90
Berlin Philharmonic Orchestra, 159 n25, 165 n13
Berlin Secession, 62, 71, 76, 77, 154 n42, 156 n28
Berlin Tageblatt, (newspaper), 162 n58
Bing, Samuel (1838-1905). Hamburg art dealer, who moved to Paris in 1871. After visiting the Far East he opened shops for Oriental art in Paris and New York. After making a report on American architecture and design for the French government in 1893, he opened his shop for modern art in Paris, in December 1895, which he called *L'Art Nouveau.* This shop gave its name to the movement in France and England, although this had not been Bing's deliberate intention. 30, 72, 150 nIV/5, 156 n27, n31
Bjølstad, Karen (1839-1931), 16, 17, 22, 28, 31, *33a,* 66, 90, 132, 136, 150 nIII/14, 158 n12, 162 n55, 165 n11
Bjørnson, Bergliot, 15
Bjørnson, Bjornstjerne (1832-1910), 12, 13, 15, 19, 21, 43
'Black Piglet' circle (Zum Schwarzen Ferkel), 24, 30, 45, 51, 146
Blehr, Otto Albert, 150 nIV/12
Blehr, Randi (1851-1938), 32, 150 nIV/12
Blomqvist's premises (exhibition rooms), 64, 117, 150 nIV/8, 166 n3
Bonneau, E., 163 n80
Bonnard, Pierre, 25, 30
Bonnat, Léon, 21, 22
Borgström, Hjalmar, 22, 146
Bradford Grammar School, 11
Braque, Georges, 97
Brecher, Gustav, 117
Brian, Havergal, 93
Brücke, Die, 95

Brügmann, Walter, 119
Busoni, Ferruccio Benvenuto (1866-1924), 45, 61, 146, 154 n43
Buths, Julius, 61, 76, 82, 154 n2, 156 n24
Buzot, Hubert, 172 n10
Bäckström, Ragnhild Juell, 145
Bødtker, Sigurd (1866-1928). Norwegian theatre critic and member of Christiania's bohemian set. 44, 64, 95, 97, 151 n26, 161 n39

Caron, Charlotte ('Madame Charlotte', 'Mère Charlotte'), 24, 25, 26, 27, 32, *34b*, 150 nIII/11, 152 n35
Cassirer, Bruno (1872-1941), 76, 77, 81, 91, 156 n28, 157 n53, 158 n14
Cassirer, Fritz (1871-1926), 76, 90, 92; 93, 101, 156 n24
Cassirer, Paul (1871-1926), 71, 76, 77, 95, 157 n53
Cézanne, Paul, 95, 102, 157 n50
Chéret, Jules, 30
Chop, Max, 92, 163 n63
Chopin, Frédéric, 11, 146
Christiania Bohemians, 18
Christiania Music Society, 20
Christiania Technical College, 17
Christiania Theatre, 44
Clews, Henry, 115, 120, 128, 144, 168 n44
Clews, Marie, 115, 120, 128, 166 n33, n2, 167 n19, 168 n44, n49, n50
Clot, Auguste, 30
Cologne Sonderbund Exhibition, 102
Commeter, 77, 156 n28
Contard, Paul, 42
Coulangheon, Jacques Arsène, 25
Courtauld Collection, 122, 167 n25
Courtauld, Samuel, 123
Craig, Edward Gordon, 91, 128, 162 n58
Crawley, Kate, 52
Cunard, Lady Emerald, 144

Damrosch, Walter, 165 n12
Dean, Basil, 124, 127
Debussy, Claude, 60, 159 n24
Dedichen, Dr Lucien, *112b*, 129
Dehmel, Richard, 24
Delibes, (artists' carrier), 86
Delius, Clare, 128
Delius, Ernest, 12
Delius Festival, London, 131, 137
Delius, Frederick Theodor Albert (1862-1934). Works referred to:
Appalachia. Variations on an Old Slave Song, 29, 60, 76, 82, 93, 94, 159 n25, 163 n64
Arabesque, An, 103, 104
Brigg Fair, An English Rhapsody, 94, 163 n64, 165 n12
Caprice and Elegy for Violoncello and Chamber Orchestra, 131
Concerto for Cello and Orchestra, 124
Concerto for Piano and Orchestra, 45, 76, 93, 94
Concerto for Violin and Orchestra, 115, 166 n34, n4
Concerto for Violin, Cello and Orchestra, 115, 166 n34
Cynara, 131
Dance Rhapsody No. 1, 94
Danish Songs, Seven, 45, 52, 53, 60
Eventyr. Once upon a time, 103, 104, 115, 135, 137, 166 n4
Fennimore and Gerda, 52, 53, 54, 94, 103, 104, 117, 118, 119, 143, 144, 163 n69, 167 n9, n19
Florida Suite, 14
Folkeraadet *(The People's Parliament)*, 44, 45, 55, 94, 147, 151 n21, n27
Hassan, 124, 127
Hiawatha, 15
Idyll, 131, 169 n9
In a Summer Garden, 94, 163 n64, 165 n12
Irmelin, 24
Jeg havde en nyskaaren seljeflojte *(I had a fresh-cut willow flute)*, 149 nIII/9
Koanga, 26, 45, 49, 75, 76, 156 n24
Late Lark, A, 131
Life's Dance, 57, 58, 61, 76, 103, 156 n24, 163 n64
Magic Fountain, The, 24, 26
Margot la Rouge, 60, 153 n35, 169 n9
Mass of Life, A, 47, 76, 82, 101, 103, 143
Mitternachtslied Zarathustras *(Zarathustras Midnight Song)*, 46, 70, 101
North Country Sketches, 103
On hearing the first Cuckoo in Spring, 103, 165 n14, 170 n27
Over the Hills and Far Away, 29, 45, 49, 61, 163 n64
Paa Vidderne *(On the Mountains)*, melodrama, 15
Paa Vidderne, symphonic poem, 15, 20, 22, 24
Paris. The Song of a great City, 49, 61, 76, 82, 154 n2, 163 n64, 165 n12
Poem of Life and Love, 115, 169 n9
Requiem, 115
Ronde se déroule, La, 47, 54, 55
Sakuntala, 15
Sea Drift, 70, 89, 97, 162 n50, 163 n64
Sonata for cello and piano, 115, 166 n34, n4
Sonata No. 1 for violin and piano, 115
Sonata No. 2 for violin and piano, 169 n49
Sonata No. 3 for violin and piano, 131
Song of the High Hills, The, 103
Song of Summer, A, 131, 169 n9
Songs from the Norwegian, Five *(5 Lieder (aus dem Norwegischen))*, 15
Songs from the Norwegian, Seven *(7 Lieder (aus dem Norwegischen))*, 15
Songs to poems of Friedrich Nietzsche, Four, 47

Songs to poems by Paul Verlaine *(Deux Mélodies)*, 60
Songs of Farewell, 131
Songs of Sunset, 90, 94, 97, 103
String Quartet, 115, 166 n4
Summer Night on the River, 170 n27
Sur les cimes *(see* Paa Vidderne)
Village Romeo and Juliet, A, 60, 76, 90, 92, 103, 153 n35, 170 n27
Delius, Helen Sophie Emilie, 'Jelka', (née Rosen) (1868-1935). The marriage register at Grez gives the date 1868 for Jelka's birth: "le dix huit Décembre nouvelle style (trente décembre vieux style) mil huit cent soixante huit'. As this was properly witnessed it seems to be a more probable date than that given on the Deliuses' gravestone at Limpsfield and in the draft of a will in possession of the Delius Trust as 26th December 1872. 29, 43, 45, 47, 49, 57, 60, 61, 65, 66, 69, 70, 73, 75, 79, 81, 82, 83, 84, 85, 86, 89, 90, 96, 99, 103, 104, 113, 114, 116, 117, 118, 119, 120, 121, 122, 124, 125, 126, 127, 128, 129, 132, 133, 134, 136, 137, 138, 140, 141, 144, 145, 153 n27, 154 n38, n43, n5, n6, 156 n22, 159 n20, 162 n52, 166 n26, n33, n2, 167 n19, 168 n38, n44, n49, n50, 170 n26, n28, n32, 171 n43, 172 n8, n10, 175
Delius, Julius, 11, 12, 13, 14, 17, 29, 49
Delius, Theodor, 12, 14, 20, 23, 29, 47
Delius Trust, *passim*
Derain, André, 97
Diorama premises (Dioramalokalet), 47, 150 nIV/8, 151 n32, 154 n40
Diriks, Karl Edvard, 75, 157 n51
Drachmann, Holger (1846-1908). Danish author of poetry, novels, travel books, plays and operetta. His poems were set to music by Delius on at least five occasions. He was associated with Munch in the 1890s and portrayed by him in 1901. 15, 45, 47, 63, 146
Durand-Ruel, Paul (1828-1922). The important French art dealer who had been the first to commit himself to handling the work of the Impressionist painters. 74, 75, 157 n44

Edwards, Bella, *40a*, 72, 73, 146, 157 n35, n36, 159 n24
Elberfeld Choral Society, 103
Elberfeld Stadtteater, 76
Elgar, Sir Edward William, 93, 132
Eliasson, Dr Anders, 43
Epstein, Sir Jacob, 172 n8
Ericson, Ida (see Molard, Ida)
Ericson-Molard, Judith (1881-1950s) 25, 26, 47, 156 n34
Esche, Hermann, 82, 159 n21

Fauré, Gabriel, 49, 60

Fauves, Les, 95, 97
Fenby, Eric, 52, 122, 127, 131, 132, 133, 144, 145, 153 n27, 162 n49, n50, 165 n17, 168 n46, 169 n49, n10, 170 n27, 171 n43, 175
Fennimore and Gerda, cover design, *118*, 118, 119, 176
Fiedler, Max, 165 n12
Flecker, James Elroy, 124
Foerder, Marthe, 42
Folies-Bergère, Les, 32
Folkwangs Museum, Hagen, 61, 66, 154 n37, 160 n31
Frankfurt Group, 93
Frankfurt am Main, Opernhaus, 117, 119
Frankfurt am Main, Stadelsches Kunstinstitut, 120, 167 n12, n16
Frankfurter Zeitung (newspaper), 127, 167 n7
Freia Chocolate Factory, 123
Freie Bühne, 157 n52
Fried, Oskar, 159 n25, 165 n13

Gachet, Dr Paul, 120
Gardiner, Henry Balfour, 93, 116, 131
Gauguin, Paul (1848-1903), 17, 24, 25, 26, 27, 28, 30, 31, 32, 47, 51, 52, 53, 75, 102, 120, 121, 122, 130, 144, 150 nIII/11, nIII/15, nIV/5, 151 n31, 153 n13, n19, 172 n8
Gauguin, Pola (Paul) Rollon (1888-1961). Son of the painter Paul Gauguin. Born in Paris, he was brought up by his mother in Copenhagen, where he studied first as an architect, but later became a painter. He went to Norway in 1912, becoming a Norwegian citizen in 1914. Apart from painting, he was widely employed as an art critic. 130, 138, 163 n77, 169, n6, 171 n47
Gemäldegalerie, Dresden, 170 n25
Gerard, Édouard, 31, 151 n30
Gérard, Édouard, 47, 156 n34
Gérard, Judith (see Ericson-Molard, Judith)
Gerhardi, Ida (1862-1927). Recognized as one of the best German women artists of her day. A long-standing friend of Jelka Delius and helped to promote Delius's music in Germany. Admirer of Munch's work and it is claimed that this was reciprocated. 45, 61, 144, 154 n43
German Academy, 124
Gesellschaft Hamburgischer Kunstfreunder, 156 n28
Gierløff, Christian, 99, 164 n84
Glaser, Kurt, 102, 165 n8
Gløersen, Inger Alver, 113, 165 n25
Gogh, Vincent van, 75, 102, 120
Goldstein, Emanuel, 98, 99
Goossens, Sir Eugene, 127
Goupil Gallery, 121, 167 n18
Grainger, Percy Aldridge, 93, 94, 114, 115, 116, 124, 127, 131, 132, 163 n71, 168 n43

Grieg, Edvard Hagerup, 14, 15, 20, 21, 25, 26, 29, 94, 103, 149 nIII/9, 156 n22, 163 n71, 165 n6, n14
Grieg, Nina, 14, 15, 20, 21, 94, 104, 165 n21, n22
Gruppe XI, 157 n52
Gunn, James, 144, 170 n26

Halir, Karol, 72
Hallé Orchestra, 11
Hals, Frans, 70
Halvorsen, Horst, 167 n16
Halvorsen, Johan, 14
Hamilton, Rachel, 24
Hammer, Karl Vilhelm, 31
Hamsun, Knut (1859-1952). Outstanding Norwegian novelist, well-known to Munch and, possibly, also to Delius. 140, 150 n19
Harrison, Beatrice, 115, 166 n34
Harrison, May, 115, 166 n34
Hauge, Alfred (1876-1901). Young Norwegian artist, known to both Munch and Delius, and a great admirer of Cézanne. 50, 59, 152 n3
Haym, Hans, 43, 45, 61, 76
Heiberg, Gunnar (1857-1929), 43, 44, 49, 50, 59, 64, 74, 95, 97, 151 n22, n26, 152 n2, 157 n47, 158 n8, 161 n39, ep5
Herrmann, Curt, 157 n52
Herrmann, Paul, 25, 42
Hertz, Alfred, 49
Heseltine, Philip (Peter Warlock), 42, 93, 114, 116, 127, 150 nIV/13, nIV/14, 168 n41, n48
Heyerdahl, Hans Olaf, 17, 19, 75, 157 n51
Heyerdahl, Hieronymous, 123
His Majesty's Theatre, London, 127
Hofmann, Ludvig von, 77, 154 n42, 157 n52
Hollaendergården, 154 n41
Holter, Iver, 21
Hôtel des Ventes, 172 n10, 176
Humperdinck, Engelbert, 92, 163 n62
Høst, Sigurd, 99, 164 n2

Ibsen, Henrik Johan (1828-1906), 12, 15, 26, 31, 105a, 43, 44, 91, 92, 142, 144, 162 n58
Impressionist, The (newspaper), 18, 19
Indépendants, Société des Artistes and Salon des, 31, 32, 65, 66, 67, 69, 71, 73, 74, 75, 76, 78, 79, 80, 81, 83, 84, 85, 86, 87, 88, 89, 97, 98, 101, 102, 113, 157 n45, 158 n1, n2, n9, n15, 159 n17, 160 n26, n32, 161 n47, 162 n48, 163 n83, 164 n84, n85, 165 n10, 176
Indy, Vincent d', 60
International College, Isleworth, 12

Jacobsen, Jens Peter (1847-85) Despite his short life and small output, Jacobsen was one of the most influential Danish writers of his time. He was also a talented scientist and translated works by Darwin into Danish. His writings greatly appealed to musicians at the turn of the century and, apart from Delius, were set by Carl Nielsen and Arnold Schoenberg. 45, 47, 51, 52, 53, 54, 103, 104, 142, 144, 147, 152 n9
Jacobson, Dr Daniel Eduard, 98, 99
Jadassohn, Salomon, 14
Jaeger, Hans, 18, 19, 140
Jarry, Alfred, 25
Jebe, Halfdan, 43, 49, 150 n19
Jena University, 102
Jensen-Hjell, Karl Gustav, 18
Joachim, Joseph, 11, 72
John, Augustus, 144, 170 n26
Juell, Dagny (see under Przybyszewska, Dagny Juell)

Kahane, Arthur, 162 n58
Karsten, Ludvig Peter (1876-1926), 73, 74, 75, 76, 82, 83, 157 n40, n47, n48
Kavli, Arne, 84, 97, 154 n1
Kessler, Count Harry (1868-1937), 71, 74, 77, 154 n29, 160 n31, 152 n58, n59
Kollman, Albert (1837-1915), 62, 77, 156 n21 ep10
Krag, Vilhelm (1871-1933). One of the leading Norwegian poets of the New Romanticism of the eighteen-nineties. He was friendly with both Munch and Delius. 25, 26, 32, 52, 142, 149 nIII/9, ep3
Krohg, Christian (1852-1925), 17, 18, 19, 22, 44, 51, 75, 95, 150 nIII/11, 151 n24, n26, 152 n35, 153 n11, 157 n51
Krohg, Oda (1860-1945). Wife of Christian Krohg and, like her husband, a painter. A central figure among the Christiania bohemians, she carried on a triangular relationship with her husband and Gunnar Heiberg, as well as inspiring feelings of love and jealousy in Jappe Nilssen. 59, 75, 104, 151 n26, 157 n51, 165 n19
Krohg, Per (1889-1965). Son of Oda and Christian Krohg. He was to become one of the most distinguished Norwegian artists from the nineteen-twenties onwards. 104, 165 n19

Larsen, Mathilde (Tulla) (1869-1942), 48, 49, 50, 57, 61, 63, 64, 86, 87, 95, 96, 97, 99, 142, 154 n1, 156 n33, n34, 157 n47, 158 n8, 161 n39, n43, ep9
Larsson, Carl, 43, 151 n20
Lasson, Bokken, 151 n26
Laurencin, Marie, 97
Leclercq, Julien (1865-1901). French journalist and author. Briefly associated with Bing's gallery and one of the founders of Le Mercure de France. With

William Molard translated some Strindberg into French. 25, 26, 32, 45, 151 n28, 174, 175
Leeds Festival, 94
Leipzig Conservatoire, 13, 14
Leistikow, Walter, 63, 76, 154 n42, 157 n52
Lemercier, Alfred-(Léon) b.1831. Proprietor of the Lemercier printing establishment in Paris in succession to his uncle Joseph Lemercier, the firm's founder. Lemercier and August, Clot, who worked for a time at Lemercier'se were Munch's major printers in Paris. 30, 74, 157 n49
Liberté, 162 n48
Liebermann, Max, 77, 154 n42, 157 n52
Linde, Dr Max (1862-1940), 61, 62, 64, 66, 69, 74, 77, 99, 140, 154 n3, 155 n17, 156 n25, 157 n41, 159 n21
London Gallery, The, 169 n5
Louvre, Musée du, 17
Lugné-Poë, Aurélien-Francois (1869-1940). French actor and manager. Appeared at the Théâtre Libre under Antoine, and at the Théâtre d'Art with Paul Fort. He later took over the latter and developed it into the celebrated Théâtre de l'Oeuvre. Here he introduced much modern work by Maeterlinck, Ibsen, Strindberg, Wilde, Hauptmann, Jarry and others. 27, 31, 53, 71, 72, 73, 156 n23, 157 n39
Lynx Ex-Artistic Correspondence, Le, 97, 162 n48, 163 n80, 164 n85

Maddison, Mrs Adela, 49
Maeterlinck, Maurice, 53
Mahler, Gustav, 151 n29
Mallarmé, Stéphane, 31, *ep8*
Manes Group and Gallery, 79, 158 n3, n4
Mannheim, Kunsthalle, 132
Manet, Edouard, 17, 18, 120
Marchant, William (d.1925), 121, 167 n18
Marquet, Albert, 25
Mathieson, Sigurd, 98
Matisse, Henri, 95
Meier-Graefe, Julius, 24, 30, 160 n31
Mengelberg, Richard, 145
Mercure de France, Le (periodical), 31
Messager, André, 15
Middelthun, Julius, 17
Mitchell, Mrs (Mitchell and Kimbell), 86, 161 n45
Moir, Byres, 114
Molard, Ida Louise Wilhelmina (formerly Ericson) (1853-1927), 25, 27, 32, 51, 156 n34, 175
Molard, William (1862-1936), 24, 25, 26, 27, 28, 31, 32, 45, 47, 51, 52, 53, 60, 97, 133, 146, 149 nIII/6, 150 nIII/15, nIV/5, 151 n27, n29, 152 n7, 153 n13, 156 n34, 158 n8, 170 n21, n22, 175
Monet, Claude, 149 nI/4
Monfreid, Georges Daniel de (1856-1929). Talented painter and follower of Gauguin. When Gauguin finally settled in Oceania he sent paintings home to de Monfreid who endeavoured to find purchasers for them. De Monfreid maintained his friendship with Delius for a number of years. 25, 26, 32, 47, 144, 151 n31
Monvel, Charles Boutet de, 25
Mordt family (see also Bell-Ranske, Jutta), 14
Moreau, Leon, 25
Morice, Charles, 51, 52
Morosov, Ivan, 155 n9, n14, n18
Mottl, Felix, 29
Mowinckel, Mrs, 49
Mucha, Alphonse, 25, 27, 30, 32
Mudocci, Eva (1883-1952), 11 *40a*, 72, 73, 79, 80, 81, 83, 145, 146, 157 n35, n36, 159 n24, 172 n12, *ep11*
Munch, Andreas (1811-84), 15, 16
Munch, Andreas, jnr., 16
Munch, Christian, 16, 17, 19, *33a*
Munch, Edvard (1863-1944). Works referred to: Collections are given against all works except graphic ones, where there are of course a number of copies. However one or more copies of these last can be found in Munch-Museet. The abbreviation OKK denotes Oslo Kommunes Kunstsamlinger, (Oslo Municipal Art Collections). Munch-Museet, which is part of this, houses all the works by Edvard Munch owned by the city.
Alma Mater (Oslo University assembly hall), 104
Alpha and Omega. Fable, illustrated with lithographs (OKK), 99, 164 n3, 165, n10, 165 n16
Arneberg, Arnstein (Lithograph), 123
Arvesen, Arve (Private collection), 21, 22, 146, *ep6*
Ashes (Oslo, Nasjonalgalleriet), 104
Bathing Man (Oslo, Nasjonalgalleriet), 117
Bohemian's Death, The (OKK) 123
Bohemian's Wedding, The (OKK) 123
Borgström, Hjalmar (Private collection), 22, 146
Caricatures, 95, 96
Consolation (OKK), 163 n77
Cupid and Psyche (OKK), 95, 163 n77
Dance, The (Private collection), 18
Dance of Life, The, c.1900 (Oslo, Nasjonalgalleriet), 56, 57, 63, 153 n26, 166 n27
Dance of Life, The (Sketch. OKK), *37a*, 56, 57
Dance of Life, The (Later version. OKK), 123
Dance on the Shore (Prague, Národni Galerie), 82
Day After, The (Oslo, Nasjonalgalleriet),

18, 166 n27
Death and the Child (OKK), 63
Death in the Sick Room (Oslo, Nasjonalgalleriet), 166 n27
Death of Marat, 1905-08 (OKK), 96, 97, 143
Death of Marat, 1907 (OKK), 95, 96, 97, 99, *107a*, 163 n7, n81, 164 n84
Dedichen, Dr Lucien and Jappe Nilssen (OKK), *112b*, 129
Delius (Sketch 1890-91. OKK), 20, 22, *frontispiece*
Delius (Drawing from *Verdens Gang*), 20, 22, *ep2*
Delius (Lithograph c.1920), *110*, 116, 122, 123, 145, 175
Delius at Wiesbaden (Lithograph), *111b*, 116, 123, 124, 125, 172 n33
Delius at Wiesbaden (Sketch. OKK), *111a*, 125
Drachmann, Holger (Lithograph), 47
Esche family portraits, 83
Empty Cross, The (OKK), 63
Evening; Melancholy (Private Collection), 54, *54*, 143
Evening; Melancholy (Woodcut), 158 n15
Fear (Lithograph), 31, 176
Fear (Woodcut), 176
Fertility (Private collection), 63
Fleurs du Mal, Les (Sketches for illustrations. OKK), 31, 104
Flight (Lithograph), 165 n16
Flower of Love, The (Lithograph), 104, 105 n16
Flower of Pain, The (see *Quickborn*)
Forest, The (OKK), 155 n9
Freia Chocolate Factory Murals, Oslo, 123
Funeral March (Drawing. OKK), 45, *46*, 172 n17
Funeral March (Lithograph), 45, 100, 101, 160 n29
German Landscape (OKK), 161 n32
German Landscape, Elgersburg (OKK), 161 n32
Ghosts. Sketches for Max Reinhardt's production. (OKK and various other collections), 53, 91, 92, 166 n3
Girls on the Jetty (Oslo, Nasjonalgalleriet), 63
Girls on the Jetty (Moscow, Pushkin Museum), 155 n9, n18
Girls on the Jetty (Cologne, Wallraf-Richartz Museum), 82
Golgotha (OKK), 63
Harpy (Lithograph), 63, 155 n9
Hedda Gabler. Sketch for Max Reinhardt's production (OKK), 91, 96
Heiberg, Gunnar (Lithograph), *ep5*
Heritage (OKK), 63
Heyerdahl, Hieronymous (3 versions, 1 and 2 OKK; 3 Private Collection), 123
History (Oslo University assembly hall),

100
Horses Ploughing (Oslo, Nasjonalgalleriet), 117
Ibsen and Nietzsche surrounded by Genius (OKK), *105a*, 160 n29
Inger at the Piano (OKK), 172 n17
Inger on the Beach (Summer Night) (Bergen, Rasmus Meyers Samlinger), 18
Jacobson, Dr Daniel (OKK), 99
Jaeger, Hans (Oslo, Nasjonalgalleriet), 18, 48
Jaeger, Hans (Lithograph), 140
Jealousy (Lithograph), 176
Jensen-Hjell, Karl (Private collection), 18, 19
John Gabriel Borkman. Programme design (Lithograph), 31
Karsten, Ludvig (Stockholm, Thielska Galleriet), 83, *106*, 157 n40
Kessler, Count Harry (Private collection), 156 n29
Kessler, Count Harry (Lithograph), 156 n29
Kiss, The (Woodcut), 118, *119*, 158 n15
Kollmann, Albert (Lithograph), 84, 161 n32, *ep10*
Krag, Vilhelm (Lithograph), *ep3*
Larsen, Tulla (OKK), 63, *ep9*
Leistikow, Walter, and his wife (Lithograph), 63
Life Frieze, The (Various collections), 24, 31, 47, 52, 62, 100, 104, 117, 123, 143, 145, 146, 150 nIV/8, 164 n5, 166 n3
Linde Frieze (OKK), 77
Linde, the four sons of Dr Max (Lübeck, Behnhaus), 69
Lovers in the Waves (Lithograph), 58, 59, 158 n15, 176
Madonna (Oslo, Nasjonalgalleriet), 166 n27
Madonna (Lithograph), *39b*, 81, 158 n15, 176
Madonna; the Brooch (Lithograph), 73, 146, *ep11*
Mallarmé, Stéphane (Etching), 31, 158 n15
Mallarmé, Stéphane (Lithograph), 31, 158 n15, *ep8*
Man with Duck (Collection of the family of Thomas Olsen), 120
Melancholy; Laura (OKK), 63, 155 n9
Meeting in Space (Woodcut), *36b*, 58, 63
Melancholy; the Yellow Boat, 1891-92 (Oslo, Nasjonalgalleriet), 143, 144
Melancholy; the Yellow Boat, 1894-95 (Bergen, Rasmus Meyers Samlinger), 143, 144
Men Bathing (Helsinki, Ateneum), 95
Metabolism (OKK), 63
Military Band on Karl Johan Street (Zurich, Kunsthaus), *33b*, 172 n17
Mirror, The. Series of prints, 47, 52, 53,

152 n5
Model by a Wicker Chair (OKK), 123
Moonlight (Woodcut), *37b*, 158 n15
Mother and Daughter (Oslo,
   Nasjonalgalleriet), 166 n27
Mountain of Mankind (OKK), 100, 101,
   108a
Müller, Ingse Vibe (OKK), 162 n51
Nietzsche, Friedrich (OKK), 82, 160 n29
Nietzsche, Friedrich (Stockholm, Thielska
   Galleriet), 82, 160 n29, n31
Nietzsche, Friedrich (Lithograph), 84,
   101, 145, 160 n29, 161 n32, *ep14*
Night in Nice (Oslo, Nasjonalgalleriet),
   151 n33
Old Fisherman, The (Woodcut), 63
Oslo City Hall. Sketches for murals
   (Workers Frieze) (OKK), *112a*, 123,
   129, 138, 169 n4, 170 n25
Oslo University Murals, 100, 101, 102,
   104, 129, 130, 143, 164 n4, 166 n3
P.A. Munch's grave, Rome (OKK), 129
Parisian Music-Hall (Sketch OKK), *35b*
Paul Herrmann and Paul Contard
   (Vienna, Kunsthistorisches Museum),
   42
Peer Gynt. Programme design
   (Lithograph), 31, *35a*
Phantoms (Drypoint), 95, 96, *96*
Poison Flower, The (Lithograph), 165
   n16
Portraits of nurses, 99
Puberty (Oslo, Nasjonalgalleriet), 18, 166
   n27
Puberty (Lithograph), 176
Quickborn. Special number of periodical.
   Cover, *The Flower of Pain*, *38*, 48, 55
Rainy Day in Christiania (Private
   Collection), 162 n59
Rathenau, Walther (Bergen, Rasmus
   Meyers Samlinger), 91
Red House, The (Private Collection), 129
Red Vine, The (OKK), 63
Reimers, Mrs Cally Monrad
   (Lithograph), 60, 146
Reinhardt Frieze (Berlin, Nationalgalerie;
   OKK, and other collections), 91, 94,
   97, *107b*, 123, 164 n82
Rode, Helge (Stockholm,
   Nationalmuseum), 99
Rode, Helge (Drypoint), *ep7*
Salome (Lithograph), 73
Sandberg, Christen (OKK), 63
Schiefler, Gustav (Helsinki, Ateneum), 83
Scream, The (Lithograph), 30, 143, 152
   n5, 176, *177*
Scream, The (Nasjonalgalleriet), 152 n5,
   166 n27
Seated Woman (Collection of the Family
   of Thomas Olsen), 120
Self-portrait (1930, Lithograph), *ep15*
Self-portrait between the Clock and the
   Bed (OKK), 171 n52

Self-portrait by the Window (OKK), 171
   n15
Self-portrait eating a 'truly magnificent
   cod's head' (OKK), 171 n52
Self-portrait. The Night Wanderer
   (OKK), 172 n15
Self-portrait in Weimar; (Self-portrait
   with a Wine Bottle) (OKK), 94, *105b*,
   160 n32
Self-portrait with a Cigarette (Oslo,
   Nasjonalgalleriet), 151 n33
Self-portrait with Lyre (OKK), *40b*
Self-portrait with a Skeleton Arm
   (Lithograph), 145, *ep1*
Self-portrait with Spanish 'flu' (Oslo,
   Nasjonalgalleriet), *109*, 116, 117
Self-portrait with a Stick of Pastel
   (OKK), 172 n52
Sick Child, The (First version, Oslo,
   Nasjonalgalleriet), 18, 19, 52, 152 n5
Sick Child, The (Third version,
   Stockholm, Thielska Galleriet), 163 n77
Sick Child, The (Fourth version, London,
   Tate Gallery), 163 n77, 165 n10, 170
   n25
Sick Child, The (Fifth and sixth versions,
   OKK), 129
Sick Child, The (Drypoint), 52, 53, 152
   n5
Sick Child, The (Etching), *36a*, 52, 53,
   152 n5
Sick Child, The (Lithograph), 52, 53
Siesta, (OKK), *33a*
Sin (Nude with Red Hair) (Lithograph),
   63
Sinding, Christian (Lithograph), 146, 171
   n44, *ep12*
Spring (Oslo, Nasjonalgalleriet), 18
Starry Night (OKK), 123
Strauss, Richard (Lithograph), 146, *ep16*
Strindberg, August (Lithograph), 81, 144,
   158, n15, 175, 176, *ep4*
Studies of animals, 99
Summer Night (Women on the Jetty)
   (Stockholm, Thielska Galleriet), 77
Sun, The (Oslo University assembly
   hall), 101, *108b*, 143, 164 n6
Tête a tête (OKK), 18
Three Stages of Woman (Bergen, Rasmus
   Meyers Samlinger), 57, 58
Three Stages of Woman (Lithograph),
   165 n10
Thüringian Landscape; (Melting Snow
   near Elgersburg). (Wuppertal Von der
   Heydt Museum), 161 n32
Train Smoke (OKK), 63
Two Music-making Sisters (Private
   Collection), 145, 172 n17
Two Young Girls on a Farm (Rotterdam,
   Boymans Museum), 83
Vampire (Lithograph and woodcut), *39a*,
   81, 158 n15, 176
Velde, Henry van de (Lithograph), 84,

161 n32, *ep13*
Violin Recital, The (Lithograph), *40a*, 73, 146, 172 n17
Wave, The (OKK), 123
Westminster Abbey (Lithograph), 103, 165 n11
White Night (Oslo, Nasjonalgalleriet), 63
Munch, Edvard: *Mein Freund Przybyszewski*, 146, 173 n19
Munch, Inger (1868-1952), 90, 145, 152 n65
Munch, Jacob, 16
Munch, Johan Storm, 16
Munch, Laura Cathrine (née Bjølstad), 16
Munch, Laura, 16
Munch-Museet (The Munch Museum, Oslo), *passim*
Munch, Peter Andreas, 16
Munch, (Johanne) Sophie, 16
Munthe, Gerhard, 164 n4
Musical League, The, 93
Musik, Die, (periodical), 92, 162 n60
Myrbach, F., 156 n30
Müller, Ingse Vibe (1882-1945), 89, 162 n51, n52
Müller, Titus Vibe, 162 n51, 169 n2

Nabis, Les, 30
Nasjonalgalleriet (National Gallery, Olso), 48, 62, 100, 113, 151 n33, 164 n6, 166 n27
Natanson, Thadée, 30, 150 nIV/3
Nay, Ernst Wilhelm, 140
Nazis, the, 140, 167 n16
Nevinson, Christopher Richard Wynne, 157 n45
Nietzsche, Friedrich Wilhelm (1844-1900), 29, 47, 59, 70, 76, 82, 100, 101, *105a*, 115, 142, 143, 144, 151 n29, *ep14*
Nilssen, Jappe (1870-1931). Norwegian art and literary critic and author of novels and short stories. A leading member of Christiania's bohemian set, he was also noted for his knowledge of France and French literature. One of Munch's closest friends and supporters. 59, 60, 98, 99, 100, *112b*, 120, 121, 125, 129, 132, 133, 134, 135, 136, 138, 145, 147, 151 n26, 153 n30, n32, 164 n87, n3, 167 n13, n14, n19, 168 n34, 169 n15, n17, 170 n22, n24, 171 n45, 172 n16, 173 n21
Nordraak, Rikard, 44
Nordström, Karl, 43

Obstfelder, Sigbjørn (1866-1900). Norwegian poet and writer of stories and a play. His writing typifies the New Romanticism of the eighteen-nineties. A close friend of Munch, he was also slightly acquainted with Delius. 52, 59, 146
O'Conor, Roderic, 25
Olsen, Thomas, 167 n16

O'Neill, Adine, 168 n38
O'Neill, Norman, 93, 165 n20
Oscar II, King of Sweden and Norway, 159 n19
Oslo City Hall, 123, 129, 138
Oslo Kommunes Kunstsamlinger (Municipal Art Collections), *passim*
Oslo University, 100, 101, 102, 164 n4
Oseberg Ship ('the Viking Queen Ship'), 113, 166 n28
Osthaus Karl-Ernst (1874-1921). Founder and director of the Folkwang Museum in Hagen. Co-founder of the Deutscher Werkbund. 61, 66, 154 n6, n37, n38, 155 n17, 160 n31
Ouvré, Achille (1872-1951). A graphic artist who became particularly famous for portraits and book illustrations, also engraving vignettes for postage stamps. He exhibited regularly at the Indépendants and at the Salon d'Automne, where he became president of the graphic section. 47, 133, 154 n37, n38, 158 n8, 169 n18

Pan (periodical), 24, 28, 30
Papus, (Dr Gerard Encausse), 27
Paris Salon, 17
Peterssen, Eilif, 164 n4
Petit, Georges, Important French art dealer who had been the rival of Durand-Ruel in taking up the Impressionists. 73, 157 n37, n44
Pettenkofer, Max von (1818-1901), 41, 150 n16
Phifer, Robert, 13
Piat, Monsieur, 31
Piatti, Alfredo Carlo, 11
Picasso, Pablo Ruiz y, 102
Polignac, Prince and Princesse de, 49
Politikken, (newspaper), 138, 171 n46
Presse, La, 31, 150 nIV/8
Proctor, Ernest, 144, 170 n26
Przybyszewska, Dagny Juell, 41, 42, 48, 145
Przybyszewski, Stanislas, 24, 41, 42, 48, 146

Quickborn (periodical), *38*, 48, 57
Quilter, Roger, 93

Raphael, 50
Rathenau, Walther, 91, 162 n59
Rasmussen, Rulle, 157 n35
Ravel, Maurice, 25, 60, 153 n35
Ravensberg, Ludvig Orning (1871-1958), 23, 100, 149 nIII/6
Reimers, Mrs Cally Monrad (1879-1950), 60, 146
Reinecke, Carl Heinrich Carsten, 14
Reinhardt, Max, 53, 91, 92, 162 n58, n61
Renoir, Pierre Auguste, 120, 149 nII/4
Revue Blance, La, 30, 31, 150 nIV/3, nIV/4, nIV/7, 153 n34

Riccardi, Eleuterio, 144
Roanake Female College, 13
Robin, Edouard Charles Albert (1847-1928). Professor of the Faculté de Medicine de Paris; member of l'Académie de Medicine. He wrote many books and was a Grand-officier de la Legion d'honneur. 67, 68, 69, 154 n8, 155 n11, n13
Rode, Helge (1870-1937). Danish poet, essayist and prolific dramatist. Rode's writings are concerned with the mystical and spiritual and represent the anti-rationalistic movement in Danish literature. 23, 51, 54, 55, 56, 57, 58, 59, 99, 103, 114, 136, 138, 142, 153 n21, n22, n28, 171 n40, n48, ep7
Rodin, Auguste, 61, 66, 144, 154 n5, n6, 156 n22
Roinard, Paul, 25, 53
Roitier, A., 88
Ronald, Sir Landon, 93
Rosen, Jelka (see under Delius, Jelka)
Rosenthal restaurant, 14
Rousseau, Henri, 25
Royal Opera House, Covent Garden, 103
Royal School of Design, Christiania, 17
Royal Society of British Artists, 169 n5

Sackbut, The (periodical), 150 nIV/13, 174
St. James's Hall, London, 49
Sammons, Albert, 115, 166 n34
Sandberg, Christen, 63
Schiefler, Gustav, 62, 77, 83, 145, 154 n44, 158 n54, 159 n21, 164 n3, 172 n14
Schillings, Max, 89
Schmitt, Florent, 25, 60, 149 nIII/6, 153 n35
Schou, Olaf, 100, 163 n77, 166 n27
Schreiner, Kristian E, 171 n41
Schuffenecker, Emile, 25, 32
Schuricht, Carl, 89
Scott, Cyril Meir, 93
Séguin, A., 88
Selmer, Johan, 44
Sérusier, Paul, 25
Shakespeare, William, 162 n58
Shaw, George Bernard, 162 n58
Simon, Heinrich, 127
Sinding, Christian (1856-1941). Norwegian composer. Studied in Germany, where he spent a good deal of his life. Composed orchestral, vocal, instrumental and chamber music, mainly in a nationalist-romantic idiom. 14, 15, 20, 23, 25, 26, 123, 138, 171 n44, ep12
Sitt, Hans, 12, 14
Slewinski, Wladyslaw, 25, 27, 32
Société des Cents Bibliophiles, La, 31
Société Nationale de Musique, La, 60
Society of Scottish Artists, 169 n5

Soot, Eyolf (1858-1928), 21, 22
Stenersen, Gudmund (1863-1934), 21, 22, 149 nII/3
Stenersen, Rolf, 152 n6
Strauss, Richard George (1864-1949), 61, 146, 151 n29, ep16
Strindberg, (Johan) August (1849-1912), 24, 25, 26, 27, 31, 32, 41, 42, 43, 48, 51, 57, 146, 150 nIII/11, nIV/7, nIV/15, n17, 151 n28, 153 n12, 162 n58, 174, 175
Swarenski, Georg (1876-1957), 120, 167 n12
Szántó, Theodor, 93

Tate Gallery, London, 165 n10, 170 n25
Thaulow, Frits (Johan Frederik) (1847-1906), 17, 19, 43
Théâtre-Libre, 27
Théâtre de l'Oeuvre, 27, 31, 53, 71, 156 n23, 157 n39
Thiel, Ernest, 82, 94, 99, 101, 160 n29, n31
Thiis, Jens (1870-1942). Norwegian art historian and long-standing friend and supporter of Munch. In 1908 he became the first director of Nasjonalgalleriet (the National Gallery) in Christiania. 23, 64, 99, 100, 130, 154 n47, 163 n74, n77, 164 n1, 166 n27, 169 n6, 172 n18
Tidens Tegn (newspaper), 166 n3
Toulouse-Lautrec, Henri de, 30
Toye, Geoffrey, 93

Uhl, Frida, 27
Universal Edition, 118, 119

Valotton, Félix, 30
Van Gogh, Vincent see Gogh, Vincent van
Velde, Henry van de (1863-1957), 82, 160 n31, ep13
Verdens Gang (newspaper), 20, 22, 44, 150 nIII/11, 151 n24, 153 n11
Verein Berliner Künstler, 24, 157 n52
Verlaine, Paul, 60, 174
Vienna Secession, 71, 72, 156 n30
Vigeland, Emanuel, 164 n4
Vigeland, Gustav, 164 n4
Vinje, Aasmund Olafsen, 15
Vollard, Ambrose, 31, 75, 157 n50
Vuillard, Édouard, 25, 30

Wagner, Richard, 11, 146
Warburg, Fraulein, 158 n12
Ward, Thomas F., 13
Warlock, Peter (see under Heseltine, Philip)
Weimar Academy of Art, 77
Werenskiold, Erik Theodor, 17
Williams, Ralph Vaughan, 93
Winge, Per, 44, 151 n22
Witte, Georg, 89
Wood, Sir Henry J., 93, 166 n31

Of this book published by

TRIAD PRESS
22 Pheasants Way
Rickmansworth
Hertfordshire
England

Six hundred and fifty copies
have been printed
of which this is copy number

Designed by Lewis Foreman
and printed by Bookmag,
Henderson Road, Inverness

Printed in Scotland

Portraits by Edvard Munch on the back end-paper

9) Tulla Larsen. 1898. Oil on canvas, OKK. RES 70.

10) Albert Kollmann. 1906. Lithograph, OKK. G/1.260-2; Sch.244.

11) Madonna (The Brooch) (Eva Mudocci). 1903. Lithograph, OKK. G/1.255; Sch.212.

12) Christian Sinding. 1912. Lithograph, OKK. G/1.399; Sch.359.

13) Henry van de Velde. 1906. Lithograph, OKK. G/1.262-94; Sch.246.

14) Friedrich Nietzsche. 1906. Lithograph, OKK. G/1.268-2; Sch.247.

15) Edvard Munch. Self-portrait. 1930. Lithograph, OKK. G/1.456.

16) Richard Strauss. 1916. Lithograph, OKK. G/1.396; Sch.460.

9

10

11

12